"Sharon's story is important beca[...] tutions should help children st[...] paternal side of the family. Too often, fathers and their families are overlooked. There should be explicit policy to identify fathers and a father's family when considering kinship care."

— *Jennifer Miller, Co-founder of ChildFocus*

"Kinship care touches everybody's life ... It is a true American archetype and a fundamental value ..."

— *Mary Bissell, Co-founder of ChildFocus*

"We need to recognize the model that gay men raise children successfully and to recognize that low-income or no-income males can provide in other ways for their children and make similar contributions that low-income or no-income single women would. To not tap into these fathers is to deprive a community of 50 percent of its kinship care potential."

— *Robert "Bob" Watt, Trustee Casey Family Programs*

"A Second Chance, Inc. is an example of the kind of formal and informal supports that kin families need to thrive ... We've got to recognize that extended family taking care of children, often have unique needs. A Second Chance, Inc. offers in its arsenal programs and services for kinship families that are tailor-made, informed by foundation research, the community, and what families and kin say that they need."

— *Dr. Patrick McCarthy, President and CEO, Annie E. Casey Foundation*

"Pittsburgh's A Second Chance Inc. is a shining example of what's possible when sentiments change and unique kinship supportive services are in place for children and those who raise them."

— *Dr. Mark Testa, the Sandra Reeves Spears and John B. Turner Distinguished Professor at the University of North Carolina at Chapel Hill, School of Social Work*

"Whether one is trying to influence policy makers (i.e., the funding sources) or whether one is trying to encourage families and communities to invest in their own growth and positive change, what motivates more than anything is helping them to see the incredible cost to individuals, families, communities and society that can be avoided by their own investment in that growth and positive change."

— *David C. Mills, Trustee Casey Family Programs*

"A Second Chance, Inc. is an agency that boldly wanted to address kinship care issues by developing a grassroots expertise to help families. The work went against the grain that the government had to be the problem-solver."

— *Marc Cherna, Director of the Allegheny County Department of Human Services*

"In the eyes of a child, being removed from your parents is an unforgettable trauma. Placed with your grandmother, your aunt and uncle, your family, eases the pain that no other type of alternative care can do. Kinship care is the right solution for so many children."

— *Marcia M. Sturdivant, Ph.D., President and CEO, NEED*

"Kinship care has had a tortuous journey, but it is coming into its own, and for this we have agencies like A Second Chance, Inc. to thank. A Second Chance, Inc. came in treating families with respect and offering them a chance to do something they hadn't been asked to do before — to be active partners with providers and with DHS, instead of the strangers they were perceived to be."

— *Julia Danzy, Former Deputy Secretary Office of Children, Youth & Families and Director of the Division of Social Services for the City of Philadelphia*

On My Way Home

A Memoir of Kinship, Grace, and Hope

Alan —

Thank you for playing you
for playing. You are awesome!

S

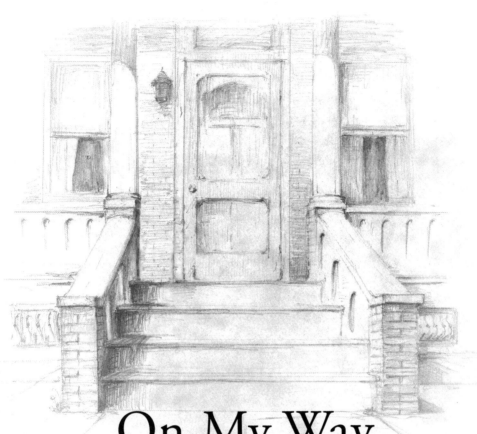

On My Way Home

A Memoir of Kinship, Grace, and Hope

Sharon L. McDaniel

This work is a memoir. It reflects the author's present recollections of her experiences over a period of years. Some dialogue and events have been re-created from memory and, in some cases, have been compressed to convey the substance of what was said and what occurred.

All photographs are courtesy of the author's personal collection or in the public domain, unless otherwise indicated.

Copyright © 2014 by Dr. Sharon L. McDaniel (ASCI)
Published in the United States by:
A Second Chance, Inc.
8350 Frankstown Avenue
Pittsburgh, PA 15221

ISBN (softbound): 978-0-9914285-1-9
ISBN (hardbound): 978-0-9914285-0-2
ISBN (eBook): 978-0-9914285-2-6
LCN: 2014901708

Printed in the United States of America on reused paper

Project Consultant: Denise Riley-Ajanwachuku, CEO
Global SOULutions LLC
P.O. Box 78 | Rural Ridge, PA 15075
da@GlobalSOULutionsllc.com

Editorial Consultants: Ervin Dyer & B. Denise Hawkins, M.A.

Artist Cover and Sketch Design: C. Barry Marron

Book Layout & Design: Jay Kadash

A Second Chance, Inc. can bring a live speaker to your event and offers bulk purchasing of this book for educational, business, and sales promotional use.

A portion of the proceeds from sales of this book will be donated to A Second Chance Charitable Foundation, a Pennsylvania non-profit, public charitable organization which supports kinship care.

Their memories have allowed me to hold on to love...
That love has allowed me to let go and thrive...

My beloved kin...

Hilda R. Baker
LaMont Toliver
Anna Mae Slaughter
Harrison Slaughter
Harriet Slaughter
Farlena Jackson
Harry Jackson, Sr.
Donald Allen
Robert Allen
Shirley Thomas
Beatrice Hampton
Evelyn Bell
Aunt Flossie
Mr. and Mrs. Sherman Knox
Willie Knox
Eva Mae Maxson

*Dedicated staff from A Second Chance, Inc.
and cherished friends...*

Mark Cleveland
Robyn Grover
Angel Manquel
Lynette Durham
Earlene Henderson
Corliss Henderson
Dr. Delorese Ambrose
Joy Dowe
Lennie Nalls
Vashti Moreland
Soror Sandy Stevenson
Soror Charlotta Saylor
Soror Cecilia Felwellen

I dedicate my work to them.

Contents

Acknowledgements

I thank those who are closest to me. Because of them, I was able to not only write my life's story, but thrive in my life's work, and continue to hope. I give honor to my father, sister, daughter, grandson, brothers, foster parents, foster cousins, nieces, nephews, fictive kin, and a host of close friends who have watched me grow up and evolve into the person that I was destined to become.

I especially want to thank my daughter for allowing me to share her with so many. From the age of 3, she shared her mother with those children and families I supported in Allegheny County and now those I advocate for across the nation. Thank you for loving me unconditionally, and for allowing me to grow as a person and as your mom—my most cherished accomplishment and responsibility.

As a professional, I have been fortunate to work with and learn from an amazing group of colleagues. They have embraced the person that I am and have helped to nurture and shape my intellectual curiosity in the field of child welfare.

To my A Second Chance, Inc. family, I want to thank my amazing and supportive Board of Directors, Community Advisory Board, Charitable Foundation Board, and staff. I thank you from the depths of my soul for trusting me to lead you each day. But most of all, thank you for believing in the vision of kinship care, and the hope and opportunity that it brings to the lives of the children and families we touch every day.

I want to thank Marc Cherna at the Allegheny Department of Human Services for his extraordinary vision, leadership, and unwavering support. In addition, special thanks to Dr. Marcia Sturdivant, who until 2013 served as the deputy director at the Allegheny Department of Human Services. I thank Dr. Sturdivant for advancing kinship care across the nation during her tenure at the department.

To my Casey Family, I thank you for the opportunity to see HOPE in action. Because of its dedicated trustees, the CEO, executive team, and staff, "20/20: Building Communities of Hope" is transforming the child welfare narrative in the U.S.

To my Black Administrators in Child Welfare family, thank you for daring to dream of a day when African-American children will be the few, not the many in our systems of care. I thank you for your national leadership as we seek to educate, reform, and eradicate the structures that harm. To my Jim Casey family, thank you for your vision of a world where 18 is not the magic age when adult life begins for our young people in care. Along the way, you have helped all of us in child welfare understand that the transition for these young adults is a lifelong process that includes family networks and the quest for a life of love, security, and health.

I am grateful to my professional colleagues who are too many to name. I thank you for embracing me and my journey. So many of you have shaped my thoughts, permitted my banter, and afforded me the space to share my dreams. Thank you all for your love, support, and belief in the vision of family first. In addition, I want to thank my reviewers Tony, Mary, Cheryl and Bryan. Your care for every period, thought, and idea further enhanced this work. I also want to thank my amazing book team: Denise, B. Denise, Erv, Jay, and Dani. My life was positively interrupted by your friendship, brilliance, care, love, support, confidence, confidentiality, wisdom, skilled knowledge, command of the written word, and your sensitivity. Thank you for being there with me the day that I found out that my 48-year-old brother died of a massive heart attack while at work. As we sat in my conference room writing the pages of this book, the unexpected gave way to a new perspective of how fragile life is and how we must cherish the people we are blessed to have with us each day. In addition, you also provided new meaning to transparency. Through necessity, I opened my entire heart and life to the each of you, and you treated the baring of my soul with such grace, dignity, and respect. For this, I thank you all.

And finally, I want to thank Doug Nelson, former president and CEO of the Annie E. Casey Foundation. With the generous support of the Foundation and matching funds from A Second Chance, Inc. Charitable Foundation, the ideas that bandied about in my head found their way into a book. I thank both Foundations for believing in a girl, now woman, who had a story to tell so that others could dare to dream and dare to find the season where their hope is blossoming.

Foreword

When A Second Chance, Inc. (ASCI) was just a dream in motion, I was by my sister's side. As ASCI moved from a plan on paper to a program for making fragile children and fractured families whole, I was there, too. The best way that I could support Sharon then was to help care for her young daughter, my niece, while my sister guided the child welfare agency into being in 1994. Today, Sharon is the agency's CEO and I am the vice president of Employee Relations and Operations at ASCI.

But long before we acquired these titles, Sharon and I were products of the system that she now works to repair. Looking back, we were among the fortunate ones. Throughout our childhood journey, we did not land in foster care, the place where so many languish without ever really finding families and forever homes. Instead, the state allowed us to be placed in kinship foster care with people who were like family. When there were no blood relatives to care for us, those who knew us and were like kin, stepped in, opened their homes and hearts, and welcomed us. To us they were like family who loved us no less.

My education about the child welfare field, kinship care, and the sacrificial service Sharon provides, came first from volunteering at the agency, and then from observing Sharon in action. It all paid off when I joined the ASCI staff. I tried to learn everything that I could about the programs, services, and supports that are so critical to the well-being of families, especially those who were just like mine when I was growing up.

Today, I continue to volunteer and learn about our unique approach to serving families in kinship foster care because I know we positively affect clients and influence the field. The past 19 years with ASCI have been a joy and, working alongside my sister, a blessing. Still, I am amazed at all that Sharon has accomplished and I marvel at the shrewd and smart businesswoman that she is. Seeing the young sister whom I helped raise, now as a CEO, is a source of pride. In that role, Sharon is fair but tough and unrelenting when it comes to ensuring the safety and well-being of both her staff and our clients.

While I am thrilled to know that through her book more people will get to know Sharon, an amazing child welfare expert, industry leader, and kinship care advocate, I was scared and reluctant when I thought about a memoir that laid bare her beginnings. I wanted to shield and protect her. Maybe even change her mind. I wondered whether she was ready to cope with the curiosity, or be able to weather the flood of emotions that are sure to come once the layers of her life, my life, and our family's lives are peeled back to read. Although just two years older, I willingly and intuitively served as her protector, confidante, and shepherd from the time that we both became girls without a mother in our lives.

Memories of my mom are fleeting now and all but dried up, but even as a young girl, what I saw, what I heard, and what I smelled of her was just enough to inspire and teach me to step into her big shoes when she died young. I remember caring for my baby doll at the same time that my mom was lovingly tending to my baby brother and little sister. I would mimic Mom's moves – cuddling my baby doll, brushing her mop of hair, and carefully placing a small plastic bottle to her lips. This must be the way that my instinct to nurture Sharon began when she and I often found ourselves alone and, at times, in the dark. When my mom died and left a hole in our lives, I didn't know any other way to respond but by us holding on to each other and by loving my sister deeply.

I'm a private person. Over the years that has meant keeping the difficult and personal experiences of my siblings tucked into the past, or only brought to light sparingly. Looking back, I couldn't let people know that my dad didn't take care of us like our mom once did. And I couldn't let them know that our father kept little food in the house, or that his hugs, kisses, and smiles were too scarce to make two little girls feel comfortable or secure. Barely 23, Dad was unprepared to work all day and then try to care for two needy toddlers. But when he needed help and turned to the child welfare system for support for his family, it never came. At the same time, strangers were peering inside our lives, leaving nothing that helped us to thrive. I believe that if they did grasp the reality of a young single male parent in peril or heard my Dad's cry for aid and guidance, the lives of his children and our family would have turned out differently. Perhaps my sister would not have been taken away to a children's home when she was just 12 and my life would not have been turned upside down when all I knew then was that my Sharon was gone. I didn't know where. And perhaps Dad would have been a part of our growing up.

Dad's girls were close. We even dressed alike. Once, when we had no clean socks to wear to school, we decided to put on some that belonged to Dad. After getting dressed, we pulled his trouser socks up on our legs as far as they would stretch. When we were done, you couldn't tell us that we weren't styling. It would have been easy to play the victim in our circumstances, but we didn't. Somehow, even with no proof, we always believed that everything was going to turn out all right. Maybe, that's because Sharon and I found God early. We knew, even then, that He was our protector in all things. God still is. In each other, we also found faith and courage.

This is my sister's testimony. Sharon's story is all about the circumstances that forced us into a dysfunctional child welfare system, one that wasn't attuned to kinship care, or equipped with strategies or practices to help family care for family or the extended relationships of those who were like kin. It is all about her efforts to make sure it doesn't happen to other children and families.

—Rhonda Wright

*Sharon L. McDaniel's Sister and Vice President for Operations
and Employee Relations, A Second Chance, Inc.*

Author's Note

It took half a century, but it was time to write the story of my encounters with kinship care, an emerging practice that falls under the foster care umbrella. Kinship care means taking care of someone as if they were kin, whether they are related by blood or not. It is what happens when the village takes care of its children. It was kinship care that helped save and shape my life. My story explores kinship care in the context of race, culture, and community. When I was growing up in the system, kinship care, as it is practiced today, was not formally recognized by those in the child welfare institutions as an alternative and viable form of care. And unlike some familiar stories of those who have emerged from the child welfare system, mine is not a tale of horror and unrelenting despair, or abuse. Rather, it is a story of commitment, tolerance, emotional connections, and sacrifice. It is a story of what can happen when a caring adult, who may not be related, makes a decision to care for and raise a child who is not their own. That child was me. It is a story of choice and an examination of how a decision to provide "kinship care" can and should be supported by larger social systems and institutions.

In telling this story, I chiefly call upon my memories of the people, events, and places that influenced my journey. When my recollections were scarce and incomplete — or for the events that happened when I was a toddler — I turned to my father and a maternal uncle who, through informal interviews, provided some glimpses into my past. But

I write about my journey through kinship care and the emotions that came with it. These pages reflect my odyssey — my mother's death, my entry into others people's homes, my college days, and the milestones of my professional career. A recounting of all these years is again drawn from my memory.

My father is simply referred to as Dad to protect his privacy. In other instances, I have changed the names and identifying details for some individuals or provided only first names to also protect their privacy. The locations of the places where I lived when I entered the child welfare system and kinship care are as I remember them. That includes McIntyre, the co-ed, state-run shelter where I was placed for six months. The facility is now defunct.

During the two years I spent in reflection, the memory of some events came flooding back. One of them was my reunion with my brother on a street corner in a Pittsburgh suburb. But other faded moments have been stitched together from conversations with friends, colleagues, and from what I found sifting through personal and government records. My goal with this book project has been both to evoke and provoke. I want people to understand what it feels like to search for belonging. And, at the same time, I want to rouse conversations about new possibilities and inspire innovative ways to improve the child welfare system.

—Sharon L. McDaniel, MPA, Ed.D.

Prologue

I am an alumni of what is now known as kinship foster care. I lost my mother just months before my third birthday. My father attempted, but was unable to raise us and by the time I was 17 and graduating high school, I had spent time in a group home for girls and lived in nearly a half-dozen homes with families who weren't my own. Some who opened their doors to me were like strangers — chilly and uncaring; others were like family, knitting me into their lives and embracing me in the bosom of their rituals and kinship. With them, I had a chance to grow up healthy and whole. I know now, that what I experienced was the power of kinship care. While mine was a challenging youth, I have emerged from a life interrupted by death, disappointment, and indifference. These things could have depleted me; but instead they became the fuel for my life's work and purpose.

Every day, thousands of children and young adults who were just like me are seeking to find hope as they attempt to survive the child welfare system. I wrote my story as much for me as for them; to be their voice and guide on their path to wholeness. This story of my life — and the lessons it offers — is to let those alumni of care, many still striving to make their way, know that their early years in child welfare didn't relegate them to being simply a case number.

I know that it is important to hear what alumni of care and family participating in the child welfare system have to say. Their messages are clear that a system needs to be responsive to all kinds of families. And, their messages are clear on why it is critical for people to speak out about their encounters and interactions with the system.

I was asked in 2012 to join with members of the bipartisan Congressional Caucus on Foster Youth. The caucus launched national listening tours focused on foster care and child welfare. During forums, I not only heard from those youth and families, but also shared my own story.

Across the nation, extended family members and those who are like family, also called kin, are caring for about 2.7 million through kinship care. And there are those children who are raised in foster care, about 386,000. Of that number, approximately 29,500 children age out or exit the child welfare system each year without finding a permanent home. Some emerge unhealed and lost as a result of their experiences and being abandoned.

We need to hear the voices of these young people and from those caring adults in their lives who stepped up to raise them in kinship care. Doing so can make a difference.

Growing up, I didn't have a voice or someone to speak up for me. Perhaps if someone had spoken up sooner, if someone had listened, my life would have taken a different turn. As an adult, I emerged as a stalwart proponent of kinship care and was invited by Congress and other agencies to inform the nation about the plight of children in the system.

Today, I know and understand the power of hearing these stories, and of listening to these voices. I know the importance of preparing a continuum of care so that new voices can be heard.

We'll always be directly in touch with the "experts"— the people who live in and have survived the system. In many ways they are the real voices of change.

It is a new day.

Alumni of care are emerging from the shadows. For years, I didn't talk about being a little Black girl with an empty belly or the daily cravings for a forever home. The forever homes where I landed were sometimes places of peace, like still waters; they weren't always perfect, but they were safety nets where love and family dwelled. Whenever I had them in my grasp, I fought to keep them.

As a child of the system, I also grappled with what it felt like being a motherless child. I entered the system at age 6, and I became an adult with memories of my mother as barren as the space she left in our lives when she died.

My father tried to hang on to his three children, but he let us go and we slid into foster care and kinship care—other people's homes. The people who raised me were real; they had problems of their own as they sacrificed and cared for me — a young girl who was full of life and worries, hope and despair, resilience and dreams, who had a song on her lips, a penchant for math, and enough will to want to become someone special.

The child welfare system that held me in the 1960s and 1970s was shaped by insensitive research and flawed and dominant cultural values. That system considered some of the families it served as ones that were lacking, different, and diminished. And as a result, it missed countless opportunities to treat children and families like mine with dignity, support, and the respect they needed to thrive and be healthy.

The lives of the young people who languished in that system and were shattered could have been mine. But it was the love I found on my journey, the embrace of people who were like family and kin, the generous grace of God, and my unquenchable faith, that kept me from wallowing in anger or becoming a statistic.

In a conversation I had with my foster grandmother in 2011, it was gratifying to learn that she remembered her "Shannie" as a giver, a girl determined to give back to those in need. I've emerged from the system and from many of life's rough places, and I have learned to cope. Even as teenager in care, I was finding my rhythm and plotting a path that would make me a steward and champion of those who had grown up in the system and those who cared for them.

I've traveled from a child in care, to a child welfare administrator, and now to a provider, educator, and advocate with a big voice. My journey and discovery are shared here in these pages. *"On My Way Home"* is written in three distinct parts.

LIFE

Part One of my book is a memoir of a little girl looking to belong. It's a narrative of what it was like to be in a system where you, your father, and siblings are invisible. It's a recounting of the pain of being taken somewhere and not knowing where you're going, the heartache of migrating through families and spaces in search of a home, and an understanding of the road I traveled to healing and advocacy.

WORK AND HOPE

Part Two details the fruit of my early professional experience. It is a profile of the genesis of A Second Chance Inc., my kinship foster care agency headquartered in Pittsburgh, Pa. Since 1994, the agency has been working to meet the unique needs of kinship care families and continues to be the only provider of its kind. It explores my collaborations with philanthropic organizations, the formation of my agency's policies toward community, staff, and how we work to keep families intact and children safe. I will share how we work to broker second chances for children and families. I will also discuss how my model helps shape national policy that benefits caregivers and elevates kinship care.

MAKING THE CASE

Part Three offers reflections for progressive change. I believe there must be lasting changes for children and communities, but how far have we come? With a focus on the field, I provide reflections. And national thought leaders, scholars, practitioners, and researchers discuss and offer recommendations for how policy, philanthropy, advocacy, and innovation can elicit those needed changes in child welfare.

Part One

Life

Someone was hurt before you, wronged before you, hungry before you,

frightened before you, beaten before you, humiliated before you, raped before you...

yet, someone survived... You can do anything you choose to do.

—Maya Angelou

ONE
The Beginning

Experiencing Loss

It is spring 1963, and Coraopolis, Pa., is in bloom.

My father doesn't notice the flowers in the front yard or even his two little children, although we are right in front of him, wandering and in need of consoling. The stately brick house that he grew up in, about an hour's drive from downtown Pittsburgh, was filled with our laughter and life. Then one day, our house stood quiet, swathed in emptiness, uninterrupted.

Inside the house, Dad is reeling. He spends his days sitting and staring, sometimes motionless, or rattling through each room like a trapped wind looking for a crevice to escape. That's what death can do when it hits home in the middle of the night. It came to our house on May 15, 1963, that year, and managed to settle in the heart and mind of a former Air Force serviceman, erasing his slow smile and easy-going ways. My dad had been well-trained in reconnaissance, and just five years earlier, he emerged strong from the service before returning home to Coraopolis and to us.

He loved my mother, and had come to her with a past that was littered with women who loved him. I don't think there was a time when women didn't love my father. As a teenager, his shiny cars were his first calling cards. His ride symbolized everything about his zeal for life that he couldn't articulate. When he was 15, the grandfather who gifted him those first set of wheels saw it coming, and decided to make his grandson wait until he was almost 16. He was thinking that giving him another year would help my dad to mature into a more responsible driver and not just be a show-off with the car. As my dad tells it, the girls flocked to him anyway. For them, just knowing that he had a car made their attraction even sweeter.

He was the Harry Belafonte of Coraopolis with his warm caramel skin and small Afro. He was smart, handsome, and he could even sing.

While in the service, Dad traveled to far-off places that were only names on the pages of an encyclopedia for his family. His world was both full and limited; he was a Black man going to exotic ports, but making sergeant was as high as he could climb in the Air Force ranks. Still, after his tour of duty, he came back with his small-town ways still intact. Sharp and adept at deciphering secret enemy code during the Vietnam War, Dad could seemingly do anything; except he didn't know how to prepare a hot meal or feed the hungry stomachs of his 2-year-old and 4-year-old girls.

Just months away from his 23rd birthday, my Dad was already a widower with a fresh hole in his heart where love used to be. He was coming undone, but he had us, his babies, to care for. All that we wanted from him at the time was love and to open up the refrigerator and find more than just frozen shrimp cocktail, metal shelves where bread, meat, and eggs should have been, and a light bulb.

Before she died, his wife cared for the children and kept the house. Now dad was a rudderless single parent in the 1960s in need of rescuing and a safety net, and he wasn't alone. The child welfare system and social services in Allegheny County, like in most metropolitan areas across the nation, were accustomed to seeing plenty of single mothers whose cupboards were bare, but very few knew how to assist the male clients among their rolls. Nonetheless, here Dad was, looking to a system that didn't know what to do with him or for him. He was not equipped for raising his children, especially after the devastating loss of his young bride. Most of the time he was offered a few referrals to the local church down the street, the Salvation Army, or to the Rescue Mission.

But his children needed more. Some days there was nothing at all to see inside our big white refrigerator but space. To little children, that white box stood like a silent, empty sentry in the kitchen.

For too many days and nights, shrimp cocktail was our supper. Most of the other food we got seemed to come when we cried hungry. It was like a signal that it was time for my father to go to the grocery store. The lack we found in the cabinets didn't give him a clue. Our crying though, seemed to get his attention, but he never rushed out in search of food. Even when he got to the grocery store, Dad wasn't sure what to buy. Was it going to be more of the shrimp cocktail he apparently liked or some corn flakes and milk? But by now, dad was spending more of his time drunk and drinking than eating.

My father's grandparents spoiled him, grooming him for a pampered life, not one where he would have to fend for himself. My father didn't have a clue about running a household and there wasn't anyone left in his life who could help him find one. Over the course of several years, in the early 1960s, since he had become a widower and single parent, his family support network was all but gone and there was no one to stand in the gap now that he was the sole parent to his children. There were no big shoes that could step in and guide a young man with two little girl children. Dad was on his own and, in many ways, my sister and I were too.

The essentials like food, furnishings, and the comforts of home, ribbons and dolls, bedtime stories, or even hugs and games, were the least of his concerns during these days, even if they were for his children. He was a young man consumed by a torrent of grief. Within a nine-month period, it had begun to wash over him. Like a tsunami, death extracted from his life those he loved and those who loved him. In June 1962, his grandfather was the first to die. His grandmother died seven months later in January 1963. It was a cruel blow, because from the time that my Dad was an infant, his grandparents had raised him as their own. The most piercing loss came within two months of his grandmother's death. His bride was gone, too. She died at 22.

Together, their deaths left dad emotionally incapacitated, adrift, and fearful of forging lasting relationships with people, especially with the women in his life. He was convinced that as soon as he got close to a woman, she would abruptly end up dying on him, too. So, he just let them come and go, passing through his life like a sieve.

While the wave of death that swept his loved ones away was receding, the ones left behind—our fragile young family—were bowing and fraying under the weight of all that grief, longing, and loss. "My mind was messed up. I was crazy. It was like I was in a daze," my father recalls. It's been five decades, but even now, my dad talks to me about the images of his dying wife on the last night of her life and how they haunted him for so long. Dad says that's also when he began drinking heavily. After all, a little liquor, some said, could put a throbbing toothache to rest or even break up the most deep-seated chest cold. So, surely, dad thought that a lot of alcohol could cure anything, right? But for him, the liquor only dulled the pain of his losses and the burdens that were his children and even his own life.

She Was My Mother

There were many women in my Dad's life who came and went over the years; I remember them even as I was growing up. Some of them came to live with us for a little while, but after my own mom died, he never remarried.

Mom was a small-framed girl with cocoa skin who caught my father's eye one Saturday night in the late 1950s. She was just standing there looking cute and holding up the wall with her girlfriends when a nice-looking boy with pretty teeth and his hair cut close spotted her at the Diamond Roller Rink on Market Street in downtown Pittsburgh.

The rink and all of the action a teenager needed could be found on the top floor of Diamond Market, a self-contained shopping and dining extravaganza.

As a 16-year-old, Dad wasn't as outgoing as some of the city boys. Life was smaller, slower, and a little more country in Coraopolis where he came from, but he was nevertheless becoming a lady's man. There were plenty of pretty teen girls with shiny fresh-done curls and swept-up hair streaming into the rink that night from all over the county. But the young lady whom he approached that evening had a first hello that he remembered. It was quiet, soft, and sweet, just like she was at 16. Before the evening was over, the two shared an Orange Crush, a silly grin, and bopped around the rink, spinning their wheels to Big Joe Turner's "Shake, Rattle and Roll." He left the Diamond with mom's telephone number on a sheet of paper in his pocket, her name in his head, and a promise to win her heart.

My mom was the baby of the family and her father's little gem. She was shaped by a life of hardship, but one softened and made richer and sweeter by family love and devotion.

Her mother, Emily Allen, cleaned the house of rich folks including one of an Italian family in Allegheny County. Over the years, her health paid dearly for the domestic work that she did. A life of perpetual striving took its toll.

She was often laden down with shopping bags brimming, usually with left over loaves of bread, a few cuts of meat, fresh eggs and milk, food her employer gave her. The day after one of their parties would also yield a bounty, usually fancy things and treats. The older Allen boys would make their way to the corner to wait for their mother, ready to give her relief as the public bus rounded the corner to deliver her back to her family. The boys watched their mother ease her tired legs down the steps of the bus, then looked forward to the smile and the hugs that she was never too tired to give. A heart attack while at work eventually ended their mother's life.

Emily Allen, my grandmother, was well into her 40s, and my grandfather, Martin Allen, was even older when my mother was born. He was a sunup-to-sundown laborer and contractor who probably laid the foundation for many of the sidewalks in Homewood, which in the 1930 and '40s was a vibrant and largely Italian Pittsburgh community.

Watching his youngest grow, my grandfather knew that his little girl would likely be his last before he died. Her brother, the youngest boy in the family, was born six years earlier. Their bond, my uncle tells me, was like a ring; it encircled them when they were children and remained unbroken as she grew up and married, and he went off to war.

Martin Allen loved all of his children, but he adored Joyce, his youngest. In 1941 when his little girl was born and in the decades that came before, he never had much except love to give his children. But he knew that his family of 10 was what made his life rich.

My mom was 12 when her mother died after living just 54 years. What her mother's weak heart wanted most to know before she passed away was that some of her oldest children would step in to finish raising their youngest sister. Barbara was among the oldest children who did just that. Together with their father, her children made sure that a young girl remembered her mother's loving ways and stayed in school. She was a good student at Schenley High, a premier school in the North Oakland neighborhood of Pittsburgh, earning mostly A's and B's in her subjects before graduating. But college wasn't in her future. Her father thought that higher education was a privilege only meant for those who could afford it. Life for this family had always meant making it. And making it had always meant working from one day to the next, keeping a roof over your head, keeping your family fed, and finding sweet relief whenever you could.

By the time my mom turned 16, most of her nine brothers and sisters were already grown and out of the house or dead. Most of them died as children and teens. Three of them later succumbed to heart conditions, another from a childhood illness, and another from pneumonia, one of the unfortunate complications that comes with poverty: misery begets misery. The sky brought with it a cold deluge the night that my mother's family was evicted from their home. My uncle—her brother—was about 5 when he stood there in the pelting rain with his young brothers and sister, and parents, watching everything that they owned turn sopping wet. The rain and cold seeped into my uncle's lungs and he died. The house they rented and were evicted from didn't even cost a lot, my uncle tells me, but "When you were as poor as we were back then, even a little was a lot to pay."

Just Say 'I Do'

At 16, my mom was easing into life, striking out on her own like the rest of her siblings. Her new life included the young man whom she met at the Diamond Roller Skating Rink one weekend. They dated for about a year before he enlisted in the Air Force and was shipped off for training in Biloxi, Miss. The Army was filling its enlisted ranks with Black men in those days, but the Air Force came calling for Dad; they gave him an aptitude test. It told them that he was smart. Then, it wasn't long before they gave him a security clearance, something not many Blacks had in the military, and taught him how to intercept enemy communication using radio code during the Vietnam War. His first deployment was to Osan Air Force Base in South Korea.

A wide ocean divided two young people in love. It would be about 13 months before he saved up enough money to return stateside to see his girlfriend again. So, while my father, the serviceman remained far, far away, my mom reignited an old flame with another lover and they were getting closer.

By the time Dad returned home on leave, the young woman he left behind had become a new mother at 19. The baby girl was my older sister. My mom's former boyfriend, who was in his early 20s, was the father of her child. He seemed to care for her, but who knows why he didn't stay around. Thinking back on that homecoming, Dad remembers the news Mom shared about her baby and the other man, and somehow determined that it just didn't matter. Dad thought that he could live with it all. He was still in love with my mom and was ready to propose.

Straightforward and simple were Dad's words. He remembers it this way: "I love you and things happen. So, what do you want to do now, get married?"

"Yes." The 19-year-olds, now a family with an infant, headed to the justice of the peace where they said their vows before my dad returned to the San Antonio base where he was stationed. Within days, he would be shipping out again for an 18-month deployment, this time to the Philippines. And when Dad returned home, this time on leave, I was the baby that he and Mom conceived.

A Time of Love and Loss: 1963

Keeping two active children both under the age of 5, corralled, quiet, fed, changed, cleaned, and happy every day wasn't easy for a 21-year-old who sometimes wanted nothing more than to leave her babies in their playpen while she window shopped at some department store in the city or just headed out, anywhere, with her girlfriends where she could again feel young and carefree. She had her third, a boy, in March 1963. Our family was living in Coraopolis, in the home where my dad grew up. His grandparents left it to him when they died. Trying to keep up with her children, and with her housework, sometimes seemed never ending. It was a good day if mom was able to stop and have a sandwich and a Tab soda or stick a couple of curls in her undone hair while her children napped.

But when night fell and her three babies were asleep, there was still work to do. It was her quiet time. On this evening, there were dishes in the sink to conquer and laundry left to wash and fold. She even managed to squeeze in some girl talk on the telephone and make her grocery list for Saturday.

Usually her days were busy and filled, but evenings at home alone seemed to drag on like a persistent yawn until her husband arrived around 9:30 at night. Mom always waited up for Dad. She had about two more hours to go this evening before he would be coming through the door tired or ready for a little loving.

He didn't want much to eat, so she decided on some leftover potatoes and a couple of fried eggs. While the big yellow yolks crackled in the hot oil, he waited and relaxed. It didn't take long for her eggs to sizzle up and glide off the seasoned skillet and for the fried potatoes to tumble easily on to two waiting plates.

Even after they left the kitchen, turned off the lights, and headed up to bed, the smell of fried food and Crisco hung in the air.

In the Midnight Hour

My mom was awakened by the telephone ringing. Her stomach was full. Fresh from a bad dream about my mother, my aunt was calling and wanted to know if her little sister was all right? It didn't matter to my aunt that it was 1 a.m. But as Mom tried to sit up in her bed, she gasped then began to choke, bringing up her last meal.

My dad remembers she had convulsions before she fell silent. He was on his feet, now. Dad shook, patted, called her name, but couldn't rouse her. That's when my father called his brother-in-law, unleashing panic and confusion that rippled through the phone line and ended up across town. By now, three of my Mom's siblings had been jolted out of their sleep, and one by one, they stumbled into the night, racing to see what was wrong with their baby sister, my mom.

The police arrived ahead of them and then the dreaded "Black Mariah" was dispatched. It was the old familiar black wagon resembling an ice cream truck that showed up at homes to ferry away the dead and the dying in those days. By the time my Mom's siblings arrived at our house, the men who were driving the "Black Mariah" were already taking my mother down the stairs in a black body bag.

On May 15, 1963, my Mom and Dad made love the night she died. She went to sleep, but never greeted the day, her husband, or her two girls and boy.

A police investigation into my mother's death followed. When they arrived, the authorities saw a young mother lying there as if sleeping. She was still shrouded in her now soiled night clothes.

The time of her death was sometime after 1 a.m. and before the break of dawn. The fried eggs and white potatoes she served before going to bed are what probably triggered the acute indigestion and gastroenteritis. The coroner's report said that's what likely ended her life. My mother was now dead after suffocating on her bile.

Barely a year after Mom had given birth to her baby boy, she lay buried in Restland Cemetery in Monroeville, Pa. No one had life insurance to cover the cost of a proper funeral and burial, but the family "got a break" on what my uncle called "an all-inclusive package." The owner of the Douglas Funeral Home knew the family and took what my uncle could pay—$600.00. For that amount, the cost of the embalming, preparing the body for viewing, the funeral service, and the burial would be covered. Those few hundred dollars were dear, but so was my uncle's youngest sister. The money was all that he had managed to save from his time in the service. My father's mother helped him plan his wife's funeral arrangements.

I was 2½ when my mother died, my sister was going on 4, and my brother was just 1. Before my sister and I could get to know him, he was gone. On the day of my mother's funeral, one of my mother's sisters wrapped him up and took our brother to live with her in the Homewood section of Pittsburgh. It was best, she told my father. *A woman needs to raise the baby; you can't do that by yourself.* And, just like that, my brother was gone. Those who gathered for the home-going service to celebrate my mother's young life were the people who were important to her. They were her brothers and sisters, a frail father, and her husband. Laid out in a modest casket in the front of the church was a petite woman who looked like she had drifted into sleep.

On the day of my mother's funeral, my sister and I didn't attend the home-going service or the burial. Funerals, the elders in our family said, were no place for young children, even when the person lying in the casket is their mother. "They wouldn't understand," whispered my elderly aunt. *They wouldn't understand. The experience would be too traumatic for little ones. They'd have nightmares and be haunted by them.*

What scared my sister and me more that day were the curious stares we received as we sat atop a hard brown piano bench during the repast. I think my family members sat us there to greet the guests. The adults, just back from the burial, flowed through what I remember as being a dimly lit home with dark walls, and filled with people and sadness.

More whispers from the adults filled the room. *They're the little girls whose mother passed away. Um, um, um! How sad.*

I wonder what's going to become of them now that their mother is gone to be with the Lord?

Who's going to take care of them?

Who would want to raise three children, all under the age of five, by themselves?

Where will they live?

And I'm sure, too, that their tongues wagged as they stood around the punch and cake table and that their inside voices spilled out on to the wraparound porch when they talked about the circumstances surrounding my mother's untimely and seemingly curious demise. While the attention that day was probably on my mom's sudden passing, I'm sure that there were those who either blamed my dad somehow for her death or were, at the same time, saddened for his loss and that of his little children.

But she was so young. She was healthy, wasn't she? She had babies still in diapers to tend to.

We weren't artwork, but that didn't stop anyone from staring and shaking their heads and pointing their fingers in pity and disbelief at my sister and me as we sat with our smooth clean faces, and legs and arms shined up with Vaseline. I didn't understand why we were there or where we were. And where was my mother?

Not Even a Memory

I'm 52 years old now. I have no memories of my mother. I can't claim a relationship with her. She is a stranger.

How can I piece together my life without knowing her story?

The story of my birth on December 19, 1961, in Pittsburgh until I turned 3 lies in a grave with my mother. Sometimes a few details of my early life tumble from my father's mind in a quiet voice. My 79-year-old uncle also holds some of those fragments, and has graciously shared them with me. I drink in the smallest detail.

He is my mother's only living sibling. She had nine brothers and sisters—John, James, Elizabeth, Donald, Inez, Barbara, Robert, Richard, Carl. My mother was named Joyce, and my uncle Carl is the only thread that I have that links me to her school days, her quiet ways, her coming of age in her father's house, her independence.

My mother's family history was born on fertile farmland in rural Culpeper, Va. And like a ribbon, it flowed from there to a spare home brimming with love, children, and hard times on the outskirts of Pittsburgh. It is that history that is my uncle's gift to his kin—remembering. He records birthdates with precision, sorts through the facts, rescues the names and the disparate dates and places from vanishing; that's when the Allen family history assembles. It's clear when I talk to him on the phone about family and my quest, that my uncle's heart still holds a precious piece of his little sister's memory—my mother—and there's just enough left over to share with me, his niece.

I was a toddler and my mother was young when she died in May, taking a part of me with her. It was that part of her little girl who smelled baby sweet and who remembers when my first tooth pressed forth and how I wore a grin most mornings when she entered the room, ready to scoop me up. I was her middle child, Sharon. My father's nickname for me was Shannie. Most everyone in the family called me that. And they still do.

Growing up, I didn't have family surrounding me to share these familiar oral accounts or even photographs of who I was, and who she was, and who we were together. Even now, I can't think of what I would have needed or wanted to ask them to share about the mother I was too young to know.

Sure, there are plenty of things that I probably should have been asking about her all of these years: how she walked and talked, what it was like being the youngest child in her big family, or what things would make her want to stop, put her hands on her hips, and have "a moment" when somebody got on her last nerve. But really, there are only two things that compel my curiosity about her: I want to know (and see) am I built like her, curvy hips and all, and do our faces, eyes, and high cheek bones bear a close resemblance?

I've been asked so many times, do you miss her or what do you miss most about your mother? It's probably because those same well-meaning and curious people can't imagine a time when they didn't know their mothers. Even if their mother is deceased, they can still remember the words that she spoke to them, that special look in her eyes, and the smell of her homemade sweet potato pies baking on Thanksgiving Day. When they remember, they have a starting place. They have a mother to recall, a context, a touch, a smell, a voice, a face, a memory.

I wish that I could tell them something, anything about what I have missed the most about my mom. If I could, perhaps I would say it's the way she parted her bangs across her forehead, or how she smelled like springtime after dabbing her favorite perfume on her wrists and in the crease of her bosom, that it's the funny pet names she gave to us children, or how she cared so lovingly for her family.

But I can't. No matter how hard I wish, those memories of her won't kick in to override the years that have elapsed or buffer the void that her death left or paint pictures of the woman who gave birth to me six days before Christmas. When I think about the absence of memories, I'm also reminded of the late Ray Charles, not so much for his music, which I love, but for what he possessed and what I still don't. The Ray Charles we knew was blind, but as a boy he had sight. Behind his dark shades, Ray could still remember what his eyes could no longer see—bright green snap peas sitting on the porch in a chipped white porcelain bowl, just-washed cotton dresses and pants waving on the line, a yellow ball of sun rising across blue southern skies, and his mother's brown tired hands with earth in their creases. I can only share what I thought I saw in my mind's eye and what I thought I remembered about a brief encounter with my mom and baby brother, father and sister, and the day that we were a family.

Like a Polaroid, it appeared in my adult mind. I'm not even sure when it came to me, but there was an image that remained lodged in my head. And before long, it became a little vignette that I would tell about my mother and family. I carried it around for years and held it close like a treasured charm that you keep in your pocket, ready to share with anyone who is willing to listen and look to see what you see. Telling it and retelling it over the years, I think that maybe it served as an affirmation—yes, my mother was real even if I didn't remember her.

I was about 2. We were all together—Dad, my sister, my mother, my baby brother, and me. We were a family. It was a sunny but cold day outside when the five of us left the house, bundled up in winter coats. My mother held my hand and her other arm cradled my baby brother. My sister, who was about 4, walked ahead on her own, not holding my parents' hands. She was a big girl, she thought. We all loaded into a small white car. I don't know where we were headed that day.

Inside, there was space enough for all of us. We were comfortable. My father was perched behind the steering wheel, one hand gripping it, and I sat behind him as he steered the car down the street and then across town. My mother was in the front seat holding the baby. This was long before the use of seatbelts and rear-facing baby car seats became mandatory; I laugh and interject when I tell this part of the story. *My sister sat behind my mother in the back seat with me.*

THAT'S IT. That's how my story goes and ends. All of these years, I thought that it was real and true, but the details, I learned, were all wrong. And in an instant, my story, my images had come undone.

Now my dad tries, but he can't remember where we were all going that day, but the car he was driving sticks out in his mind. "It was a jacked-up Ford," he says of that white car he drove. Yes, the family piled into the car, but the vague image I've had of the woman holding my hand was actually my father's girlfriend with their newborn son, not my mom and baby brother.

"I never owned a car when I was married to your mother," my dad revealed when I interviewed him for this book on my life.

For so many years, that image of our family together—mother, sister, brother, and father, traveling on that sunny day, belonged to me. Now I don't even have that.

Living Without Mom: 1965

There's just one more memory that I have held on to and sometimes share. Like the other one, it too, is fleeting. It connects me, though, to my family. It also reminds me of the family secrets that set my father and ultimately our family on a meandering path to dysfunction.

This image and memory begins on Christmas Day back in 1965.

My father, sister, and I were living on the North Side of Pittsburgh, in a home that was sparse and motherless. A white couch sat in the living room; it was the first room that you got to once inside the front door. A small kitchen table with a few chairs around it sat in the pale-green kitchen. The rooms were spacious and the homes were lovely on the North Side neighborhood where mostly hardworking families lived, struggling to make ends meet. Our family seemed to rattle about those rooms with little in them. Our beds were mattresses on wooden floors. My sister and I shared one in our room and my father had his own room.

My paternal grandmother, Hilda Baker, stood at our front door with Christmas presents pressing her arms wide. She had come from Washington, D.C., about five hours away by car. The gift-wrapped boxes were for my sister and me. It had been a year and a half since my mother died and since we saw my father's mother, but there she was, a short elegant lady wearing a look of concern and a stately camel-haired coat.

Even as we sat surrounded by shiny wrapping paper and boxes, I wished that day that my little brother could have been there with us. It comforted me to believe that like us, he had gifts and toys and was also enjoying Christmas that year in 1965 at his new home with our Aunt Inez, my mother's oldest living sister. But still he wasn't with us. I wanted so much to see him and would ask about him constantly. He was just

15 months younger than me and I know that if life and circumstances had given us a chance to be together, my brother and I would have been the best of playmates and maybe even the best of friends growing up. And I know that I would have been a good big sister.

Because of my grandmother, Christmas came to our house in 1965 when I was 4, but so did discord and disappointment, which were brewing in the room, down the hall. They told my sister and me that they were going to have a conversation, but my dad and grandmother were going at each other on this Holy day and the subject was his children. Their welfare was at stake and my dad was to blame. My grandmother's words and his words erupted out of the backroom where they were meeting — *Taking care. Raising those children. They're mine. Home.* Why. Dad, my grandmother said, wasn't doing things right since his wife died; my grandmother admonished him.

If my grandmother had her way on that Christmas Day, she would have convinced my dad that she should take custody of my siblings and me, raising us in Washington, D.C., where she was a high-level executive secretary in the federal government and lived well in the nation's capital with her husband, a military officer. But on that day, after the gifts and the words were doled out, my grandmother vanished from our home and our lives. It would be years before we heard from her again.

I learned that my grandmother first approached my dad about her desire to be the caretaker for his children following my mother's funeral. But before my dad could tell her no, my grandmother's husband did. He was not my dad's birth father and didn't share my grandmother's desire to bring three small children into their lives at Fourth and Taylor Streets, a comfortable home on a corner lot, in a middle-class section of Northwest Washington, D.C. Her husband was adamant. And so was my dad. My father told my grandmother that he didn't want his young daughters separated. Somehow, he recognized then that his girls needed each other.

The notion of bringing her grandchildren to live with her in Washington was what eventually drove a wedge through her marriage; my grandmother confided this when I visited her as an adult. Once divorced, my grandmother reached out again to my father, this time, about wanting to take only me to raise. By then, she knew that my brother and I were her only biological grandchildren, not my older sister. Again, my father said no to what he imagined would be an unfortunate separation, even though he struggled daily to hold on to us under his roof.

It wasn't until I was 10 and my sister was 12 that we first learned the truth about our fathers.

A Father's Past

Love and adoration welcomed my dad from the day he was born, but secrets and betrayal followed him.

When my grandmother Hilda gave birth at age 19 to her bouncing baby boy in 1941, he quickly became the son that her father and step mother never had but desperately wanted. But unfortunately, my grandmother became an outcast. Getting pregnant out of wedlock was nothing but a disgrace. And for my grandmother's people, being proper and good was utmost. Much of this I know because my grandmother chronicled it in the unlined handwritten pages of her memoir that I later found and read.

After all, her people were somebody. They had jobs and money to buy things and comfort. Feeling pressured to maintain their image, the family decided to hide my grandmother's pregnancy. It was the next best thing. And it's what many Black families would have done, too, whether they were well off or not. My grandmother described getting pregnant young and being unmarried as the worse form of family betrayal that could have beset her clan.

As they believed, the family name and image had to be protected. For my grandmother's parents, that meant raising their daughter's son—my dad—as their own.

Since his birth, my dad grew up believing that his grandparents were really his parents and that his biological mother was actually his sister. And as "siblings," my father and the woman he thought was his sister never developed deeper bonds. They only lived for a short time in the same household and because the true circumstances of their relationship were hidden away, and because she was 19 years older and traveling in different circles, a gulf developed between them.

When I discovered my grandmother's memoir some years ago, a young women's despair and sense of shame poured out. My heart ached for her. Grandmother wrote about regret. Not being born a boy, she said, was reason enough for her not to be liked while growing up. Absent from her writing, however, were any references that she had of the woman who gave her life. She never knew her. Like my own mother, my grandmother's mom died not long after she was born. When her father remarried, he and his wife raised my grandmother. Things didn't get much better for her. Embedded in her story is my own. The same parallel history, a generation forward.

On most days, it seemed, my grandmother wanted nothing more than to change schools, flee her family, her home, and life as she knew it in Coraopolis; never to return if it meant escaping the treatment she received at the hand of her stepmother. But instead of running away from the life that she had, she stayed put, and rushed into the arms of trouble—a neighborhood boy who would father her son.

My grandmother never spoke of that young man, my father's dad, and I never asked her about him when I grew up and we talked. I guess that I wanted to spare her from dredging up memories of a rocky past and some of the pain that came with it.

Sadly, I lost my grandmother's memoir during a move to a new home, but still hold on to the gift and memory that she gave me by chronicling her young life.

Since Grandmother Hilda had had my dad so young, and much of her early life was thrown out of order, she spent years tidying up her choices, taking pride in being a model of respectability and determination. Her manner was prim and her speech was proper. She had spent decades proving herself, and it paid off. She had become somebody.

Even as a lively 72-year-old graduate student in English at the University of the District of Columbia, my grandmother was still striving to learn, and achieve, and reach back. On campus she tutored and used her time with students to prod and mentor them about the importance of speaking well and clearly. She wanted my dad to do better and if he couldn't she certainly believed that she could.

It wasn't until I was an adult that I really got to know my grandmother and admire her sophistication, strength, and style, some of the things that made her special to me.

The Price of Steel: On Being Black

In the 1920s and '30s, my father's family was considered prominent. A coveted job in a Pittsburgh steel mill helped give them the means to create a stable, comfortable life.

After World War II, the mills became a magnet for Black men. A great tide of Southern Blacks washed into Western Pennsylvania and other points north for a chance and for a way out of poverty. But for Blacks like my great-grandfather, Fred Lee, these jobs came with good pay and heart-breaking discrimination.

The money my great-grandfather made in the steel mill made him upwardly mobile. It also bought his family a home, some peace and quiet in a nice neighborhood, and a tip-top, second-hand powder blue and white 1955 Ford Crown Victoria for his grandson.

The brutal work of the steel mill also gave the family new aspirations. Steel wasn't going to be his grandson's life. Dad remembers the warning his grandfather gave him growing up. It came with his rite of passage:

"Do anything else with your life, but you are never to work in the steel mill."

Steel made rich men out of Pittsburgh's Whites. My step great-grandmother, Mary Lee, probably knew more about the industry's barons than anyone.

Mary Lee cleaned their estates and served as a surrogate to their children, who often had everything but a motherly hug and some supervision. In fact, when the son of one of those steel magnates was just a little boy, it was her job to look after him when his own father was nursing a bottle of alcohol, my dad recalls.

That little boy and my dad became playmates while in my step great-grandmother's care and for a time those boys—one Black and the other White—grew up like brothers.

Someone to Watch Over Me

My grandmother died in 1991. My father always called her Hilda — never mother. Their relationship was always strained and polite and void of visible affection. There were no hugs. The emotional and physical embrace my father needed growing up came from his grandparents. But it was at a price. They doted on him and spoiled him, instead of telling him the truth about whose he was.

Looking back, Grandmother Hilda was right about what she said that Christmas Day when she came to visit us on the North Side, bearing gifts. My father couldn't take care of us, raise us, or keep us safe. He tried, I think, in his way. But the three of us were all a part of a losing battle, trying to survive the best way that we knew how.

My father continued to work the night shift at UPS, sorting and hauling packages. Although only 4 and 6 years old by now, it seemed we stayed home alone most nights—sticking close together, keeping the doors and windows locked, and chasing away the boogey man if he came calling in the middle of the night. Quickly, my sister was emerging as the parent and protector that I needed but didn't really have.

Tired from working and hung over from drinking, Dad could usually be found stretched out upstairs across his bed until it was time to get up for work and do it all again the next day. I'm sure that it wasn't easy being 23, alone, and raising two little girls. But there weren't family members he could turn to at the time, no matter how desperate he felt most days or how he wrestled with what to do to keep and maintain his family. Usually my sister and I kept watch over each other until he came home. That was his plan, but one evening the routine changed when he brought over sitters. They were two teenage girls who were apparently friends. We had never met them before.

As soon as my father left for work, and the door closed behind him, our evening with our new sitters seemed to be off to a good start. We began playing games, the sitters seemed nice and together our laughter filled our home. Soon, one girl turned on my father's old phonograph player and, at the same time, the other began watching our black-and-white floor-model television. But it wasn't long before I asked the sitters, "What's for dinner?" Then suddenly the mood changed as quickly as a clap of thunder on an otherwise sunny day.

"Oh, you're hungry, OK, I'll feed you!" one sitter yelled back as she huffed and shuffled off to the kitchen to see what she could prepare without too much effort. When she opened the cabinets, it was actually on a day when some food was inside.

As this sitter busied herself in the kitchen, I hurried back to the living room to continue playing the board game I started with my sister and the other baby sitter, who seemed much nicer than her friend. As we sat playing on the living room floor, it wasn't long before I smelled a wonderful aroma coming from the kitchen so I hurried to see what was cooking. The sitter scowled at me when I peered in. It didn't matter. I was determined to ask what was in the pot on the stove despite her bothered look. My sister was just as hungry as I was and also wanted to know what smelled so good, but she was too shy to ask. So, I asked for the both of us. I was excited, too. Tonight was going to be our opportunity to have a hot home-cooked meal for a change.

"It's spaghetti," the sitter in the kitchen shot back at me. I clapped and grinned. "Spaghetti is one of my favorite meals," I said. She ordered me out of the kitchen and back into the living room. It wasn't long, though, before I made my way back to the kitchen. That's when things turned ugly. She again saw my face at the door of the kitchen and slammed her stirring spoon down on the side of the stove like it was a small bat. That clang and the sight of her knotted up face reached me before she belted out a final warning: "Didn't I tell you to leave me alone and go in the living room and wait?"

I didn't come back. I gathered up my sister from the living room and we went to play out back. We were still hungry. Waiting for the sitters' call to come back inside didn't take long, but it seemed like forever. When she summoned us, we dashed back in the house. We were ready to sit down at the table, but instead, the one who was cooking complained that there was no bread to go with the meal. She demanded that my sister and I go to the neighborhood store and buy a loaf.

It was fall and night had already begun easing in around 6 p.m. Until then, the only darkness that my sister and I had experienced alone was inside our house. But there we were, a 4- and a 6-year-old, forced out into the night to buy bread. Together, we would be like a shield against whatever two little girls may face in the dark. We locked hands and set off on our journey, walking quickly. Those three blocks stretched out before us like three thousand blocks and we didn't let go of each other. It was tough turning the corner because we couldn't look back and see our house in the distance. For the first time, we felt our aloneness in the world. And we sensed that to make it, we'd have to stick together. We made it to the store. Once inside, we found the bread, put our change for the loaf on the counter and left.

There were paper plates and clear plastic tumblers on the table. We couldn't wait to eat but we weren't prepared for the huge amount of spaghetti and sauce the two sitters heaped at once on our plates. One serving probably could have fed two adults, but we were just little girls who wanted something warm and filling to eat. We decided to just dig in. With our heads down, noisy slurps went up as tomato sauce dripped from our chins and sprinkled our shirts.

But soon reality set in for us, my sister and I didn't know when we would get another meal so we didn't complain even when the sitters towered over us demanding that we "eat it," as they heaped the pasty strings of spaghetti and slices of white bread on our plates. Sitting at our small kitchen table, we tried as best we could to eat all the spaghetti that our stomachs could contain.

We weren't used to having much to eat, but now the sitters were making the sight of food a nightmare. Like a game gone badly, we didn't ask for more but the refills kept coming. The sitter who didn't cook stood by the stove looking, sometimes snickering, but not saying a word. Was this their way of punishing us or paying us back for just being hungry children who wanted to be fed?

Our eyes filled with tears and our cups filled with more and more water. Her attempts to force us to eat and drink more didn't stop. She didn't touch or twist our arms in the process, she did it all with her yelling and scary face. We were on the brink of bursting. The sitters made us eat the entire pot of spaghetti and drink what seemed like gallons of water before it was all over. The hot dinner that we had longed for earlier that evening, soon ended up on the kitchen floor as vomit. It became the sitters' mess to clean up before they sent us to bathe ourselves, and then to bed. We didn't put up a fuss about our bedtime; we went willingly that night.

Dad heard about our night of trauma first thing the next day. We begged him not to bring those girls back. Dad said that he understood, but he didn't tell us who would be coming to watch us now, if anybody. He still didn't have a plan for care for his little girls during the times when he wasn't home. So, once again, my sister and I found ourselves home alone, hungry, and with no adults to watch over us most days. My sister did the best that she could to take care of me, but she was just a child, too, who needed looking after. I listened to her and almost always obeyed. She was the oldest. I entered school when I was 4 years old and it was the stern voice of my sister that roused me in the morning. Getting up and out of the house on our own—sometimes with breakfast cereal in our small bellies or nothing at all and dressing for Pittsburgh's cold gray fall days in summer cotton and a sweater. It was just life as we knew it.

While we didn't know who, someone was watching us. Someone reported our father to the child welfare system. Before I left school one day, my teacher informed me that I had been selected to participate in a special event. I was invited to a special lunch with a reward of candy. The teacher sent a note home to my father informing him about the event. Dad picked out a pretty, yellow spring dress for me, too thin to wear on a chilly day. The night before I was supposed to go, my father fixed my hair, greasing and plaiting it in three sections. My father wasn't at home the morning that I went off to school for my big day. Trying to imitate a big girl, I grabbed a pair of my father's sheer black trouser socks, pulled them up my legs just like a pair of ladies' stockings. I'd seen my father put them on plenty of times before. On they went, sagging under my yellow dress and swimming inside my black Mary Janes. My outfit was complete.

The day was going to be just like my kindergarten teacher told me that it would be. Excited but curious, I left school at lunchtime with a White man dressed in a rumpled suit and tie. He drove us to a nearby restaurant. When we sat down, this strange man smiled and let me know that I could order anything I wanted, and then he began peppering me with questions about my family life and home. *Do you have toys at home to play with? Are you getting enough to eat? Are you happy? Tell me about your father. How are you treated?*

In between bites of my hamburger and French fries and swigs of my shake, I answered this man's questions. I was in kindergarten. I don't remember if I told this man that perhaps my father did have people to look in on us occasionally, but that on most days and nights, my sister and I felt abandoned and alone in the little world that we created. He jotted down my words in his notebook.

For a while I wondered who this man was, but he never said that he was from the child welfare office or from any other organization, or why he wanted to meet with me. But whatever the reason, I knew that it must be OK to be there with him, my teacher knew where I was, and my father had received the note from the school saying that I had been "selected." So I answered his questions as best that I could, ate my lunch, and looked forward to my prize. And as promised, I returned home that day with a bag full of candy that I gladly shared with my sister.

TWO
Finding Home

Knowing What's Real

The notion of home was strange to me. There were always four walls surrounding me and a roof over my head even if they didn't belong to my family, but from age 2 to 5, home was however my father defined it or my sister would attempt to create it for us.

With eyes shut, there would be days when I thought about what it must be like inside of a permanent home, a real home. It would be the kind the characters on *The Adventures of Ozzie & Harriet*, and *Leave It to Beaver* had. They filled my vision and our television screen every week—my eyes drank in images of homes, moms, dads, kids, and fun. I didn't see White or Black, then, just smiling happy people.

It felt good to dream about family even when memory and fantasy collided, as they often did:

Ummmm. Sweet cornbread is still browning in the oven, but in my mind, it already tastes good. It's a part of the bounty that we are about to receive. We haven't long returned home from Sunday morning service. The heels and hats come off once inside the front door and the anticipation of a

27

family meal hovers. Sunlight filters through a pitcher of just-stirred lemonade.
In the kitchen, rich brown gravy is simmering on the stove next to a pot of
steaming collard greens and a skillet filled with hot oil crackling. It's waiting
for chicken to land and fry up golden.

Fantasy—if only I could see my mother emerge from that bustling
kitchen wearing a look of contentment after eyeing all that she has
prepared for her family. She would have tiny beads of perspiration on
her forehead from standing over a hot stove in a small kitchen. And she
would be wearing the crisp apron she reserved for serving her family
Sunday dinner. Some memory—these are scenes that belonged in someone else's home; some of them were my caregivers when I was growing
up and some lived on Hollywood sets.

Life With Father and Miss

In 1966, when I was 5, I wanted to know, "Why me?" Why couldn't
those dreams of home be mine? The other children in my first-grade class
at Conroy Elementary School and in the neighborhood seemed to have
it all, at least the things that I thought mattered as a little girl—mothers,
fathers, sisters and brothers, sometimes even a dog or cat, and they lived
together under one warm wonderful roof in a place called home. They
had kinfolk who celebrated being family with all the trimmings—birthdays with presents, hugs, and evenings huddled on the sofa around the
floor-model black-and-white TV that they probably bought from Sears,
Roebuck & Co. Their lives were like a fairytale, but far better than the
ones I saw in my picture books.

Even at 5, I think I realized that the way we lived in my father's
house wasn't the way that it should be, and it surely wasn't the life that
my friends had, it seemed. My childhood longing was for a traditional
family that I could call my own. It was what I wanted more than life
itself—a family to love, care for, and protect me.

Then came my father's announcement one day: we would be moving
in with another family. He met a lady, she had a daughter who was a

few years older than my sister, a home, a family—we were processing it all. The words were still sinking in even though we had no idea what to expect from a family. In our little world, family meant the two of us—my sister and me. We were together most of the time, taking care of each other.

Dad's new lady could mean a mother figure for us. We hoped for a real bed to sleep in, not a mattress on the floor, and regular meals. We prayed for someone, a caring woman who would comb our hair in the morning before we went off to school and tuck us in the bed at night. Could this mean a normal childhood, where parents take care of you, not the other way around? But at the time, we couldn't have imagined that the woman who would introduce us to that normalcy would also be the one who ushered us into a family tradition, a sense of shared history, culture and belonging, and the joy of knowing generations of kin—all the important things that families are made of. Before long, the parents of the lady we called Miss became our grandparents; her three sisters, our aunts; and their children, our cousins. We were even embraced by the family's matriarch—she was Miss' grandmother.

In the days and weeks before we packed up the few belongings and clothes that we did have, my sister and I allowed ourselves to dream of the place where we were going and the people who lived inside that home. Like a mother, my sister was the one who usually made sure that we ate something if there was food in the house. She kept my face clean, making me wash it even at night before we went to sleep. My sister saw to it that we took our baths; we usually shared a tub of suds and water. Though we may have been the hungriest, loneliest children on the block, we stayed clean.

It was looking like the opportunity had arrived to be a part of a family that was bigger than just the two of us. Along with it came the chance to just be little girls. Until now, we were busy being little survivors masquerading as children.

The move would mean a new elementary school for us and a new life on Pittsburgh's South Side, in a community called Beltzhoover. To those who lived there, it was Black suburbia. Dwellers were proud of their yards, their homes, and all that they had accomplished. We lived in a three-bedroom apartment in a row house that sat above Mr. Tillman's bar, the neighborhood spot where my father met his new girlfriend and where neighbors drank, ate, and hung out. From the street, we followed a cement walkway down through a courtyard to get to the new place. It was attached to three other brick dwellings. Getting there, we saw children playing and it wouldn't be long before I'd make them my friends and cousins. Once inside the door of our new home, we first flowed through a tiny kitchen, then into the dining room turned playroom. I don't ever remember us actually eating in that room. It was just another pale yellow and dull white room like the others in the apartment but filled with board games, boxes, Barbies, and other young girl toys. The living room was in the front of the house and the bedrooms, including the one that my sister and I shared, were down a hallway and to the left.

Looking around—everything was in place and had a place in this neat and tidy apartment. Being there, I remembered that clean smelled good, but, most important, I saw food in the kitchen and in the refrigerator. And on our first evening, I watched the last rays of sunlight filtering in below the roller shades, bathing the living room in a pale peach glow. I thought surely, this must be heaven.

I looked around and for the first time I was old enough to realize all of the pieces seemed to be under one roof: a mom, a dad, and siblings. It was a family. I eased into this place and space, excited, but still unsure. I didn't really know how to act, or even what to call my father's girlfriend—mom or Miss? My father never sat my sister and me down to discuss any of these things or give us guidance, but here we were, just willing and eager to give our new family and home a try. I decided to call my father's girlfriend Miss. I grew to know her as a woman who was warm, giving, and with a kind, big heart. She had a 12-year-old daughter who enjoyed having me around, even when I was underfoot, like the 6-year-old that I was then. I called her my cousin.

Miss was also exotic. She was the kind of woman men wanted to be around. At Tillman's Bar, Dad would sit and sip his beer while drinking in her loveliness—a face the color of chocolate dappled with gold undertones and almond-shaped eyes that sparkled. He liked petite women and his hand glided easily around her small model-perfect waist.

In her mind, the world of striving that Miss knew all but vanished when she stepped over the threshold and into the world of means where she worked every day. The good life was close enough to touch and surely she could have it someday, too. That came with her thinking that she was better than and more than just a domestic. Like her makeup and jewelry, Miss was never without flair and sophistication. She brought it home, she took it to Tillman's Bar, and even to the grocery store on Saturdays. Her fine good looks and the stylish hair she wore, cut on an angle, are what made people look twice at Miss.

When we arrived at her house, we took in our surroundings, surveying all we saw—a television, a stereo, rooms with furniture, pictures on the wall, and scatter rugs on the floor, and a bedroom of our own with twin beds. Her daughter had her room and Miss and my father shared a bedroom. The wealthy Jewish family that Miss worked for made sure that their housekeeper was the recipient of many of their fine lovely hand-me-downs. Sometimes she got their gently used furnishings and appliances, even beautiful dresses that belonged to the woman of the house, and at least a tray or two of the lean roast beef, colorful *petit fours*, and other food left over from their weekend parties. On almost any day, we could open up the refrigerator and see shelves that actually had bread, milk, eggs, peanut butter and jelly, chicken, and so many other good things on them.

But for me, being in her home also marked the first time that I felt pretty and enjoyed what it felt like. *You are sooo cute, you're such a pretty little girl...* is what Miss and her daughter were always telling me. I would just smile and blush. Hearing those sentiments were new to me, I had never heard *pretty* and *Sharon* together in the same sentence. When I looked in the mirror, the little brown-skinned girl starring back at me was just me, I thought. Nothing more. My father, I don't think, ever called me cute or pretty. But climbing on to a stool in our tiny galley kitchen, ready to get my wild knotty hair combed and done, I probably felt better than cute. I felt beautiful—inside and out.

My cousin enjoyed combing my unruly locks and parting them and greasing my scalp with blue-green pomade that smelled sweet enough to eat. Mine was the kind of big hair that begged to be a part of something greater for our first Halloween together as a family. And Miss and my cousin had plans for it—my hair wasn't going to be tucked under a witch's mask or peeking out behind the plastic face of Snow White with her molded black tresses. Instead, my cousin went to work unleashing the cornrows she wove across my head, fluffing out the hair with a pick. And just like that, I was sporting a fierce and fabulous Afro. And for that Halloween, I went as political activist Angela Davis.

Days like that left me feeling lifted up, buoyed, and so special, but at the same time, my sister felt herself getting smaller and on the margins. My sister had been used to playing the role of the mother to both of us. Before we moved in with Miss, she was the one who got me up most mornings, dressed me, and shielded me from the things that she thought posed a danger to us both. And as the little sister, I listened and obeyed her, at least most of the time. My independent ways were budding; but experience had taught me that she knew what was best. Since coming to Miss' house, though, the dynamics were quickly changing. This home already had a mother; she was kind but demanded respect and obedience. My sister bristled and struggled as she saw her role shrink and soon dissolve. All of my sister's moxie wasn't going down without at least a little fight and some grumbling every now and then.

For me, I just tried to get along with everybody and did my best to steer clear of the adults in my new world and their concerns as best that I could. I wanted to focus on being carefree and on discovering what being a real family was all about. So far, it looked like we didn't have to worry any more about being home alone. And despite my sister's turmoil over recognizing who was really in charge in the house, the days that she and I spent hungry were now in our past. Being here in our new home was all that we had imagined it would be. Everything, I thought, was finally beginning to look up for us and for my father. And before long, our family had folded into theirs. And it wasn't long before their grandchildren became my play cousins and we'd looked forward to heading to their home in Pittsburgh's Oakland section for Sunday afternoon dinners.

Grandma's Sunday soul food feast was a meal that took hours to cook if you counted the baking and other preparations that she started on Saturday evening. Once everyone arrived, the hugs, hearty laughter, and banter about the day's sermon and life, were an anticipated prelude and just as much a part of this family's ritual as sitting down to eat and saying grace. It would take at least 30 minutes to just carry out and assemble all of the food across the lace-covered dining room table. With all of the serving bowls and platters brimming with candied yams doused with nutmeg and cinnamon, hot homemade rolls catching melting pats of butter in their creases, the finest fried chicken, barbecued spareribs, macaroni and cheese, and potato salad, there was barely room left on the table for her white China and fancy green glasses of sweet tea.

I'm not sure if anyone noticed me doing it, but there were so many Sundays at Grandma and Gramps when I would sit looking around the table at the extended family members gathered there and just begin to rock back and forth in my chair, contented beyond words to be in their presence and to be a part of something wonderful.

Happy, I would just begin humming as I ate. Actually, my humming, which was low and lighthearted, replaced the singing that I did until Gramps put an end to my habit.

"The dinner table is was for eating and fellowshipping, not for horsing around," he said in a stern voice.

Everything that Grandma prepared was good to me, but time spent with her wasn't just about the food. It was about serving up the ritual of family and bringing her kin back together and to their roots on Sunday. Grandma's mother was the matriarch of her family before she passed away and her house was the first meeting place for Sunday dinners. Big Mama Hunter allowed me to call her my great-grandmother, too.

Growing Pains: 1967

Our family was about to get bigger.

Dad knew that his girlfriend was pregnant with his baby when he decided to move us in with her, but that didn't stop him from stepping out on Miss and drinking too much. But according to Dad, Miss wasn't the woman that he thought she was when he decided, after only a few months, that he and his young children would live with her. She wanted more of his attention and presence, and a commitment, but Dad just felt pressured and overwhelmed.

After a while, his rumblings, and drinking, and creeping began wearing the entire family down and out. The frequent run-ins my sister continued to have with Miss and her daughter just stoked the flames in the house that was about to ignite. And watching it all unfold and unravel, I knew that our days here were numbered.

Things inside these walls were still neat and tidy, but now they didn't look so pretty through my 6-year-old eyes. Life at home became like a game of dodging bullets, only for us, it was the dreaded threats of eviction that Miss felt forced to level at my father and that we hoped wouldn't hit us. With each passing week and month that we were able to escape being ousted and put on the street, I breathed a sigh of relief and tried to go on living and being a kid, but that was becoming tougher to do. I believe that Dad's girlfriend, who was about to give birth, wanted to do the right things by keeping her new family intact. So, she tried for a little while longer to put up with my dad and with us.

And me, I just decided one day to go to my best friend's Patty's house and never come back to mine. It was a random act from the simple mind of a first-grader for whom a stable home wasn't a way of life.

I hadn't packed clothes or anything that day, but instead of coming home like I was supposed to, I tagged along with Patty, a girl who sat next to me in class at Beltzhoover Elementary School. She thought that it would be great fun if I came with her and moved in. I had never been to Patty's house before, but I liked her and it sounded like a good idea. By day, her father was a smelly fishmonger at G.C. Murphy's and by night, he was a wrestler known as "The Hurricane." Patty's mother stayed at home and was there every day when her daughter arrived home from school.

From where I lived, walking, you could get to Patty's house in about 10 minutes. Patty lived in a single-family home with three levels. When we got to Patty's, the two of us played and did our homework. I saw her parents cooking together and when they were done, they called Patty and me to the table for dinner. That's something that we didn't do at our house. I liked what I was seeing in Patty's home.

After dinner, I smiled and asked if I could live with Patty in their home? It seemed like it would be an easy "yes" for her parents to make, but they gave me a surprised but sympathetic look before asking where I lived, and delivering me back to my house after dinner. It was the mid-1960s and there was nothing traditional about our family makeup—my father was a young widower with two small children; he lived with a woman that he wasn't married to. But nonetheless, the same rules applied when it came to not telling your family business to strangers. I was just a young child who took matters into her own hands that day when I went in search of a family who could care for me. I never told Patty's parents what life was like where I lived or about what it was before we came here, but my father thought that I must have laid bare our lives to these strangers. I didn't. That's why I couldn't understand my punishment that evening or his accusations that I betrayed our family and brought strangers into our life when I ran away.

Sisters squabbling over whose turn it was to comb and style Barbie's long blond hair sometimes led to a doll with a missing head if one of us didn't get her way. And commandeering crayons or claiming the same page in the coloring book that we had to share was reason enough to argue or worse, pinch an arm and make one sister cry. But in my father's eyes, his girls should get along at all times. Our lives really didn't have rules to mold us, but Dad expected his girls to be obedient. And when we weren't and he found out, my sister and I knew what to expect from his discipline—standing in the corner for about five minutes, with our arms stretched out to our side and with our palms open, and facing upward. To a child, the time spent standing in that pose seemed to drag on forever. And if our arms dropped we had to do more time in the corner. This act of discipline seemed peculiar to me even then, but if I knew the beating that awaited me for running away to Patty's that day, I would have marched to the corner on my own, without being told.

The first and only beating Dad ever gave me came that night after I arrived home from Patty's and my sister and I began playing with our dolls. There wasn't any dessert. Dad was at work when Patty's parents brought me back home, but, by that time, Miss had already called my father at work and let him know that I hadn't come home after school, but had returned safely. Miss' daughter was beside herself, laughing and taunting about the "big trouble" that I was going to be in for running away.

When Dad got home, things were quiet and he ate dinner as usual. I didn't think any more about being in trouble and still didn't grasp what I had done wrong, even as I headed into the room where he was about to punish me. Dad had never really been a disciplinarian to his girls, but on this occasion, Miss probably made Dad think twice about the level of punishment that was needed to fit my escapade. She thought that running away from home deserved much more than a few minutes in the corner and Dad was persuaded.

When I entered his bedroom, he told me to take off all of my clothes before tying my wrists with a small rope to the arms of a wooden chair. He proceeded to do something that evening that he would never do again. He pulled out an extension cord and whipped me about my legs and butt.

I screamed and cried for him to stop as the cord stung my flesh. Dad didn't utter a word. Outside the door, my sister cried, pleading to Jesus to save me.

When he was finished, my father wept.

And when I woke the next morning, my tears had dried and my lesson was learned. It was going to be just another school day even though I wore last night's welts and bruises under my knee-hi socks and cotton dress. I don't think that anybody knew that they were there but me.

Goings and Comings: 1968

In the midst of our churning lives, a new baby arrived. When my father's second son came into the world, he seemed to be the glue that we all needed to meld us back together. I even began glimpsing glimmers of light and laughter filtering back into our lives and home, but it wasn't long before my thoughts turned to the first baby boy that I knew. I was too young when my brother was taken away to have had any concrete images of him, but in my senses, his memory still lingered. My father had a new son now, and his presence represented a new beginning of sorts for our family.

But for Dad, some things just stayed the same. He was surrounded by his family, but alcohol and leftover emotional pain seemed to sit like dark weights on Dad's young shoulders. And there was no escape for my sister and me, either, on those days and nights when his emotions erupted and spilled over on us. Even as children we worried and flared up sometimes too because we didn't know what life was going to serve us from one day to the next. But we were powerless to complain or yell stop. So, we went on living in limbo—wondering whether we would be put out of the house or whether we would be able to stay another day, a week, or a month.

Inching toward two years, we were still managing to stay together as an extended family under one roof. Coming to our new home brought with it the first glimpse of what my sister and I called a real family and we were tickled when we arrived and had the opportunity to become a part of it. We were enjoying the good days and, just like that, the bad days crept up behind and chased them far away.

It was a humid summer evening when we learned that our time was finally up.

Sitting with Miss on the brown velour living room sofa waiting for my father to come through the front door, all my sister and I could feel was lonely, scared, and worried and simply angry. My father couldn't tame his penchant for chasing women. And because of it, he managed to snatch away all that we had come to know and enjoy about our new family. The place that we called home for nearly two years was teetering and breaking. Even more than toys and little girl things, all I remember wanting during those dim days was to find peace and quiet. I didn't want to worry about anything that the grownups in my life were doing to themselves and to our chances of finding happiness and a permanent home. But it was too late.

That evening, we weren't allowed to go to our room and climb into bed like we usually did around 9 o'clock. Instead, we sat in our sun dresses and sandals, still huddled on the living room sofa, waiting with Miss. By now our slow quiet tears and worry had given way to intermittent sleep. It was way past our bedtime. In the corner of the couch near where my sister and I sat, our belongings were bundled in a plastic trash bag and ready to go. Dad's keys rattled close to the door around 2 a.m., startling us as he strolled in through the kitchen and back to the living room. He didn't expect to see a pensive girlfriend and his droopy-eyed girls dressed and waiting on the sofa at that hour. This time, Miss was determined to make good on her threat to end things with my dad and put us all out of her house. Miss told my sister and me earlier that evening that she had tried. She cared about us, but was sorry. Dad and his girls had to leave.

He had barely gotten his foot inside the place where we sat waiting, still scared but sleepy, when Miss pulled him aside and gave him the news. He would have to go that night.

It was as if he knew what was coming, and he didn't put up a fuss. There was no arguing from him.

Where we went didn't matter to her. Miss let him round up his shirts, work uniforms, and shoes and some other personal belongings before showing him the door he had entered just 20 minutes ago. It didn't take long for my dad to leave this place, grabbing up his things, including his children. Together we stepped outside under a still dark sky and into the backseat of my father's car parked on the street. That's where we slept until the break of day.

My father had no idea where we would go. But he enlisted the help of his friends, some from among his Tillman Bar crowd. The next day, it was to the home of another of his women friends. We stayed with her for about three days before we were again on the move.

Dragging behind him like two small sacks of laundry, we showed up at another door and then the next. One belonged to a relative. He left us at this place like he did at every stop. He'd never stick around once we got settled inside. Dad was off to one of his jobs—washing dishes at a restaurant downtown or working at UPS. Or maybe he had been spending time with one of his friends? We didn't know or care just as long as he returned for us.

All of those who gave us shelter probably felt sorry for the two little girls my dad had with him. Our traipsing across town and bouncing from place to place was seemingly never ending, but in reality, it probably lasted about a month.

Each new day brought uncertainty and the weariness that comes from constantly being on the move without a home. If we had a road map for our journey then, it likely would have been marked *You are here: somewhere and nowhere*. We had no idea what was going to happen to us and where we would lay our heads on any given night.

The only reward of being evicted in the summertime was that at least the weather wasn't cold and school was out. But summer break was nearing an end. We didn't know if we would be going back to school or when or if we would again see the friends we made in our old neighborhood.

We kept up the pace—moving, moving—for about two months before my father finally found us an apartment.

Our new place was small and unfurnished, but at least it was ours and we could stop drifting for a while. For the first time since we were put out, my sister could fully resume her unofficial role as my caregiver. Life for us seemed to be rewinding, landing us back in the same place that we were in two years prior—alone, hungry, and unsupervised most of the time. These days, my father's absences were growing longer—maybe he was working more, spending time with his lady friends, we didn't know.

At least we had a roof over our heads and a mattress. My sister and I shared a mattress that lay in the middle of the living room floor with no box spring or bed frame on which to place it. At night, we usually found ourselves curled up together on it, awake, wondering, and speaking into the darkness about when things would get better for us and when we would find a family again.

Our neighbors were watching. Their eyes were drawn to what was happening inside of our place. What they saw needed to be fixed. In their way, they wanted to remedy the situation of two little girls whom they saw were unkempt, alone, and hungry on many occasions.

When they looked on my father, they probably wondered why a woman wasn't in the home or by his side. They saw an able-bodied man come in and out of the apartment. There was no mother there. And finally one day, a few of the neighbors rallied together, knocked on our door, and asked my father to step out into the hall. I tried to listen near the cracked door as they confronted Dad and delivered their sentiments and persuasion:

"We think that your girls need help in there. They're always home alone."

"Who feeds them when you're not around?"

"If you can't take better care of your girls, we'll have to call the child welfare agency and they can have those little girls removed from your home. We don't think you want that?"

I guess that confrontation shook Dad and he didn't want to lose his children. He sprang into action that week, thinking that he was doing the right thing when he decided to send us off to live with a single female cousin who, like him, was also about 24 years old and who didn't quite know what to do with two little girls.

Rough Transitions: Homewood

Our cousin and new caregiver was a young person who had struck out on her own but who didn't yet have much to show for her independence. What she did have was apparently the best that she could afford. Her cramped first-floor apartment would be our home. We shared it at night with mice and with other small bugs that even crept out during the day.

She turned her empty dining room with sliding pocket doors into our makeshift bedroom. It had a flimsy full-size bed inside. There may have been one lamp for the whole apartment and it never seemed to cast enough light, especially when we wanted to go to the bathroom in the middle of the night. The darkness even seemed to hang over us in the daytime. But we were glad that it kept us from seeing what we heard just outside of our bedroom. The thin wall the dining room shared with the kitchen seemed to amplify the tiny feet of mice scampering across the cold linoleum floor or gnawing their way through my cousin's kitchen.

My sister and I shouldn't have been here in this strange place, but being home with our father, who couldn't care for us at the time, wasn't the right place, either. With every passing week, my cousin would call and ask my father how much longer she would have to play babysitter to his children. But despite the burden on her, she managed to keep us fed, get us up and out of the house, and off to school. In the six years of my life, and in my sister's eight years, we had already been on the rolls of three different schools in three different sections of town. But no matter where we landed, I loved to learn. I enjoyed sitting in my second-grade classroom surrounded by splashes of bright primary colors, receiving nice books that had never been opened, and learning how to count using chunky wooden blocks. Coming to school was also a relief from being hemmed in my cousin's tiny dwelling.

In our classroom we sat next to Black and White children who wore well-scrubbed clothes and faces. We were too young to know about being ashamed on those days when our dresses weren't ironed or as clean as they should have been or when our tattered pants were in need of a needle and thread. We mainly kept to ourselves anyway. What was the point, we thought, of making new friends when we didn't know if the following week would mean another journey in search of the next home and another school enrollment?

One day, when we were still living with our cousin, my father showed up at the house with Miss. Perhaps she and my father had gotten back together? No, they were here today to visit us and to bring some clothes for school. When they arrived, there wasn't much good for them to see inside the place where we were living. From the looks on both of their faces, they knew that we needed to leave, but it took another month before they came back and took us away from there. Because Grandma and Gramps lived just a few blocks away from where we were staying, their home became the refuge we sought from our cousin's four walls.

THREE

In Search of a Forever Home

A Welcome Table

The people who gathered around Grandma's table for Sunday dinners were family—her grown daughters, their children, husbands and boyfriends—about eight in all. They considered us extended family even though my sister and I weren't tethered to them by blood. Dinners and gatherings were the traditions Grandma's family had known for generations. For them, coming home and just being together were a part of the fabric of their lives—tightly woven, resilient, and familiar.

On Sundays, family gathered for food and for fellowship. And when their afternoon together was over, this family would take helpings of both away. When it came to the food, Grandma would dole out the leftovers after dessert, scooping up a little of this and a lot of that onto paper plates and containers before covering them in wax paper or wrapping them up in aluminum foil. Inside each bundle and on each plate were elements of the savory downhome cooking shared just hours ago around the dinner table. Each person also took away delicious memories of that day and of family who would help sustain and lift them up until they could come together again on another Sunday, if not sooner.

Painting a Portrait of Kin

When we came to know Grandma and Gramps, they were probably in their mid-50s, still spry, working, and living alone in the house where they raised their own daughters and where they probably would retire someday. Grandma was not big and sturdy, but just right. I loved to see her all dressed up, which seemed to be almost every time that she left her house to go shopping, to her club meetings with a group of ladies who called themselves the Jolly Wonders, and definitely to church. Even when she was around the house relaxing or cleaning, she still looked good and tidy in her crisp cotton house dresses that snapped shut in the front and matching bedroom slippers.

This was a woman of virtue. She had a deep religious conviction that took root in her heart when she found Jesus while still a young girl. Jesus must have given her an easy smile. At first it fooled us kids until we learned quickly that she didn't take any stuff and didn't miss a beat. Her watchful eyes saw everything. We joined in with the grandchildren in jokingly calling Grandma "the fuss budget," when we had to do and re-do everything from placing our shoes out of the way so that nobody tripped over them, or putting things that we used back in the same place where we got them. Everything in order is what she taught.

And her husband, tall lanky Gramps, must have stood at least 6'4." We called him our gentle giant. Unlike his wife, he never quite found a church that he wanted to wade into on Sunday mornings, but he still professed to be a believer. On the seventh day, Gramps was content with keeping the pillow warm while grandma went off to be with God at her church in the Hill District. He could rest assured that the wife he adored and respected would remember him to the Lord when she knelt at the altar. If anyone's prayers could reach above, it was surely hers. She meant business and got things done heavenward and at home.

Even as a good, traditional, no-nonsense man who made it known that he wore the pants in the house; Gramps was just fine with letting his wife lead and do most of the talking. Gramps' own words were spare, but when he spoke, his friends and family sat up and took notice. He could confidently debate and, with authority, recount the news of the day with friends and family using the powerhouse vocabulary he gleaned largely from the endless Sunday newspaper puzzles he tackled each week. Some would have said that Gramps wasn't a learned man since he didn't have a college degree, but I always thought that he was one of the smartest people that I knew.

When he'd come to the table or sit in his easy chair in the living room, the point of his pencil would tap, tap, tap, gently until the letters and words his mind searched for flowed. But most of the time when you saw gramps, he'd be wearing that pencil between his right ear and the crease of his slim neat head or he would just hold his No. 2 in his right hand while the left one rested thoughtfully on his forehead. Sunday crossword puzzles were a labor that he loved. His work on them wouldn't come to an end until Monday after dinner. That's when he put down his pencil and declared victory until the next weekend.

But family and the work that he did for a living were his real-life prizes. Gramps just did what he knew was best for his life and right by his family. He loved setting out early in the morning for work full of pride and zeal because he knew that his family depended on him. So, he worked hard, and earned a good living with a comfortable home to show for it.

A House Becomes a Home: 1969

On the day that we pulled up in front of Grandma and Gramps' house on Ward Street in the Oakland section of Pittsburgh, it wasn't Sunday and we weren't here for the soul food feast. We were here because this time, Dad finally had a plan for our lives. He wanted his girls to have stability, something he discovered along the way that his girls needed. But it was also the very thing that he couldn't seem to provide, at least for any long stretch of time. Fortunately for my sister and me, the people that we called our Grandma and Gramps were here now for us and they would provide.

We were here to stay. We had found our "forever home."

Grandma and Gramps wanted to raise us as their own and we would be living with them. When we heard the plan, I looked at my sister and she looked at me with wide eyes and a smile, something that I didn't often see on her face in those days. The news was unbelievable and unexpected; but almost immediately, my mind took off dancing with hope that every day with Grandma and Gramps in this house would be filled with the same peacefulness and joy that I knew on so many Sundays around the dinner table and during sleepovers.

Letting us go to be raised and cared for by a family who loved and wanted us was the best gift that my father could have given his girls. This time it looked like Dad had finally found a way forward for his family. I guess that this was his attempt to make straight the ragged pattern that our young lives had taken since our mother died five years ago and he was left to raise us.

I was seven years old and my sister was turning nine. We needed to be wrapped up in all of the love and goodness that Grandma and Gramps had to give—they knew it and so did my sister and I. We were determined to make our new home in this familiar place work and last as long as it could.

Who knew on those days when we played "tag you're it" in their big back yard or made our way through this room and that room on those weekends when we visited that we would someday call these spaces our own. That's why, when we got there, we didn't have to wonder which way to go, where most things were, and what they looked like. We were already familiar. We knew where the bathrooms were and which toilet was temperamental; and inside which kitchen drawer Grandma stashed the bag of small hard candy and the melt-in-your mouth peppermints that she usually gathered up by the fistful and dropped into the zippered pocket of her church purse, next to the fresh white handkerchief she carried. We even knew the gentle wheeze that escaped from beneath the upholstered sofa seats enshrined in clear heavy plastic; and we knew the pattern on the wallpaper in the hall and the off-white paint that adorned the three bedrooms.

Jewish families in Pittsburgh hired Grandma to keep their manses masterfully cleaned and their children lovingly attended to. And at the end of each workday, Grandma caught the bus and returned home to her own immaculate dwelling in Oakland, in the center section of Pittsburgh.

Grandma and Gramps' house had an eat-in kitchen where breakfast and lunch were served. In the dining room, the table was always at the ready for guests. It was also the gathering place for dinner that didn't get served during the week until Gramps arrived home from his work hauling coal to local schools and businesses. When we arrived to live with our new parents, they gave us the large lovely bedroom at the front of the house. It was where Grandma and Gramps slept before we came. They moved down the hall into the middle room to give us space to spread out and enjoy growing into young ladies. And the third and smallest bedroom in the back of the house was kept ready for guests. The finished basement is where Grandma's wide-bellied wringer washing machine stood. There wasn't a dryer, so Grandma would move damp pants, shirts, and undergarments, socks, and dresses to the clothesline where they finished drying and catching the sun and breeze on bright clear days.

Along the block, good neighbors surrounded us. And not long after settling in, the children who lived in those houses became some of my new best friends. When the other kids wanted to know what I was doing living in Grandma and Gramps' house, I just said that they were my grandparents and that this was my new home. As I was out and about with the neighborhood children, my sister usually kept to herself, content to be quiet and reserved most of the time. She seemed more comfortable testing the waters of her new surroundings, but me, I just dove in wherever I went.

For the first few months at our grandparents' house, every day was like Sunday—full and festive. It took some time for it to sink in with us that we weren't leaving after dinner or at the end of the weekend like we usually did. Even as we settled into a familiar place, we learned to be watchful and observant of our grandparents' ways and how things were done in their house. Rules were a new concept for us. Until we moved in with Grandma and Gramps, rules were only loosely defined when we lived with my father or with Miss, but we were quick studies and looked forward to being told what we could and couldn't do. It gave us boundaries and made us feel as if someone actually cared about the direction of our lives.

My sister and I stayed attentive during those early days, determined yet eager to grasp Grandma's wise words and learn the art of cleaning from someone who made it their livelihood. Having rules meant asking permission, now, for just about everything we wanted to do, including leaving our front yard to play with a friend across the street or watching some of our favorite shows and cartoons on television.

Living with Grandma and Gramps also meant learning about some of the household routines that we would be expected to do on our own when we were older—how to strip the beds or apply "hospital corners" to sheets so that they looked neat and taut and hung just right. For now, making our beds every day, even on the weekends, was required in this house.

We had a routine. Dinner was at 5 o'clock and my sister and I were responsible for setting the table. Here, weekday meals were a family affair even when there was just the four of us—Grandma, Gramps, my sister, and me—around the table. Conversation and moments of sharing our days and good news were staples at the dinner table, just like the meat and the potatoes. Grandma and Gramps believed in conversation during the dinner hour, absent of background noise. So, the television, the radio in the kitchen and in the living room would be clicked off. Sitting together, we provided the music of our lives and the stories as we ate. But Saturdays were casual times when we didn't gather together at the table, and usually just ate leftovers for dinner somewhere in the house.

When it came to chores, Grandma assigned them seven days a week. And on Saturdays when we didn't have to dash off to school, we still tumbled out of bed early, managing a smile, even though we wanted nothing more than to stay tucked under the covers just a little while longer. But we had cleaning to do. Episodes of some of our favorite Saturday morning cartoons— *H.R. Pufnstuf* and *The Perils of Penelope Pitstop* had to just go on without us, and so did meeting with our friends on the block, until we finished our chores.

Whether it was sweeping the kitchen, taking out the garbage, our chores rotated. When we got older, around 11, we were given ironing to do once a week and we did our own laundry. But when we were starting out in the house, Grandma discovered early that I didn't have a knack for washing dishes. That's when she reassigned that chore to my sister who would instead climb on top of the little plastic stool Grandma gave us so that we could reach the sink. I couldn't seem to get plates clean enough so, I ended up drying them.

Whatever chores and rules were handed down, I just wanted to please and comply. We didn't want to break our grandparents' hearts or find ourselves out of the house or on the street again. Every day that we were in their home, we were just grateful to be surrounded by people who wanted us enough to take us in and who cared enough to treat us as if we were their own. They were our family now.

Taking Care of Business

So much was happening all at once in those early days, it seemed, but they were the kind of changes that kept us hopeful and happy. We were settling in and life couldn't have been better. The prayers that I had prayed for a family and home had been answered. I was blessed, clothed, clean, well fed, and loved by two people who became like kin.

Not long after my sister and I arrived, Grandma decided to give up the "day" work that she did in other people's homes so that she could become our full-time caregiver and stay-at-home grandma. This meant that she would now be at the center of our daily lives, keeping a bird's-eye view on all that we did, watching us as we grew, making decisions for us, speaking for us, dressing us, feeding us, caring for us—all of the things that we had lacked, but needed for so long. Coming for Sunday feasts had given us a head start on being a family. And with each passing day and month, we were growing even closer.

Grandma was willing to play with us and at other times she was the no-nonsense housemother to two girls under 10 who could be giggly, inquisitive, a bit rambunctious, and sweet. Having raised four girls, two of them twins, Grandma had done this all before, but her mothering to young ones had been decades ago. This was the late 1960s.

When Grandma could have been thinking about kicking up her heels and finding a place on her porch to ease into her rocking chair for a long spell, she was thinking about enrolling my sister and me in music lessons and dance classes, and finding us the best schools. She wanted to do more for us than just be our grandma.

No matter how loving, Grandma and Gramps were, they were not our biological kin, which meant that they didn't have the authority to enroll us in school without my father's signature or legal documentation. We lived with Grandma and Gramps, but in the eyes of the state child welfare system, the two little girls that they cared for were just dependent children. Grandma and Gramps were doing for my sister and me what Black families had done instinctively and quietly for centuries—take in kin to keep them together when they were down and out or needed a home. They were the relatives who would make a way out of no way to find a room or a place at the table for another hungry mouth, the motherless, the jobless, the penniless, the sick, and the dying, so that their kin wouldn't have to turn to the state, the streets, or worse.

This time, Grandma had the added burden of trying to get the state to recognize her as our new legal caregiver. But this was 1968, when the child welfare system nationally was struggling to find its own position on practices governing dependent children like us and the families who couldn't care for them. Grandma and Gramps were caring adults who could provide a permanent home, but they just weren't biologically related to my sister and me.

There was no real discussion of a permanent living arrangement, just foster care. Grandma and Gramps, who were legally becoming our foster parents, had limited contact, at the time, with either the courts or case workers when they tried to navigate through the child welfare maze in search of answers and resources for the two girls they brought into their lives and home. But Grandma got things done as she always did. As her new foster daughters, we were entitled to medical and dental benefits and Grandma and Gramps received a small monthly check to help cover the cost of caring for us. I remember her telling us with relief that she now had "papers that allow us to take care of you."

What a happy day that was.

Well, if those papers that Grandma waved in her gloved hands and beamed about made us more of a family, then we were truly grateful. My sister and I just knew that our fear of being uprooted again and back with Dad was slowly vanishing—we were home now and not going anywhere.

The Jackson Five and Dreams Come True

My sister and I didn't understand the word "foster care" and we weren't too concerned about it, either. We just knew that Grandma and Gramps were taking good care of us, even if we weren't their flesh and blood. We would sometime overhear Grandma on the telephone referring to us as "her foster children" when she was trying to arrange for things like our medical care or for a new pair of free glasses. But under her roof, we were her grandchildren, just like the others that she had and loved.

Grandma showed us that only the best was good enough for my sister and me when she took us to the more upscale department stores in town to shop for pretty dresses and clothes for school and play. She didn't think twice about walking pasy the local discount stores where most kids in the neighborhood got their clothes. Those kinds of store, she'd say, weren't for us. I chose one of the new dresses my Grandma bought me—it was my favorite with yellow and white ruffles—when she made my dream come true. Grandma was taking my sister and me to see our heartthrobs, Michael Jackson and the Jackson Five! I knew that I must have been Michael's biggest fan, but so did my sister and every other pre-adolescent girl in America.

In just a few months, life had changed so much for us. Here I was, a beaming third grader who just a few months ago was homeless and helpless, now sitting in prime seats that evening in Pittsburgh's Civic Arena waiting for the concert of a lifetime to begin. And just when I thought an already perfect evening couldn't have gotten any better, Grandma surprised us after the concert with dinner at McDonald's. You must understand that visiting the Golden Arches then was a rare treat for us; Grandma didn't believe that anything on the menu was worth us eating or her paying for when there was a perfectly good and healthy home-cooked meal in her kitchen. But that night, our dinner out was just about having fun and letting her girls devour Big Macs and French fries.

After my father delivered us to Grandma and Gramps, he eased away, only coming around for an occasional visit. We would still see Miss when she came over for Sunday dinner, but my father would not be with her. Since we were living with her parents, now, I began to call her Aunt instead of Miss. She and I were now connected as kin. We were family.

Sometime during those early months with grandma and gramps, I'm not sure if I found peace or peace found me, but now that it was here, the questions I asked often about my brother seemed to diminish. Thoughts of him, though, never left my mind. I just told my 7-year-old self that he must be happy, too, and that we would see each other again, somewhere, one day.

I Hear a Symphony

In third grade, teachers must have thought that my favorite word was "why?" I wasn't rebellious, then, but I could be relentless in my inquisitiveness and challenges. My mouth sometimes got me punished at school and sent home one too many times for my Grandma to tolerate. I was a little girl growing up, but in many ways was reeling from a disrupted home and school life. But Grandma had devised a remedy.

A strict, controlled environment, that's what Grandma said that I needed along with some no-nonsense Catholic nuns who "are not going to put up with your sass!" After the second semester of third grade, my Grandma enrolled my sister and me in St. Richard's Parochial School, a Black, Catholic school in Pittsburgh's historic Hill District. For a time, August Wilson, who would go on to become an award-winning playwright, was also a student here.

Sending both of us to a private school was a major financial sacrifice for Grandma and Gramps, but it was worth it, they said, even if it meant using the monthly allowance they received for our care and housing on school tuition. It wasn't easy when we arrived at St. Richard's. Having bounced like balls from school to school over the years, we struggled academically to make up lost ground. But clad in my new school uniform in this place of privilege and order, I buckled down and worked hard on my lessons, determined to prove that I belonged at St. Richard's.

After breakfast at home, we would stand outside our door and wait to hop on the local transit bus that made its way onto our street, and ride the 15 miles to St. Richard's. Like she usually did, Grandma worked everything out when she convinced the local bus driver to stop for her two girls in front of their door instead of up the street at his "real" bus stop and route.

Grandma knew best. Transferring me to St. Richard's was the right thing. When I got to the school, I didn't have a choice but to listen to the nuns, be quiet, and do my work. By now, Grandma had also enrolled me in modern jazz dance classes at the Selma Burke Art Center in Pittsburgh. Violin lessons came next, thanks to one of my classmates who played in the acclaimed Ozanam String Orchestra. Since 1965, Sister Francis Assisi Gorham, a diminutive White nun with the tenacity of Goliath's David, used the music of Vivaldi and Beethoven and Brahms to raise up budding Black violinists from Pittsburgh's historic Hill District.

In the 1930s, Harlem Renaissance poet Claude McKay referred to the Hill District as the "crossroads to the world." In the day, it was a place that flourished as a center for African-American music, art, and business. Growing up there, I learned about some of the Hill legends who came before me: musicians George Benson and Stanley Turrentine, and another famous one, singer Lena Horne, who, for a while, called the Hill District home. So, when we raised our violins to our chins and made our music, we fit right into a tradition where music and culture were passed along like gifts.

The first time I saw and held a violin was the day that I went with my classmate to her music practice with Ozanam Strings, an afterschool music program and performance group. The next thing that I knew, Sister Francis told me to pick up and play one of the pint-sized violins sitting in an open black case. It didn't matter that I had never slid a bow across the strings or couldn't read music; all of her students had learned to play the instrument just by listening, being immersed in the sound of music, and performing. I hurried home excited and asked about the possibility of joining the orchestra and taking lessons. In that instance, I almost forgot I went to the music practice that day after school without even asking permission. But Grandma gave me her blessing, anyway, because she thought the experience and the discipline of learning music and an instrument would be good for me. It turned out that I had real musical talent, too. I continued to play through high school and on my own until my freshman year in college.

Being a musician in the orchestra was a lot of responsibility and work for a young person in those days. I traveled from home by bus to get to the required three-day a week practices that were usually held in the basement of a Catholic Church, or elsewhere in the city. Sister Francis, who was a musician herself, faithfully taught us the classics, but from time to time, she would slip in some pop tunes along with the movie scores from *Shaft* and *Star Wars*. And once a year, Sister Francis would take her young but serious musicians on the road to perform in Atlantic City, Chicago, New Orleans, and even at New York's Carnegie Hall, where we would play with musical legends like Canadian trumpeter and band leader Maynard Ferguson, and legendary jazzman and composer Count Basie. In my last year of high school, I competed for and won the sought-after position of Ozanam Strings' second violinist in the orchestra, second only to the concert master and the first violinist. And at school, things for me were also looking up. Being at St. Richard's helped get me on track academically and it was a place I enjoyed and where I thrived as a student. But after seventh grade, my sister and I had to leave this place when we learned that Grandma and Gramps had an opportunity to move into a new house across town. The house was a gift from their daughter and new son-in-law. The woman who I now called my aunt (formerly Miss) had moved on with her life after her relationship with my dad dissolved.

At first I took the news about the move pretty hard as I thought about the friends and the environment I would be leaving behind. This house represented a good and permanent place—a fresh start that for years was uninterrupted. But then I realized that I really didn't have a reason to be sad or afraid of leaving our house this time. Things at home weren't like before. I knew that we would be safe and cared for as long as Grandma and Gramps were with us. After that, I began to look forward to the move and to returning to a familiar community and a neighborhood where my grandparents' children and my cousins lived—back to Beltzhoover.

We had another lovely house, a bit smaller than our old one. This one had a washer and a dryer, which meant that we didn't have to hang our clothes on the line to dry anymore, but for Grandma, old habits were hard to break. Her clothes still hung on the line. Our dining room was formal, the way she liked it. My sister and I shared a bedroom.

As Long As We're Together

While we were back living in a familiar neighborhood, both of us were entering the eighth grade and yet another school. When we enrolled, it was like being in the middle of the pack since our middle school concluded with ninth grade. But the good thing was that we already knew many of the students who attended. Getting to know some of the new girls was a challenge, but not one that I had much interest in taking on back then. I just tried to have fun with the people that I knew, worked hard to get good grades, and focused my attention on the violin and all that the Ozanam Strings program had to offer. The school orchestra and the chorus became my refuge from the day-to-day drama of being a middle school girl.

Then one day, I don't know when it happened, I looked up and I noticed boys—I liked some that I saw and they started liking me. Then there was Grandma who managed to squash my excitement and any of my talk of boys and house parties with classmates. No, Grandma wasn't hearing any notions that took me physically beyond her listening ear, her keen gaze, or our front yard. To her, my budding social interests, especially in boys, amounted to just "nonsense."

At 13, I remember my first attempt to date behind my grandmother's back and where that got me. The object of my young affection was an older boy who was also in the Ozanam Strings. It wasn't long before my grandma discovered who he was. She found his name along with cute little hearts encircling it and love notes scribbled in one of my notebooks. That was the end of my little crush. Grandma came to orchestra practice one day, confronted the boy, and told him that her granddaughter was not old enough to date. Beyond talking about musical notes or the violin, the boy had nothing more to say to me.

My 15-year-old sister, on the other hand, was permitted to at least see boys socially, but only if they came to our house. Until she turned 16, my sister still wasn't allowed to go out on a date. Those were the rules in our house. Grandma did her best to orchestrate those visits when a young man came to call. And at other times, telephone calls my sister had with a boy were monitored; and when a boy came over to see her, Grandma hovered and supervised.

When it came to raising us, Gramps was fine with staying on the sidelines like a good assistant coach watching his players in motion. All he demanded, though, was that my sister and I respect Grandma at all times and obey. He was aging and graying, but he still remembered what it took to get his own four daughters from puberty through the teen years, and the angst, the tears, and ranting that came with the process.

But it was Grandma who wanted to hold on tight as my sister and I itched to unfurl our maturing wings. As Grandma tried to keep our emerging social circle narrow and manageable, we got absorbed into hers. Before we knew it, my sister and I were becoming Grandma's regular companions during the hours that she spent at her Jolly Wonders Club meetings or frequenting their card parties and fish fries. And by this time, as her friends died off, we had accompanied her to more funerals and gravesites than we could count.

As our kinship family, Grandma and Gramps sought to raise us no differently than their own children. They did not see us as strangers, but as "daughters." As such, they applied the same discipline to our lives as they had to their own teenage daughters. However, the boundaries created for us had reached a tipping point for my sister. She just wanted to taste freedom. And by now, she had made up her mind that the rules weren't about to change in our house and she was willing to run away to get loose. Her family didn't know, not even me, but my sister had a plan.

It was Memorial Day weekend and, after some exhaustive negotiating, we convinced Grandma to allow us to attend a friend's party that Friday night. Doing some negotiating of her own, Grandma gave us until 11:30 to return home that night, which to her was a compromise between my 11 o'clock and my sister's midnight curfews. We took Grandma's deal and got dressed to the nines for the party.

Although we were allowed to attend the party, nothing much seemed to please my sister any more. Not even me. We bickered and even tussled each other to the ground some days. I really didn't think she liked me any more. I remember how our relationship got bruised one day and never really seemed to recover after our foster grandmother shared a letter that she received one day from our biological grandmother, Hilda. I never learned what her motivation was for sending or sharing that letter. After all, I was 10 and my sister was 12 when we were told that we didn't have the same father. The news shocked and disturbed us. But after that revelation, I made up my mind that I wouldn't let it change my feelings for my sister. She was still the most important person in my life.

My sister had made it clear that she didn't want her little sister tagging along to the party that night, but I tried to put that behind me and look forward to a good time. I could hear the beat inside as we climbed the steps to the front door. It was going to be a happening party, I thought as I strutted in behind my sister. Girls in culottes and mini dresses and guys and girls in bell bottom pants were working up a sweat as they stepped hard in platforms and rocked to Parliament's "Flash Light." A few fellas in the corner with no dance partners were making their own fun as they belted out the chorus and waved their arms in the air. I danced and made the rounds, talking to some of the girls and guys from school and the block. When I stopped and looked around the crowded living room, I couldn't see my sister. Then this good-looking guy in a fly red double-knit shirt and denim bell bottoms asked me to dance. I plopped my cup of soda down, slid my purse up on my shoulder, and we were doing the bump. When the music stopped, I eyed the clock on the wall and again looked around for my sister before heading to the kitchen. There she was huddled with her girlfriend. When she saw me heading her way, I got the same angry get-lost look that I had been seeing for weeks now. I didn't care, we needed to leave. I just wanted to make sure that we had enough time to walk the 20 minutes back home and still make our curfew. We had a deal with Grandma and I was determined that we would honor it. But here my sister was, acting like she had lost her mind. It was already close to 11 o'clock and time for us to say our good byes and start our walk back, but my sister announced that she wasn't leaving the party and told me to go home without her. For a minute, I was just dumbfounded. Not go home? What was she talking about? We had to go together. All I could think of was Grandma's rules, the curfew, and the big trouble that we were going to be in if we didn't leave right then and show up at home together by 11:30 p.m.

I begged my sister to leave with me, but she tuned me out and didn't budge even when I reminded her of how far we had come since those troubled days growing up and that we couldn't risk the good life that we had with Grandma and Gramps. But the blaring music on the stereo, not the urgency in my voice, filled her ears. She sat slumped in a chair at the kitchen table in her flowered, sleeveless mini-dress. In the next room, The Jackson Five were crooning "I'll Be There" and kids were dancing slow and close.

Still stunned by her news and what I was about to do, I left the party, and my sister, behind. My walk home was a dreary, lonely journey. Confused and scared, I cried uncontrollably as I turned the corner, nearing home. All I had were questions—what was I going to do without my sister if she didn't come back home? What was I going to tell my grandparents? I knew that I had to protect my sister as she had protected me all of those years growing up, but now, I just didn't know how. I didn't want to lie.

As I eased my key in the front door, it was already midnight. We were a half hour past our curfew and Grandma and Gramps were up waiting in the dining room for my sister and me and for an explanation. Once inside, crossing from the front door to where my grandmother paced the floor as she puffed on a Virginia Slims cigarette, was another long walk. As they waited up, Gramps sought patience in his crossword puzzle.

They looked eagerly at me standing there in the entryway to the dining room and immediately noticed her absence. "Where's your sister?"

I knew the truth, but nothing came out of my mouth after that but lies. I told them that we got separated at the party and I couldn't find her when it came time for me to leave. I made up what I thought would be a plausible story just in case my sister decided to come to her senses that evening and come home. It didn't matter much what I said that night about my sister's whereabouts, the questioning from my grandparents was unrelenting as their concern escalated. My own lying and worry eventually got the best of me. I broke down and told grandma and gramps the sad truth. My sister wasn't coming back home. She hadn't taken a bag with her, but she had run away.

At that moment, hearing my own words made me angry and scared as I realized what her not coming home would mean. And before I knew it, heated words and emotions leapt out of me that I had never unleashed in this house. Worried eyes stared back at me from their two worn and stunned faces. By now, I was shaking inside and yelling at Grandma at the top of my lungs. I let her know that she was the reason that my sister was not standing beside me in the dining room facing them. Your meanness drove her away, I shouted. That's when Gramp's tall frame reared up from his chair, reached down for my face and slapped it hard. In an instant, he silenced me, and I stumbled back.

My face stung and my mind raced as I began to wonder how we let our lives and family spin out of control. There weren't many answers, but here we were in the middle of the night, in a sad emotional heap. Looking back, I wish that we could have talked together as a family instead of at each other those months. And I wish that my sister hadn't felt that she had no alternative but to leave home and leave me. Maybe raising my sister and me came with more frustration and confusion than Grandma and Gramps remembered when they were twenty-something parents rearing their children in the 1950s and 1960s. Perhaps, adolescence was a tamer phase and life was simpler, with fewer distractions for young people. It was the 1970s and maybe my sister and I were just a bit more independent and worldly than the generation that came before us? I don't know, but looking back, I wish that as a family, connected through kinship links and the foster care system, we could have had intervention to save us from unraveling. Wasn't that what our case workers were supposed to do?

I hadn't seen or heard from my sister since I left her behind at the party that Friday night. So, on that Monday, which was Memorial Day, all that I could think about first thing in the morning was finding my sister. It was as if the events on Friday night that seemed to topple me now didn't matter. Finding my sister did matter. So, on that holiday, I left the house without permission, determined to search for her. It didn't take long to think about where to start looking because she didn't have many friends. Her best friend's house was the first door I knocked on and wasn't surprised to learn that my sister was inside.

"She's been here since Friday," my sister's friend told me. As I headed up to the third floor of the house to see her, feelings of happiness and sadness marched ahead of me now that I knew that my sister was safe, but also realized that our family life with Grandma and Gramps was quickly coming to an end.

My sister sat on a twin bed in her friend's room looking bewildered, but she was adamant about me leaving her alone. I wasn't listening and instead tried to convince her that we needed to be together. Apparently, my sister never explained to her friend's family that she had just run away from home. And when I asked them if I could stay, too, they assumed it was for a sleepover. That's when I picked up the telephone to call Grandma.

This was it. I shared the good news that I had found my sister, and then I let Grandma know that neither of us would be coming back to her. My place, I decided, was with my sister.

But even then, the chaos wasn't over for us. In fact, it was just beginning. Her friend's parents were clueless that my sister and I had run away until the police notified them. Grandma and Gramps had reported us missing, but there was no going back to live with them. Even if we wanted to, Grandma and Gramps wouldn't have us. We weren't welcome any more in our forever home.

Our foster grandparents were legally responsible for us. The state child welfare system made it so, but neither our caseworkers nor the family court were connected enough to know that our shattered situation at home was their clue to step in and help us find resolution without dissolving. During the more than seven years that we were with Grandma and Gramps, my sister and I rarely if ever saw a caseworker. Now, here we were with no place to live.

When you fail at Grandma's house, it's like someone has turned off the lights, shuttered the windows, and rolled up the welcome mat. Grandma's house is "that" comfortable place where an embrace awaits and where most of us hasten to when tough times tag along and when trouble finds us. Until now, Grandma's house had been our best chance and we thought our last resort. Unfortunately, we didn't consider the consequences that would come when we decided to push back against the family who was raising us as if we belonged to them.

My sister had a number and address for my father that she always kept close. She reached out to him in desperation. At the time, we needed a place to stay and it looked like it was going to be back were we began, with our dad. After picking us up, the police transported my sister and me to my father's place.

When the Past is Present

Here we go again.

By now, my dad had built another life of his own and with yet another woman, but he let us come to stay anyway. The woman he lived with had two children of her own and was also pregnant with my father's baby. She made it clear that she wanted nothing to do with my sister and me. When we got to Dad's place, I couldn't help but look around my father's apartment and think now about all that we had just left behind—a lovely, good and loving home, all of our belongings, and caring grandparents. All of the great outfits that Grandma bought me were back there in the closet. We arrived at Dad's apartment with just the clothes on our backs. Our sudden move also meant that we didn't even get to finish the last week of school before the summer break.

It was June and the days were warming. And now, here we were cooped up in a cramped apartment with too many people and with two adults who would have been just fine if my sister and I had faded into the woodwork. When we landed a few days ago on my father's doorstep, he once again had the chance to do the right thing by his girls, but, instead, he allowed us to slip through his fingers. He had chosen his new family, others, over my sister and me. To him, it was acceptable to care for and raise children who were not his own when those he brought into the world and claimed as his own became someone else's responsibility.

By now, I had learned what family was, and I didn't see a hint of it in this place. But today was about coping. I couldn't dwell on yesterday and what was, or look too far ahead, either. As a child growing up with a fragile safety net, I learned that life lesson well. So, I resigned myself to just make the best of living here until or if things changed. I realized there were mountains that I couldn't get around.

Dad's girlfriend and I didn't get along, and I did my best to stay out of her way. I quickly found a new friend in her brother who was around my age. He lived below us in another apartment. I also played with some of the children I met in the neighborhood or just stayed inside, sleeping on the sofa or plopping down there to watch television. This was how my summer began.

We had only been in the apartment a few days when my sister left one morning to start the new summer job that she had lined up when we were still living with Grandma. Dad was also heading out that morning for his work. I stayed behind, watching them both go off to start their day. Too young to work or do much of anything else, I played or sat on the stoop, pondering my young life as it was.

But I didn't last the week in this place. My end began with a question—"Are you Sharon?"

When I looked up from the stoop, a White woman in a crisp summer dress was standing there. She had pulled up in front of our building, got out of her car, walked toward me, speaking my name and asking more questions. Is your father home? I said no and told her that my dad's girlfriend was upstairs. Back in the apartment, the two women talked and while inside, the woman who greeted me outside, had also spoken on the phone to my father. I was certain that he knew what his girlfriend had done to get me out of their lives.

What could have happened, I wondered? What did I do wrong that made this strange woman take me away? I had to go with her, she told me. Nobody stopped her. I wanted to know where I was going and why I had to leave. This woman, who had unexpectedly stepped into my life that morning, was the only one giving directions or telling me anything. My father's girlfriend kept her mouth shut, busying herself in another room as I moved about the apartment, stunned, as I gathered up a few of my things.

I was leaving and my family wasn't present and the person who knew me wasn't saying a word. The boy from downstairs that I played with was the only one who reacted. He was upset and begged to know what was happening and where I was going with this stranger. I didn't know what to say to him but good bye as I headed out the door with the woman who came for me.

When I reached the front stoop and looked back, there was no adult standing there. My father let me go. And this time, I couldn't reach for my sister. Nearly all my life she had been by my side, unwavering in her roles as mother, protector, and friend. Where was she? Was this going to be a short-term absence from her or would it be forever? No, she must be joining me wherever I was being taken. My mind raced. As I stood on the sidewalk, it was like I was invisible, fast becoming a memory.

Along for the Ride

The woman eventually told me that she was a social worker with the child welfare agency and that I was being taken away temporarily to a special place while my father and his girlfriend could sort things out about my living arrangements. I ended up in shelter, a called McIntyre. My stay there, she said, should only be about 90 days. My ears heard forever.

I climbed into the backseat of her car and sat on the right, next to the window, silently staring out beyond the familiar concrete and trees and sidewalks and people that I knew. And even as I was being driven away from the South Hills where I was living, somehow I wasn't afraid. I couldn't imagine the place in the North Hills where I would be, but I knew that the woman behind the wheel wouldn't hurt me. When my sister and I were with our grandparents, we rarely saw a case worker, but Grandma told us about them.

It only took us about 45 minutes to get through the city and onto a pleasant country-like setting, pushed back off the highway.

Looking into the rearview mirror, the social worker finally spoke again to me, announcing, "We're here. This is McIntyre." I got out holding on to my little bag. Silently, we walked briskly to a large main door with a buzzer. She spoke into the call box giving her name and mine. A voice inside acknowledged us and the door's sensor released a startling buzz before clicking open.

When I stepped inside the shelter, I left summer on the doorstep, and entered a cold place. Most things inside looked a bit worn from all of the children who had passed through these rooms, but you could tell that someone tried to bring a few human touches to the public spaces in the institution. There were curtains and rugs, and the bright orange chair cushions in the sitting room off the lobby. They offered some color and life.

We met the woman who was the supervisor. She acknowledged me with her smile and then the three of us walked across the linoleum and parquet to what could have been called a processing area. And with a quick goodbye, the social worker who delivered me turned and left. I gave my name to the woman at McIntyre who accompanied me from that point. By now, I had a file that would be filled with the results of the physical examination that the nurse gave me not long after I arrived. At my next stop, the house parent handed me a set of neatly folded, white twin bed sheets along with a couple of white bath towels and wash cloths soap and some toiletries. The final stop before seeing where I would sleep was my favorite. The house mother took me to a large clothes closet called inventory. It's where the girls at McIntyre were allowed to pick out brand new things—about three changes of clothes from the racks and shoes from the shelves. We didn't wear uniforms, here.

A House Is Not a Home

McIntyre was a co-ed shelter and state-run facility of sprawling green acres and mature oaks atop an attractive hill. We were all the same—dependent boys and girls and teens who landed here because we didn't have mothers and fathers who could care for us. Those of us who were brought here from across Allegheny County, also had this in common—we were all in need of someone to love us.

Even with its worn vinyl floor tiles and motherless kitchen, the shelter really wasn't a bad place for children to be while the problems our parents were having caring for themselves or us got fixed, or until another suitable home was found. At least, that's what we were told about why we were in shelter. There were no physical bars at the windows here or massive gates hemming us in. We were free to roam among the cottages or dormitory-like buildings. But for many of us children, the uncertainty of not knowing if or when our families would come for us often kept our minds on lockdown. At McIntyre, I was assigned to Cottage 6. Each cottage was single-sex and identified by a number. I lived with the 13- to 15-year-old girls.

Oddly enough, when I first saw my roommate, she reminded me of myself. She was warm brown, round, and short. But on that first day, she was just chilly with little to say but a casual "hi." I later learned that my roommate was probably rankled after being told that the room she had to herself for the past several months now had to be shared with me, the new girl.

Now, decades removed from my days at McIntyre, I remember it as being like a fireplace without a fire—it was a pleasant place to look at, and it loomed large, but it was without warmth. Compared to the cozy home where I lived those wonderful years with Grandma and Gramps, McIntyre was almost clinical with its white paint clinging to its behemoth cinderblock facades and scent of disinfectant wafing up from every corner. Inside, no amount of comfy futon-like furniture, bedtime snacks from the kitchen, or laughter could have made it otherwise. But back then, McIntyre was still needed. Otherwise, children who had no refuge from their storms and no kin would probably have ended up on the street or worse.

Being brought to McIntyre for the first time on that summer's day, alone and with no hint of goodbye in the humid air, was totally unexpected, but it wasn't the first time I had been plucked out and uprooted from family and home. Those patterns that I knew growing up somehow made my present at McIntyre not the jarring and frightening experience that it could have been during those early days. By now, I knew what it was like to be on the move and in transition. It was those early lessons that taught me, as a 13-year-old in shelter, not to dwell much on what was going to happen next in my life. I just tried to be a kid.

But there were some things that not even my past could have prepared me for, now that I was in shelter and separated from my family, my sister. Thoughts of her kept me up at night and so did my constant tears. I was trapped between my anger and my sorrow. And when night fell, there was no escaping the two-headed monsters that haunted me—feeling abandoned and unloved.

In those early days at McIntyre, just the sight of another girl, bounding back to our cottage from a wonderful weekend visit with her relatives or a potential new family who wanted her, stirred pain and disappointment as I wondered, what about me? I even asked one of the house mothers why no one was calling for me or coming to take me back home? Surely, my sister must be worried and wondering where I am. We always stayed together.

The house mother had no doubt received the same question countless times from the girls she cared for in Cottage 6. She couldn't give any of us girls a reason, but in an instant, her words to me poured out like pillows of comfort — *"Baby, who wouldn't want you? I would take you home if I could."*

I clung to the house mother's words like a blanket and to the warmth in her heart like it was the passport I needed to leave McIntyre, go home with her, and live happily ever after with a loving family. But the reality of her not being able to take me home eventually set in, and I continued to wonder if anyone would?

The next time I searched for answers, I turned to someone I couldn't see but knew—God. I was angry and demanded even more answers—why did God let my mother die and leave me with a father who would abandon me and not show me love when I needed him most? And I'd ask God, what did I do as a child that was so dreadful and unpleasing that I deserved to be forced to live in a shelter? He didn't deliver the answers I went seeking on those lonely nights, but in the midst of my tears, he did send me peace and rest.

When It's My Turn

Our house parents worked incredibly hard to keep life inside McIntyre as normal as possible. We had home-cooked meals, movies, and fun group activities, and even shopping trips downtown. And they provided a routine and schedule for us to follow. We woke up around 7 a.m. to the house mother's call or tap at our door—"OK, wake up." After that first call and no one stirred, they usually granted a few precious minutes more to snooze before passing through again. The last call usually came at 7:15 a.m. Those on the early breakfast shift, however, usually knew to spring up first so that they could meet the food service delivery truck, set the table, and help get the food started.

And like at Grandma's house, we even had assigned chores here at McIntyre. The women who cared for us also wanted to keep our minds occupied so that we didn't have time to dwell on life without our parents and families or the circumstances that brought us to this place. But no matter what services and support the house mothers rendered, the one thing that they couldn't do for us was replace the love of family.

These were caring adults and trained caregivers who tried to help us cope with life in shelter, but their presence in our lives was always punctuated by their rotating shifts and days off. They were near to us, and people like Ms. Byrd, the shelter supervisor, were even dear, but somehow never close enough. The other girls thought that our Ms. Byrd was just plain mean. I saw a big Black woman who was as stern as she was stout, but my Ms. Byrd had a soft spot in her heart for me. She kept us girls in line and the shelter running smoothly. I can't recall a time when Ms. Byrd had to impose a heavy hand in Cottage 6, even when my roommate wielded a fire extinguisher and aimed it one day at my head. I ducked, she missed, and we made up.

McIntyre wasn't a place brimming with crisis, and we weren't bad kids who were out of control. We were simply dependent.

One of my favorite places to spend time was in front of Ms. Byrd's office, which reminded me of a pharmacy or bank with its sliding glass window in the front. Ms. Byrd was seated behind the glass, inside the office, always on watch and in charge. Like clockwork, I would show up there at her window ledge. Propping up on my elbows, I'd lean in and talk and laugh with her. But we could never really get close. It was as if that thin pane of glass that separated us physically also put a limit on our emotional connection.

Living at McIntyre was everything that Grandma and Gramp's house was not. While in the care of my foster grandparents, my sister and I needed permission to even go to the corner or across the street, but here in shelter, children were in their own world living independently, but with supervision. We were youngsters giving each other advice on life and living as we knew it. We were each other's counselors.

These were my peers—the girls of Cottage 6—and they became like family. We were in the same age group; we even looked a lot alike. Sure, the circumstances that played out in our life stories varied, but we shared a common thread—young girls left dependent without a permanent home and parents or a family to raise them.

Huddled together on top of our beds or sitting in the shade, crossed legged on the grass, adolescent dreams were repeated from mouth to mouth and heart to heart. We chattered endlessly about that hopeful day when we would be told that, yes, somebody, our parents, some family, some mother, wanted us.

As my days at McIntyre flowed into months, I did what other children in my situation would; I adjusted. I learned to join in with the other girls as they shared precious snippets of information from well-meaning house parents about news of when they could be scheduled for a weekend home visit or if their chances of going to live with a new and permanent family looked promising. But, as new girls entered McIntyre and others left us for their journey back home, we learned one of the most important lessons of living life in shelter—don't get too close to moving targets. That meant sometimes living with your emotions cloaked—it didn't always work, but it was supposed to be the best protection against the pain of separation in this place. So, when new girls came to live at McIntyre as they did every month, we would embrace them, but we couldn't risk getting too close. We knew that someday we could be heartbroken when it was their turn to leave.

Like me, the residents of McIntyre juggled hope and uncertainty about whether the stay would be short-lived or if we'd end up being long-timers. It didn't help that the assurance and information we needed to ready our minds and spirits for a future with family and kin, or the day when we would leave McIntyre, came to us in dribs and drabs and usually without confirmation from any legal authority or social worker. I was in month four of living at McIntyre, and still no social worker had contacted me. I hadn't been to family court, or heard any news about my sister and father, or had a word from my foster grandparents. But apparently, behind the scenes, plans were being made for my future.

It arrived second hand and was still unofficial, but the house-mother repeated the message that she heard being bantered about—I may be going to live with my foster aunt and uncle. A month later, I learned for sure that I was leaving McIntyre. But even as the counselor gave me the good news, I could hardly believe it when she said, "Sharon, your family is coming for you!" They were the daughter and son-in-law of my foster grandparents and just special people; a young couple in their 30s with two children of their own.

But where were they? I wanted to know what was taking them so long come for me. Somewhere between month four and month five at McIntyre, I began to grow tired of waiting for that day to come, if it ever would. Around that time, a friend in neighboring Cottage 8 was hatching her plan to run away from her restlessness and McIntyre and persuaded me to join her. I'm usually the one leading things, but this time, my emotions were leading me. I couldn't see beyond my anger and sadness and was in search of relief.

Running away could put an end to my waiting. Anything seemed better than just counting the days and expecting news to come about family and my departure. No one had given me any updates about my pending placement with my foster aunt and uncle or what was in store for me. That would have made all of the difference. But I was tired of thinking about the situation. By this time, I had convinced myself that

I could run away at 13 and start a whole new life on my own with just the belongings I had at McIntyre, and with no job, no money, and not even a high school diploma. I was still an eighth grader. But I was desperate and disappointed and those things just weren't important to me at the time. Finding peace, a family to support and care for me unconditionally, was foremost in my mind.

The View from the Top

I was on kitchen duty that chilly Saturday in October when my friend and I decided to make our escape.

I eased on out the back door of the kitchen pretending the garbage bag holding my belongings was the morning trash I was assigned to take to the dumpster. My heart raced one minute and quivered the next as we began our descent on the sloping hill that led to an embankment and then to the highway below. After 15 minutes, we were still making our way down the side of the property with our loaded bags in our hands. When we finally reached the bottom of the hill, we realized that we hadn't thought about how we would make the leap from here onto the congested highway below. That ribbon of highway would lead us to the interstate and to what we thought was freedom. For now, it stopped us in our tracks.

Looking down on the roofs of moving cars beating it down the two-lane highway was enough to make me think again about our escape. My life at McIntyre may have been in limbo, but at that moment, I was grateful to still have choices—risk jumping off the embankment and possibly dying that day or just turn around, make my way back up the hill, and never look back.

To my friend's amazement and agitation, I left her standing there, alone with her decision. She pleaded for me to come back. But instead, I climbed up the side of the hill and eased into Cottage 6 through the same back door. And she went forward.

If I had jumped, lived, and fled on that Saturday, I wouldn't have been at McIntyre two days later on that Monday morning to receive the news I longed for—I would begin home visits with my foster aunt and uncle starting at the end of the week. One of the counselors had pulled me out of class to tell me this. Excitement followed me back to class that morning, and within minutes, anyone who would listen knew the plans for me that weekend. And by that evening, nearly everyone in Cottage 6, especially the house-mothers, was overjoyed for me. Looking back, I'm not sure how I got my excited heart to keep up with my head between Monday and Friday. But I did.

By the time Friday at 5 p.m. rolled around, the suitcase I packed days before was standing at the front door of the cottage, ready to be carried over the threshold and to a familiar place. I was more than ready, too. That evening, the whole family had come for me. These were the people and faces that I knew from weekends when I would sleepover at their home, or babysit their children. This was the family who sat with me around the dinner table on Sundays at Grandma's. My foster aunt was one of Grandma's four daughters. She and my foster uncle and their children were the extended branches of the people who raised me. Together, we had become like family. It had been six months in July since I had entered McIntyre and had seen anyone who knew me. When my family arrived, the only gifts that I had to give them were hugs, smiles, and my heartfelt gratitude for opening up their home to me.

This was a homecoming. The only person missing, though, was my sister. I wanted to ask where she was and if she knew that I would be coming to live with them, but I didn't dare bring the matter up. Who knew how they would have responded to my curiosity and surprise when I didn't see my sister there? Instead, I stayed quiet, choosing to relish the moment and being home.

Everything else under their roof in the spacious two-story home was as I remembered it. Every room was furnished and decorated. And in my cousin's room, there was a new twin bed just for me. She was a little girl, younger than me, and who looked forward to sharing her space and even to taking on a "big sister." My other cousin was a boy, a year younger than me.

For all of my excitement that led up to that weekend, the evening was rather uneventful. The family went about their business, falling into their Friday night routine, but leaving me a little space to get re-acclimated and unpacked. Later that evening, though, we gathered in the family room to watch a movie on television. I couldn't stop thanking them for taking me in and giving me another chance at having a home. My foster aunt and uncle let me know that theirs wasn't a tough decision because I was already family. As we sat there eating buttered popcorn and drinking soda, they let me know that it was foremost in their minds for me to be safe and to have a place to stay.

The next day was Saturday and I got permission from my aunt and uncle to hang out and roam in the neighborhood in search of the friends that I had made there. I went knocking on some doors to meet up with a few of the girls and guys. They were glad to see me back on the block. But before we could get down to the business of playing, they wanted answers: "Where have you been all those months? Where is your sister? Who are you living with now?" and so much more. I had spent months in shelter eating lots of comfort food and unknowingly adding pounds to my short frame. Since my friends saw me last, I probably had gone up at least four dress sizes. There were even rumors swirling that I left the neighborhood because I went away to have a baby and then put it up for adoption. Nothing could have been further from the truth. I was still a virgin, but that was none of their business. None of the stories and questions the kids stirred up that weekend was going to spoil my time back home with my family. Reconnecting with my friends was brief and bittersweet. In that moment, I realized how concerned they were about my sister and me. There was so much that had happened to us. Those kids would never understand and I couldn't begin to explain why I had spent last summer in Cottage 6 at a shelter while they went off to camp and summer school, packed into the family car for vacation, or ran for ice cream when the truck's bell clanged, making its way down our street. How would I begin to tell another youngster about two sisters whose young lives had been interrupted? I didn't understand it myself. I just knew that it all made me sad.

That weekend, I couldn't stop the clock from winding down.

The great visit with my aunt and uncle and cousins was coming to a fast close and, by Sunday, I was growing despondent. I didn't want to leave. But when I returned to McIntyre that evening around 7:30, it was my turn to bound in and beam as I made my way through the front door at Cottage 6. Knowing that my foster aunt and uncle were working as quickly as they could to make living with them permanent and real, my mood lifted and I came back to shelter confident and hopeful. I was warned, however, that there were still mounds of paperwork for them to complete and more home visits to schedule, but having spent time in my aunt and uncle's home in those early years, could work in my favor and hasten the whole process along.

By mid-week, my counselor at McIntyre again had great news for me. Because the first weekend home visit went so well, my foster aunt and uncle wanted me to be placed with them immediately. Like today, they were the kind of caring adults who knew me and wanted to raise me even though they weren't my blood relatives. I was being given a second chance at having a forever home, and was finally leaving McIntyre, the place that had sheltered me for six months.

On that day, thinking about moving forward was complicated and emotional, as I had to also say farewell to the place, the life, the routine, and the people I was leaving behind in shelter. I didn't know how to share why thoughts of a new life and starting over, even in a familiar place, was making me anxious. The placement would mean living full-time in a home with adults, not in the quasi-independent world that the girls at McIntyre created for themselves. There would be new rules and routines to get used to and younger children in the house who would be looking up to me. When I was with my sister, I had always been that younger, needy person. But whatever it took to stay in my new forever home is what I was going to do. I didn't ever want to worry about finding another home. But most of all, I didn't want to end up back at McIntyre, dependent, and in Cottage 6.

Then, of all things, I started to worry about the many hair supplies that I had amassed over the months and who would step in as the unofficial resident stylist when I left. At McIntyre, the girls knew that they could come to me for a new "do," a touch up, some curls, or a trim. Oh well, I thought, they'll find someone else and I'll have other hair to style—my little cousin and my friends in the neighborhood.

FOUR

Living in the New Normal

Going Home

A few stuffed animals and, of course, my arsenal of hair care products—Bergamot Hair grease, both the green and the blue kind, brushes with black plastic bristles, a straightening comb, and of course Marcel curling irons, the kind the professionals used—were among my belongings.

Then there were my clothes. I didn't have many, maybe enough outfits and underwear to last me for a couple of weeks, but they all fit well inside the customary, green, heavy-duty garbage bag. That green garbage bag, while drab and essential, was a proud sign that the girl carrying it was on her way out of McIntyre—heading back home or to a better one than she left. An image of that green lumpy bag slung over one shoulder was usually the last image that I would have of the girls who left Cottage 6 before me. I was usually the one in the background and out of sight, longing for my turn. But on that evening, I was the one walking across the threshold and out the front door with my bag and my new family beside me.

My heart and mind that evening had been in celebration mode, but my arrival was without fanfare. No hugs enveloped me once we got back to the house. But then, I wasn't entering a stranger's house.

"Come on in, Shannie," my uncle intoned, as we all piled through the front door. "You're back. This is home, now," he said. And normal quickly followed those words as everyone drifted into their usual routines. My friend, Sheila, from across the street, made up the only welcoming committee that day when she stopped to visit and say that she was glad that I was staying this time.

The newest member of this forever home was here to stay, and life in this household just went on as it usually did—there was homework to do, television to watch, household chores, cooking, relaxing, laundry, and living. The bedroom that I shared with my young girl cousin waited for me upstairs next to a blue bathroom at the top of the stairs. Our room was in the middle of three others. My male cousin, who was slightly younger than me, had his own room. Once I acquired more outfits, I made the small den upstairs my clothes room. It was also a thoroughfare for my aunt and uncle on their way to and from their bedroom.

My first hours were spent unpacking my small load and relishing being home. I emptied the green garbage bag of my belongings, putting everything away inside the closet as neatly as I could since I shared the space. Some things went on hangers and other pieces of clothes, like some of my play tops, were folded, also neatly, before being tucked in my side of the dresser drawer. My few stuffed animals landed in a row at the head of my bed. They fit right in.

After eyeing my small amount of clothing, my aunt and uncle decided that a few new pieces were definitely in order. Like her mother, my aunt wanted her girls to be outfitted with pretty dresses and nice clothes from the better department stores, too—the bargain basement and discount shops just weren't going to do the trick.

I lived here now, but when that first Sunday afternoon rolled around, I couldn't help but think and smile—I didn't have to leave, like before, when the weekend was over. Instead, I attempted to find my place and ease in to it. Household chores made my transition a little easier. What

I knew about making beds and keeping house, I learned from Grandma and I knew that she would have expected it of me, even if her daughter, my aunt, didn't. I knew how to clean, make beds, and wash and dry my own clothes. Saturdays here didn't mean chores. There was no early rising to tackle dusting, and scrubbing, and cleaning as the sun was just getting comfortable in the sky and by the time my favorite Saturday morning cartoons were airing. I had time to sleep in and hang out with my friends or find a comfy seat on the sofa for the morning line up of TV shows. And likewise, Sunday didn't usually mean church for this family. That never would have happended at Grandma's house; she taught me well. Church and chores were a part of me and what I did. Both were familiar and among the things that gave my life meaning and stability. I even found some comfort and calm in cleaning. So, these things remained a part of my routine.

In this house, I was the only one rising and dressing, and making my way to the house of the Lord early on a Sunday morning. Church was my refuge, the special place where I communed with God and found a sense of peace. Before I went to live with Grandma, church hadn't been a part of my life. But because of her, I learned the value of worship and prayer. And along the way, my faith in God became the mainstay of my existence. I didn't always understand why I was left without a mother whose face I couldn't remember; a little brother I didn't have a chance to know; a sister who was not by my side; and a father who had, in his way, tried to hold on to his family, but let it slip away. But I knew that I could count on God on Sunday and during the rest of the week.

With my low-heeled patent leathers, knee-highs, and in one of my best dresses or skirts, I would walk from our house on Industry Street, up to Climax Street, the main drag through Beltzhoover. And 20 minutes later, I was at the corner of Chalfant Street and Delmont Avenue ready to step inside South Hills Baptist Church where the Rev. Cornelius Carter was the pastor. I sang, I listened, I rocked and clapped, I prayed, and my spirit was at rest when I came here.

I grew to love the Rev. Carter and his wife. He was a family man whose sermons usually reflected those virtues in clear, concise, and teachable moments. When he stepped into the pulpit, I sat back and grabbed hold of what this quiet, genteel preacher had to say about things like love and morality. And from the Rev. Carter's pulpit to my pew, his sermons on forgiveness and his familiar refrain that Jesus would "make everything all right," seemed always meant for me.

But the man of God who succeeded the Rev. Carter when he stepped down, well, he was definitely the "whoopin and hollerin" Holy Ghost and brimstone kind who needed a white hand towel to mop his forehead and dab the rest of his face. Our pastor, the Rev. Michael Dickerson, could sing like nobody's business and was quite the showman. When you left church on Sundays, it was easy to recount the Rev. Dickerson's sermons, not so much for what he said, but for how he delivered them. Sometimes he'd toss his small towels with abandon as we watched them cascade down in front of the pulpit like manna. Or the Rev. Dickerson would leap up then walk across the wooden benches in the sanctuary when he was on fire and driving his three-point sermon home.

I came to South Hills Baptist for the music, too. It was dynamic and I wished that I could have been a part of its fabulous choir, but my time after school and on weekends were taken up with dance at the Selma Burke Art Center, and my rehearsals and performances with the Ozanam Strings. After my six months in shelter, my aunt and uncle had to re-enroll me in these activities.

Smooth Places

For much of the time, life in the care of my aunt and uncle was warm and sometimes even wonderful. But there were many times when those otherwise smooth places that families shared and enjoyed and where parents and their children met turned bumpy and contentious. And I didn't know what to do when that happened, so I busied myself with a list of chores that I made up as I wished for answers.

If only there had been a handbook with instructions for dependent children like me, someone transitioning from shelter and their own troubled families to a forever home. At the time, I was also struggling with how to live again outside of an institution and even talk to the adults who now cared for me like their own. But there was no one to intervene and guide my aunt, uncle, cousins, and me on our way to becoming family.

Nevertheless, I was hopeful that living with caregivers in their thirties would allow just what my emerging teen years needed—some fun, some freedom, and structure, but not too many rules.

My sister and I had spent great weekends at my foster aunt and uncle's house babysitting and playing with our cousins, sleeping over and getting up late, and just hanging out with a couple who was much younger than our grandparents and who allowed us a bit more latitude to stretch our wings. Then one June day our lives were interrupted and my sister and I were gone—me eventually to shelter and my sister, well, I didn't know where she lived the summer that I was taken away.

But here I was on my own, now trying to figure out how best to make life with my new family work from one day to the next. If my sister were here, she would have known what to do. This home is where I wanted to be, still there were days when I felt like a stranger in a lovely, familiar place.

When company came, my aunt and uncle never had to make a mad dash to primp the pieces in the living room or shove clutter in the closet or in other places out of sight. Despite having three youngsters in the house, they kept the place spotless: the living room, just off to the right of the front door, was always ready to receive and entertain guests. Even the coordinating pillows on the sleek comfy living room sofa never needed plumping or arranging. Most all of the furnishings in this young, family-friendly household were modern, fresh, and stylish. My aunt cleaned house like her mother and took great pride in her efforts, but it was her guests' generous praise for her décor that made it all worthwhile.

Most of the rooms in my aunt and uncle's house were outfitted in wood paneling. The kitchen, straight down the hall from the living room, was the exception. Its walls wore beige designer paper for a backdrop. That color made the kitchen's stylish golden brown appliances pop. And just off the kitchen was the den, the place where we could sit and relax on the sofa or love seat and watch TV as a family. The dining room was our other formal space. You reached it through a doorway that led from either the den or the living room.

Most of our living was done on the second and third floors. The only reason to go down to the unfinished basement was to do laundry. And our backyard, with its hills and mounds, was also a place that didn't get much use. But the house's large front porch is where I often entertained my friends from school and the neighborhood, or where I would sit and draw.

My sister and I should have been together in this house, I often thought. We had always been together. During those months in shelter, I had grown accustomed to the residents of Cottage 6, their counsel, their comfort, and even their chatter; much like a family, but they never could beat what she and I had together. But as much as I wanted to leave the confines of McIntyre, transitioning from the other young people I had grown to trust, it wasn't going to be easy co-existing with the adults in this family now that I was in a forever home. All I wanted to believe was that the adults I lived with could also be trusted and counted on to be present for me the next day and the next; and not leave me.

Under One Roof

There was one thing that I knew for sure: I needed stability in my life and a family to take care of me. Those were important things and had been out of my reach for far too long. I was ready to do whatever was needed to hold on to what I had been given—a second chance. Even if it meant sometimes silencing myself or steadying my tongue when I wanted to talk back to my new family, or stifling my emotions so that they didn't seep out of me like poison and ruin the day; I did it. And none of that was easy to do as a teen girl who could carry a big attitude when she wanted to.

On many days, the best place for me was in the confines of my room where I sought refuge from the things that plagued me and sometimes from the family that cared for me, even if I found little relief. My aunt's moodiness could drive me there—as it often did. The walls of my room served as a ready shield for when she would rant and find fault with most everything we children did or on days when she bounded between sunny and just leave-me-alone when her 11-7 shift at the post office was over.

But there was more to my aunt's hot and cold moments that trickled down on us like a faulty faucet. The issues that gnawed at her were bigger and ran deeper than her work at the post office, her kids, and me. One day when she came home from work, tired, she announced that I would be in charge of preparing the dinner meal for the family. I couldn't believe what I was hearing and resented this chore. Did she think that because I lived with her mother, one of the best cooks in town, that I knew how to prepare meals, too? I didn't. My sister and I helped out in Grandma's kitchen, stirring and mixing or measuring, but she didn't spend time teaching us to cook and we didn't ask to learn. But again, I did what I had to do to comply in this forever home. If there was one thing that I learned as a child growing up without much stability or safety nets, it was not to rock the boat when you want so much to stay and belong.

As the head of this working-class family, my uncle kept a watchful eye on his nest. But he also usually kept a closed mouth when it came to managing and disciplining his son and daughter, and me. That was his wife's responsibility. My uncle was a steamfitter in his early 30s. He had proudly become one of the first African-Americans in Pittsburgh to be accepted into a local journeyman program where he learned his trade. In many ways, my uncle reminded me of Gramps, a self-made man who put family first.

He, too, was wise and reserved, and never one for idle talk. And this otherwise easy going man was unflinching when it came to extolling the virtues of academic achievement and ensuring that all were on one accord with that belief. He set the bar high for the children in his house and he created incentives for reaching that place. With the fastidiousness of a scientist, my uncle handled each of our report cards and pored over them. No grade went unnoticed and lesser ones—below a B — had to be explained. And top grades—A's and B's—were rewarded with $5 and $2 respectively. For a C grade or below, we weren't rewarded. We were lectured, instead, on being average.

"Let me hear it," my uncle would say slightly annoyed, but patient as he stopped on a C grade. "Tell me what happened in this class and what you did to earn this mark?"

We were glad that at least he was willing entertain a reason for it being on the report card. This was our cue to make a case for why we got a C. We told him that it reflected hours of study and hard work and even efforts to engage his help with our class work.

At times, it seemed like earning top grades on my report card was out of reach, but I wasn't one to give up. I had been a smart curious student even if my formal education was spotty and lagged in some places.

Finding My Rhythm

The days of going to school at McIntyre in a trailer outfitted with books, a desk, and a teacher who met with me each day for one-on-one lessons were over. There were no classrooms filled with other children at McIntyre. I was returning to a building made of brick and mortar and filled with lots of classrooms, and students that I didn't know. I was just starting Prospect Middle School and, I was entering ninth grade and starting out as an upperclassman at the school that also included grades 7 and 8.

Prospect Middle was a public school situated next to a mainly White middle-class neighborhood. It was where children from our section of Beltzhoover were assigned but my aunt knew that it was also a school that came with a good reputation, money for resources, and fine teachers.

By age 14, my academic transcript already contained the names of seven schools, if my education on the McIntyre campus was counted in the mix. Looking back, I wonder if the time spent in the trailer school represented half a school year that I missed. I don't even know if

I was working on grade level when I was in that trailer or just plodding through remedial courses?

It didn't help that I hated reading. Picking up a book and having to sit quietly and alone turning pages wasn't something that I looked forward to after my teacher gave us those instructions. And even after delving into a book, capturing the meaning of the words and passages on a page confounded me when it came time to tell my teachers what I had just read. But not so for math, the subject I excelled in and loved. In my mind, numbers and solving the math problems that blazed across a chalkboard excited me. I seemed to learn best when my mind, my eyes, and my hands were in motion.

Nonetheless, I wasn't giving up on reading or on any of my other subjects. Between my school work and trying to overcome and adjust to a new home was proving to be more than a notion at the start of 9th grade. My school work ebbed, flowed a little but never quite soared. And by the time first-quarter grades were tallied, my report card told the story. Dread and taking those grades home were all that I could think about after school. Home was the place where my uncle preached that "hard work and studying equaled the honor roll." At report card time, my cousins were accustomed to bringing home nothing less. That's what my uncle expected of them.

Neither my aunt nor my uncle was college educated despite the fact that their parents wanted so much to call their son and daughter a college graduate. In fact Grandma, my aunt's mother, wanted all of her daughters to go to college and earn degrees, but they didn't. Instead, Grandma found other things about her girls that made her proud. Long before my uncle's people got schooled and earned their degrees in the North, they were a proud farming family from Mississippi. His parents knew early that going to school and getting educated held the best chance of escaping a life of poverty and the trappings that came with it if you were Black. But despite those leanings, college wasn't in my uncle's plans. As a young man, he wanted to strike out on his own to work and make money, unlike his siblings who stayed in school and all graduated from college. Their mother was a school teacher.

But when he became a father, my uncle delivered much the same message to us that he heard growing up. He talked to his children, including me, about academic excellence and good grades being stepping stones to a good life after high school. Because he never experienced it for himself, my uncle couldn't provide a specific map of the route that would get us there. He had decided to go directly to the steel mill.

But on one afternoon when he returned home from the dentist, my uncle spoke words to me that forever illuminated my academic journey, especially on those days when I wanted nothing more than to extinguish the fire for learning and success that I thought was inside of me.

"Obstacles are those frightful things you see when you take your eyes off your goal."

These were the words my uncle told only me that day. They were first spoken by the wealthy industrialist and Ford Motor Co. founder Henry Ford. Fortunately for me, my uncle found Ford's words on a poster that hung on the wall of his dentist's waiting room. Decades later, I keep those transcendent words close and set them in motion when my path grows cloudy.

His hope for us to do better and to go further in life than he did was constant. So, it was not a surprise to me that when he saw my first-quarter report card, my uncle delivered a kind but sobering directive when I eased it into his waiting hands. The report was filled with disappointment and more than a few marginal grades.

"We make the honor roll in this house," he said, looking down at the report card and then back up at me. For him, anything less was considered a failure.

With a made-up mind, this member of the family wasn't going to disappointment my uncle again. The pressure was definitely on, now, to bring up my grades. I was the oldest child in the house and if the younger ones were going to see me as a role model, I wanted them to also look up and see a smart and motivated student like they were. It didn't take long before they did. That next quarter, I did my best to follow my uncle's prescription—I worked hard, studied hard, and went to my uncle when I had questions. And by the next quarter, this girl made the honor roll for the first time. What a sense of relief it was. I felt like I was finally turning an academic corner, especially knowing that I had come to middle school not working on grade level. By now, I had caught up and was able to compete with my classmates. Doing well in school also made me feel an even greater sense of belonging in this family. That school year I continued to bring home A's and B's and make honors most of the time; when I didn't, I'd gear up, hunker down, and work harder the next quarter.

As the months passed, I started to get into the groove of being in this home. I even stopped worrying so much about landing back in shelter because I said or did the wrong thing. This was home now. I was a part of the family and convinced that my aunt and uncle were committed to me. It felt good knowing that, but at the same time, their troubled marriage didn't go unnoticed. Their tension, which they tried to keep hidden, chipped away at my newfound happiness.

Most of the time, my forever home was a peaceful place, like still waters, at least on the surface. But the longer I was there, the more I could sense the storm between my aunt and uncle. It wasn't the mundane kind of friction that found its way into most any marriage at one point or another; it had roots that ran deep. In fact, it had been brewing long before I arrived, but the two did their best to shield us children from their rain. We would never see them arguing, but their relationship was struggling. They even stopped liking each other. For the children, they stayed together and tried to make things work. They managed and kept up this routine until each child was grown up and out of their nest. They were family. I had been placed in their care, but I had landed in the middle of something as my own rough spots were still festering.

There were many days when my aunt's sparks landed on me. Without warning, she could turn chilly and indifferent toward me just because I was there. And, because at the end of her shift, she didn't know where to dump her displeasure with her job at the post office and didn't know where to plant the airy dreams of a young mother who wanted to do something different, more, and better with her life.

While I had been invited to live in her home after she and my foster uncle completed plenty of forms and underwent background checks to get me, perhaps my foster aunt saw me as "the other child," or "the outsider." Whatever she perceived about my existence in this house, it made me the unfortunate target of her anger. Like an arrow, her torrid words or very look found me when I was most in need of her kindness and understanding. Trying hard in my way to be good, keep the peace, and get along with everyone in the house, I was probably more sensitive than I otherwise would have been to her apparent discontent, but all I wanted to do then was be "the good foster child."

Even back then, I could sense that my aunt and uncle were a couple and family in need of rescuing, but I was helpless to do anything more than observe them in decline. Then I decided to shut down and retreat, determined not to let my actions or very presence stir up more trouble or contribute to a family breakup.

In those days, the only time that I really surfaced around the house or offered anything to say was when we all gathered around the dinner table or when I was doing my homework in the evening and needed to ask my uncle for help. Other than that, I kept pretty quiet and to myself, hopeful that things would continue to work out for me in this house and for my aunt and uncle.

I also tried to focus on balancing the good with the bad, knowing that my good days outweighed the bad. One Sunday, the Rev. Carter preached that message, too. My safety net—a forever home—wasn't a perfect place, but it was there to sustain me. The support of my pastor was also there for me. Still, the fear of a lack of permanence and the threat of disruption held a tight grip on my heart and mind. During that first year in my forever home, those were my greatest worries —just like with my mother—one day the home would just be gone.

The first year that I was with my aunt and uncle, I conquered middle school and emerged a much better student than when I entered. In fact, I had become an honor student. I was excelling at violin and really going places with the Ozanam Strings. I had missed being away from the other musicians and friends when I was in shelter. Orchestra got me out of the house and took me on the road, across the city and sometimes even to cities across the country to perform.

It was 1976 and my life couldn't have been better. For the past two months I had been living with my foster aunt and uncle. And during that time, I finally heard from my sister and found out where she was living. Shortly after I entered McIntyre Shelter, my sister left my father's apartment where we were staying. She had reconnected with our biological uncle, my mother's brother, and was being raised by him and his family. I loved our uncle so much and was happy for my sister because she was in a good home surrounded by people who cared for her.

My sister and I were talking again, periodically by phone, and she would sometimes visit me at the house. It bothered me that months of absence had flowed between us. I sensed that our relationship was not as warm, loving, and close as it once was; nonetheless, I was glad that we were again connected. Decades later, my sister confided that she didn't rush into my new life with our foster aunt and uncle because she felt that they didn't want her, too. She also thought that I had it all, the good life.

That fall I was 14 and sailing into 10th grade at South Hills High School, also in the Mt. Washington section. It was close enough to walk to from my house. As I eased into my new life with my foster family, my uncle and a few other members of my biological family showed up from time to time to help keep me grounded and tethered to my roots. My sister and I looked forward one year to traveling with my uncle to our family reunion in Virginia. It was a happy time and the chance to discover just who was who. Among the clan were the curious ones who needed time to warm up to the two strange teenage girls who were at my uncle's side. We were dressed in blue, cotton, flowered-printed dresses and sandals, our uncle introduced my sister and me as Joyce's girls. Images of family flickered on a projector, but I only knew a few of their faces. My uncle had been the keeper of my mother's memory and the one who made sure that her daughters' lives were also knitted into the family where she came from. As we made the rounds, I took in the tapestry of people, many short and deep brown, but I didn't concern myself with searching out familiar things or about lingering on their features, or voices, or hair, or hands, or faces. My eyes widened, though, and a smile filled my face, when my uncle introduced me to relative after relative including one who was a school teacher, and another who was a principal. They were a sight to behold. In school, I had at least one Black teacher. Most of those who taught me, though, had been White nuns and lay people who believed in their Black students and who made us believe that there was nothing that we could not learn and achieve. On that day at the reunion, I was filled with a warmth that must have been pride; I relished the thought of my family members also being professional educators.

As the day went on, I was also surprised to see two people I knew from Ozanam Strings gathered among the crowd of relatives. I wondered why they were here with my family. To my surprise and theirs, we discovered that we were related—cousins.

When I returned home from the reunion, a part of the spirit and joy of being connected to a circle of family came with me.

Growing up in foster care already set me apart from nearly all of my friends, but the teen years could still be prickly and tough for all of us. At times, though, just striving to be as close to perfect as I could, became overwhelming and made me anxious. But I hoped then that being good would earn me favor and allow me to hold on to a family and to a home. I couldn't afford to lose them. And with time, love, and a growing sense of belonging, I began to relax and live life most like any other teen girl. I weathered peer pressure, too, and the other challenges that came with the high school years and with growing up. Opportunities and temptations—drinking, sex, smoking marijuana, and partying—were all around me. Many of my classmates and friends had already dipped their toes into many of those activities before I even began to think about them. When we lived with Grandma and Gramps, Miss' basement was often the place where my sister played hostess and partied. She spun the records, and made money, charging friends a $1 just to enter and $2 to fill up on chicken and soda. Living with my aunt and uncle, my time and focus was on playing the violin and on my dancing. As an honor student, grades were important to me. So was being good, but I still wanted to have some fun with friends. I made sure that at the end of each school week, my homework for the following Monday was completed before I even asked my foster aunt if I could go out on a weekend or join friends at a party.

In my high school years, Kennywood, an amusement park not far from downtown Pittsburgh, was the destination. It was the place to be seen, picnic, and meet up with boys. I can still taste the warm doughy funnel cakes and smell the Potato Patch Fries. Choosing what to wear for our descent on Kennywood and getting ready for my date was an important and fun ritual. By May, I was lining up a date weeks early for the big spring picnic and shopping for an outfit. For daytime, I was usually strutting my hot pants and platform shoes. Palazzo pants or a flouncy, flirty summer dress was in order for evenings at Kennywood when I would meet a guy under the big clock tower in the park or cozy up with him for a boat ride under the moonlight.

But one weekend, when I was in the twelfth grade, I really wandered into the mix. When my best girlfriend learned that my aunt and uncle were going out of town for the weekend, she immediately saw an opportunity for a party without adult supervision. At 16, I wanted instead to prove to my aunt and uncle how responsible I could be while they were away; I would take care of the house and watch over my two younger cousins. That Friday night, as we waved goodbye to my aunt and uncle as they drove away, heading to Akron, Ohio, my girlfriend had already been hatching party plans. The venue later that evening, she said, was going to be my house.

I was on board and when ready, called her to say that the party was officially started. I invited a few classmates that day who eagerly accepted. This was going to be my first house party even though I didn't have a dime to buy refreshments or own records or tapes to play. Never mind the details; my best friend assured me, "I've got everything under control." The party was going to be a huge success.

On that October evening, around 7 p.m., my guests started trickling in. I didn't invite too many people, just a few close friends from school, but as the evening wore on and the music was pumping, the house swelled with about 30 kids who spilled out onto the front and back porches. My 15-year-old male cousin was among the partiers that night. His 11-year-old sister stayed upstairs in the bedroom watching television. My girlfriend handled the music, her cousin brought the drinks. Before the party got started, I had already decided that I wouldn't be drinking. I knew the toll that alcohol had taken on my family over the years. I didn't want it to get me in its grip. But that didn't stop my guests from toting red plastic cups half filled with Mad Dog 20/20, cheap but potent booze.

Before I knew it, someone had shoved one of those cups in my hand, too. I didn't have to drink this first time, but I did. My curiosity had won out, my promise went out the window, and my lips were on the red rim cup. I only took in a few sips before I called it quits. It didn't take me long to get tipsy and to realize that this wasn't something I'd probably do again.

When my aunt and uncle returned home, I made sure that there were no tell-tale signs that a teen party had occurred in their orderly house, but I always suspected they knew what I had done. But they never let on or even scolded or punished me. I may have gotten away with it, but I knew that throwing another party without their permission wouldn't happen again. Instead, I wanted to continue making my aunt and uncle proud and setting a good example for my little cousins.

Born On This Day

At South Hills High, I had found my social niche. And in my neighborhood, I found my first real boyfriend. I was 15. He was a basketball player with tall lanky limbs and broad shoulders. My aunt and uncle approved of him and so did my best friends. Grandma, who wouldn't let my sister and me go out with boys until we were 16, still would have said no to my request no matter how nice this boy was to me or where he came from. But I was living in my aunt's house, now. She was cautious, but her rules on dating were more relaxed than her mother's would have been. My relationship with my high school sweetheart lasted a year.

I guess Grandma knew best. I learned that I wasn't ready for the kind of relationship that he seemed to want. Control was his game, but I wanted to have fun, feel special, and be happy going out with one of my school's star players. By the time I got to the eleventh grade, our relationship came to a much-needed halt. I felt like I had escaped after he tried to put me under lock and key. It was such an uncomfortable situation to be in, but I didn't say anything to the adults in my life even as I struggled to make sense of what I was experiencing and feeling. All of the closeness and the things that I mistook for romantic attention and his like for me were pure obsession and control. What did I know at 15? His interest in me fast became like a pillow that smothered instead of one that provided comfort.

Resentment rose up in me like a fountain as he tried to make me feel small. Whenever I went out with my friends and we weren't together, my boyfriend wanted to know about it—where, why, when? At every turn, he tried telling me what I could and could not do, or who I could talk to. I may have only been a sophomore, but I had sense enough to know that I needed to get out from under this relationship. My gold standard for relationships was Grandma and Gramps. They didn't exchange harsh words or hateful looks, only wrapped each other up in love and respect that seemed to stay sweet and fresh even as they grew old.

"Can we start our relationship over and just be friends?" I asked my boyfriend after mustering up my nerve. "No" was his emphatic response. So, I broke up with him.

At 16, and after that experience, I kept things light with boys, and channeled my focus on graduating that year, my dancing, and my music. I had even joined the cheerleading squad in the 11th grade with my sights set on the varsity captain's spot.

After trying out and scoring the highest in the competition, Ms. K., who managed the cheerleaders, told me that leading the varsity squad would go to someone else. Some of the judges told me later that I had scored high and should have been Ms. K.'s pick. When she offered me the opportunity to lead the junior varsity cheerleaders instead, I turned Ms. K. down. I guess that year, she wanted to have girls out front cheering who were tall and thin or light and bright. None of them looked like me. I was short, brown, and round; still, my routines were tight and near flawless. In my senior year, though, I tried out again for varsity cheerleading captain and made the cut, with my hips and all, but opted instead to be the captain of the Dance Troop.

Otherwise, getting to age 16 and nearing the completion of my final year at South Hills High was as normal as my life had ever been. At school, the competitor in me enjoyed vying with Crystal, a girl, who was No. 1 in math. I was always just trailing her and now I was racing to move ahead. This was my life now. Dancing, cheering, and closing the gap with my math competitors; high school was going well. I was in a happy place. December was here. I would soon be celebrating my birthday and Christmas. How was I to know that those happy days would be snatched away and destined to be memories?

It was Saturday afternoon. It was my birthday. But in our house, birthdays weren't over-the-top occasions or even very festive. Turning a year older was a rather subdued affair. Eating cake and ice cream and getting a chance to open cards in front of family and friends. That was usually it. On this birthday, I wasn't looking for anything special. And, besides, with my birthday falling so close to Christmas, any present I got would usually have to do double-duty. My girlfriend Sheila jokingly called those kinds of gifts "two-fors," short for two-for ones. The cake cutting at home was scheduled for later in the evening, so I had all day to catch up with friends.

I had just finished putting a perfect crease in a pair of new wool pants when my friend phoned and asked me to come for a visit. We were so close that we called each other cousins. His house was a place where I had been dozens of times. It was a safe comfortable space, one where we laughed crazily about school, gossiped, and wiled away the hours talking about our favorite singers or the latest "Soul Train" dances.

I walked the few blocks to his house, and a winter wind whipped around my face and licked at my uncovered ears. I lowered my head to shield myself from the elements and kept going. It was a nice, lazy day and I soon would be in a warm place with my friend, wrapped in memories and good times.

He greeted me at the door. "Hi, Sharon," and welcomed me in. I threw my jacket on the sofa.

I was surprised when "my cousin" told me another friend was there and that he wanted to talk to me. I had not seen or been in contact with this guy for a while. In fact, we had lost track of each other. I knew that he had graduated and like many high school friendships, you remember people fondly, but when you don't see them every day, you drift into different worlds and spaces.

Standing on opposite sides of the glass and wood coffee table in the living room, we exchanged pleasantries. And he seemed bothered and uneasy. I almost didn't even know what to say to him, so I was even more stunned when this guy said he needed to talk to me and then asked me to follow him upstairs.

"Okay."

His urging seemed a bit curious and I was a little uncomfortable, but I walked up the stairs behind him.

I knew him. We were friends, had gone to the same high school, and had sat at the same cafeteria table and knew many of the same people. So, I didn't fear him. But maybe, that day, I should have.

Seconds later, we were upstairs in my "cousin's" attic. My friend closed the door and pushed so close to me that the smell of alcohol on his breath assaulted my face. He never said a word.

He shifted his weight and the full force of his body pressed against me. I struggled, but he was too strong. He landed on me and I felt as if I had been knocked outside of myself.

He pinned me down. My fingers splayed, then tried to claw, and then folded tight as the rest of my arms and body felt immobilized. Stumbling, he forced his hand to the top of my pants, yanking them down, then off. I could barely breathe now. He put the other hand over my mouth. I could not scream. Then, he used his hand to pry my legs apart. He rose up and shoved his lust inside of me. I couldn't bear it. I felt like I was there, but what was happening to me was so brutal and ugly I couldn't allow myself to think that it was me. It was happening to someone else.

When he let me up, I pulled on my clothes and swatted at my tears as my confusion boiled to anger. I made my way out of the room, down the stairs, and grabbed a broom handle I saw propped in a corner. I was going to bash him with it. I wanted to wield it so hard that he could feel its blunt force; I wanted to give him the same stunning pain he had just caused me. I wanted to hurt him like he had hurt me. But I thought better and left the broom handle on the floor, thinking that I didn't have a chance of fighting his big frame. My cousin wasn't around when I was running out of there. In fact, I didn't see anyone or anything on my way out the door. Flooded with tears, humiliation, and loathing, I walked fast, though aching, back down the street to my house. This time I didn't even notice the chill and the wind pushing about me. All I could think about was getting home. None of the family was there. I went to my room and just sat on the edge of my bed in silence. When I could stand up again, I put myself into a hot shower and stayed standing there, trying to wash and scrub away everything that just happened to me in the home of a friend.

In that moment, I realized that not only was my virginity gone, my voice was too. I threw it away. What had happened to me was a shame and a violation that I could never speak of with my best girlfriends. Nobody would ever know what had happened to me in that attic. Not my aunt or my uncle, not even the police because I decided that day to clean myself up, guard my secret, and somehow go on living my life so that others around me could do the same.

Although the victim, I made the sacrifice.

If I had opened my mouth and told, families would have been shattered, a neighborhood would have been turned upside down, and another 18-year-old Black man, although guilty, would have surely ended up doing jail time. And me, I was remembering the half year I spent in shelter; I thought of the repercussions of outing my perpetrator and how it could possibly mean being removed from the home that I had waited so long to have. In my heart, I knew that my aunt and uncle would have believed me and would have fought hard for me to be heard and for others to believe my story, too, if I had chosen to tell it. Yes, I was stirred up inside, but I didn't want to rock the boat and be labeled the problem foster child. Every day was a reminder that I was the one without a safety net. I was the one who needed a family and a roof over my head. The possibility of losing my family and my home as a result of saying that I was sexually assaulted would actually have been more horrible than the rape, I concluded. That was a chance that I wasn't willing to take. So, I said nothing.

Even as a high school student, I understood the limited power of child protective services and the law. And who would have believed me? I felt like a David, but I couldn't slay the giant. I was a young, Black, female, foster child. My voice couldn't cry victim. Who would have heard it? Who would have listened? Who would have done something about it? I was the most vulnerable member of society.

There was no choice for me, then, but to try and cope. This was another one of those hurts. When they came before in my life, I would attempt to break them down into small manageable pieces, like trying to swallow a big, bitter pill. I had done it before when no one kept me from slipping away and into shelter. Suck it up, I told myself, and try to move on with your life. Right then, however, I wanted nothing more than to get through the next few hours of that day. I knew that I would have to find a smile to wear that evening to my birthday celebration. My aunt and uncle and cousins would be gathered around the dining room table with candles on a cake and cards, waiting to sing happy birthday to me. This was December 19—the day I turned 17.

The Price of Emancipation

Since the New Year, I had been cramming so much thinking into the weeks and months that I checked off and circled on my desk calendar. The things that I deemed important in my life — final exams, graduation, and senior prom — were looming large after the winter of 1978. I wondered what my life would look like when I left my forever home. Could I make it on my own when I had to? Could I return to this place?

While going to college wasn't something that we discussed at home, the expectation of doing well and being well educated was ever present. Attending college, though, was in my thinking and I knew that my foster families always expected good things to come from me when I finished high school. Growing up with Grandma and Gramps in the Oakland section of the city, the University of Pittsburgh's sprawling urban campus was a familiar sight. I could glimpse its iconic 42-floor Cathedral of Learning in the distance and often encountered its pride of students moving back and forth between classes. I didn't know if I would end up there one day, but somehow I knew that I would go to college.

In high school, during my senior year, my dream took hold: I wanted to help children who had grown up like me, and who were grappling with finding their voice. As a teenager, I knew I was smart and wanted to achieve, but my adolescent voice at times was muzzled by the despair of living so much of my life in other people's homes or paralyzed by my circumstances. And even when I managed to find my voice and get it unleashed, it usually ended up being misunderstood. I didn't doubt that other youngsters felt the same way. By going to college, majoring in the right field, getting clinical practice, and gaining counseling skills, I could be their big, clear voice to the world, sharing the plight of children in foster care. In those final few months of high school, sitting in those classrooms, dreaming is when I knew instinctively that what I had to give to those children would be borne out of my own experience.

Everyone needed people in their lives like Grandma and Gramps. For kids who have been separated from their family, having kin in their corner, people who cared about them would be a must. These could be blood relatives—or others who were like family—to stand in the gap, claim them as their own, and snatch them back from a life in the system. And I suspected that there were those who probably didn't get that second chance at life, and family, and wholeness, and stability, and peace like

I did. This was the future that I dreamed of, but I never shared it with anyone. It nurtured my thoughts, but I never spoke the words out loud.

Before I knew it, the constant urging of zealous teachers who came at me with their good intentions and what they thought was sound advice for my next life and college career had filled that space.

"You're a strong math student, you should major in engineering," my teachers advised. "It's a field that needs more women, especially Black women," they told me, even though I wasn't the least bit interested in being an engineer. At 17, I couldn't declare what it was that I wanted to study in college, but I knew what I wanted to do with my life. Still, I went along with what people thought I could be because I hadn't articulated to anyone what I would be.

The road map for getting to where I wanted to be from where I was as a high school senior wasn't always clear. So, I hoped and prayed that someone would come along to guide me. God answered.

My help came at the beginning of this journey. It was Cynthia, an African-American Penn State graduate and recruiter who made South Hills High a part of her swing through Pittsburgh in search of promising African-American students. Standing nearly 6 feet tall, in cocoa skin, and sporting close-cropped hair, Cynthia touched our school's handful of Black graduating seniors.

It didn't take long for Cynthia's warmth and energy to sell us on this Big 10 University, which none of us had ever seen or visited. Watching Penn State football on television on Saturdays probably didn't count, but it was as close as we had gotten to being there. Within days of her first visit, my love affair with Penn State had begun to sizzle. For now, Cynthia's words were enough to start us dreaming in navy blue and white, the university's colors, and feeling like hot stuff after telling us that "1 out of every 10 college graduates in the United States is a Penn State alumnus." We knew that we wanted to be among that number one day.

She was sent by the university and was on a mission to fortify its anemic African-American ranks with new young bloods who were college-ready, and who could last beyond their freshman year. A minimum GPA of 3.2 and SAT scores of at least 750, Cynthia said, is what the university was looking for in its next freshman class. With my grades, I knew that my chances of getting in were great. Traveling nearly three hours each way from Penn State's main campus in University Park, Pa., to Pittsburgh, Cynthia visited our high school often. And over time, we grew to know a woman whose compassion and care extended beyond her job description and did more to win our families over than the glossy Penn State marketing brochures and giveaways she dispensed from her blue and white Penn State shoulder bag. We felt that she really wanted us to be Penn Staters. That's why it was my only college choice.

Cynthia guided us through the admissions process and made sure that our essays were written and all of our paperwork was completed. I was like most of the African-American students who Cynthia courted at South Hills High—first-generation sons and daughters of parents who wanted bright futures for their children, but who could only do so much to help them apply to college and then get there. Some parents never had the chance or the money to go to college, but from our small group at South Hills High, three of their children—daughters—had been accepted to Penn State and would be carrying the dreams of their families forward.

A New Day Dawning (1979)

On December 1, 1978, I had my acceptance letter in hand even before I was graduated from high school. I was halfway to where I wanted to be. But despite my good fortune and busy life as a high school senior, the rape remained a dark shadow. With time, the memory got buried a little deeper. But it shoved its way to the front of my mind when I wasn't busy making college plans or when I wasn't completing term papers and mid-terms, or playing the violin. On some days I couldn't push it far enough away, but the burden of carrying my secret was as constant as breathing. Its residual pain can still ooze out, even today, just in smaller lighter fragments that I can manage and then put away.

But during that spring, something as simple as searching for a prom dress and a date to the dance could make life bearable and seem normal again. The new boy that I was seeing was going to be my date for the senior prom, but he picked the worst time to get himself in trouble with his parents. As punishment, he wasn't allowed to attend his own prom. His hard-headedness meant that I wouldn't have an escort for one of the most special nights of a young girl's life. But thank heaven for girlfriends. One of mine came through, offering up her brother as my prom date. It turned out, though, that he was not only looking for a prom date but also for a new girlfriend. That's when I had to make it clear to him that he was only going to be my date for the evening, nothing more. Once we got that straight, we had a wonderful time. I looked lovely and my corsage smelled sweet and sat up high. The evening was full of fun and dancing, and as special as it was, prom night passed too quickly.

This was my senior year of high school and also a year of new beginnings for my sister. She was turning 19, had become a new mother to a baby girl, and was about to become a wife. Her new life would take her far away from Pittsburgh and from me. But in the time that we still had together, I would be by her side, making sure that she looked stunning on her special day. She was a bit smaller than me, but my sister wore the clothes that I picked out for her from my closet—a knee-length burgundy skirt and a white blouse with gold threads running through it, ruching adorned the front. She carried a small bouquet.

A white towel tucked inside the neck of her blouse served as a shield against the makeup. Everything had to be perfect. After curling her hair, I went about dipping sponges and swirling brushes into a pallet of foundation and pressed mocha powder. Some blush dusted her cheeks. A soft red shade of lipstick covered her mouth and shimmering eye shadow finished her look. I went from makeup artist to maid of honor at the small private ceremony at Bethany Baptist, then a small church on Tioga Street. The uncle who raised my sister was a member at Bethany and another uncle performed the ceremony. The man my sister was marrying was in the Army with immediate orders for Germany. They remain happily married today. Following the wedding, my sister and her baby lived on their own until she joined her husband in Germany about a year later. That's when she and I had to again say goodbye. From the time I was 13 until I turned 23, my relationship with my sister was a series of reunions and separations. It started when I was taken away to shelter and she went to live with our uncle. Then there was my foster home, and her marriage and move abroad.

When I graduated from high school on June 11, 1979, several family members were among my well-wishers. On that day, I was both leaving high school and the child welfare system. It was my formal emancipation from foster care. Full of newfound feelings of independence, I resolved then to look forward, not back. I had had limited contact with my father for more than two years now. In my 17-year-old mind, I thought moving forward meant not reaching out to have his involvement in this rite of passage. So, I just didn't take the time to invite him to the graduation.

In the auditorium at Soldiers & Sailors Memorial Hall, in the heart of Oakland, about 277 students marched across the stage—the boys in royal blue and the girls in billowing white gowns into new beginnings. I ranked 76th in my class. Standing on the stage in the auditorium, with the tassel on my cap bobbing, I sang my heart out one last time with the honors choir. We offered up a medley of songs for our parents and families. I can still remember singing "A New Day Dawning." Most of the lyrics I've forgotten, but that song's title spoke to what I was hoping and believing for my life back then.

After our names were called, and the principal conferred our diplomas, and the commencement ceremony concluded, I waded through the sea of waiting arms and people. I found my proud uncle in the crowd standing with the rest of the family. He was beaming brightly for me and all that I had achieved at school and all that he had done to help raise me. As we left Soldiers & Sailors, I walked on proudly in new white shoes that were beginning to pinch my toes and clutched my diploma and the certificates that I had won during the ceremony, but it took only a moment for my aunt to flatten my soaring spirit. She spoke in a space where only I could hear her and pronounced, "We have done all that we were supposed to do for you."

Her words stung and left me unable to speak. I felt dumbfounded. Had I been a burden to her all those years? Did my uncle feel that way, too, I wondered? My time was up, but I took some comfort in knowing that the start of college was around the corner and I would be out of her house.

Even on paper, the rules and the state showed that my time in foster care had ticked down. I had "aged out" of the system. Those were the words that my caseworker used in explaining the mandatory process of being untethered from my caregivers when I graduated from high school. The thought of it made me a bit fearful and anxious, like plunging alone into the darkness, and hoping that someone would flip the switch so that I could see what was ahead. Rick believed in me. He was my last caseworker before I left the system. Even though I was only 17, Rick saw me as a survivor. I had been resilient and, a good student with a positive attitude and a thirst for learning.

"You were never one of my problem children," Rick confided, "I know that you will go far. I have a feeling that our paths will cross again or I'll hear about the good things that you are doing," he told me. That thought made me happy. He saw my life transcending the limits of South Hills as I fulfilled my dream of working with children. I was glad to have Rick in my corner. He was the kind of caseworker I wanted to be—caring, attentive, engaged, and supportive. As I worked with him on my financial aid forms, Rick instructed me to declare myself as an independent student so I could receive the maximum benefits for college tuition, food stamps, and other resources I would need to survive without support from home. But he couldn't prepare me for what it felt like to be independent or how to make that transition from being a dependent kid to a college student without a safety net.

Child welfare claimed that I, and thousands of other foster children like me, was ready to be emancipated—ready to be set free, to soar without falling, to make grown-up decisions and to make my way in the big world outside of South Hills and Pittsburgh. I couldn't help but wonder if I was going to be free or if the system was going to be free of me?

For a couple of months, at least, I would be working, and would still have summer to enjoy. From the money that I made during my summer job, I purchased the things that the Penn State checklist told me that I needed to outfit my dorm room and take to class. This would be the last summer that I would spend with my family before leaving for college. Wrapping my mind in memories, I relished the fact that I had made it to the end of this period in my life. Two caregivers—my foster aunt and uncle—helped me get to that point. As a new life for me was beginning, and with a clean slate, I felt compelled to say good-bye to those who had loved and cared for me, and to also make amends.

In the weeks before I left for Penn State, the one thing that I asked of my foster grandparents was their forgiveness for any hardship I had caused while under their roof. I remembered that at their age, it could not have been easy bringing up a teenager. And I was sure that my last act of defiance and anger before leaving their home hurriedly was probably a big disappointment. Still, I always felt that Grandma and Gramps would always be in my life. A family get-together brought Grandma and me together one summer afternoon. As I sat next to her on the front porch of our house, I offered her thanks and asked for forgiveness. She smiled at me and squeezed my hands tight. As generously as she and Gramps had given so many things that sustained and nurtured me when we were a family, they graciously forgave the young woman they once cared for and remained among my loyal cheerleaders well into my future.

When I thought about Miss, my father's ex-girlfriend, it seemed that she had seen something in me that she liked. She wanted to see it blossom and thrive. When we came to live with her, I didn't know what to call the woman who loved my dad and who shared her home with us. She was a mother of two—one child was my half-brother—we began as strangers. But Miss and I shared something akin to an umbilical cord. From that link, she connected her family with me and helped give birth to new opportunities and chances that I enjoyed. She was my foster grandparents' daughter, my foster aunt's sister, one of my best advocates, and one of the few adults that I trusted, especially as a teenager. I called her aunt and she was family.

Wading Into the Blue and White

Soon, I'd be among the 33,000 other undergraduate and graduate students who populated this bustling mini-city called Old Main Campus at University Park, Pa. The thought of going to one of the largest universities in the nation was mind blowing, and we couldn't wait to experience it. In 1979, the year that I enrolled, Penn State's African-American student population was as tiny as a colony of ants on an elephant's back, hard to find unless they were gathered together in one place. At that time, Black students numbered about 1,308, just 2.4 percent of the total enrollment. But, somehow, this was still "Happy Valley" to Penn Staters and the other devotees of this picturesque, close-knit college town that was steeped in tradition.

Our ranks were small in comparison to the majority of students on the campus, but what I learned after getting here was that even those slight gains among Penn State's Black-student population had been hard won. Black student activists would press the administration often and as fervently as they could for a stronger presence on campus. They wanted to see more Black undergraduate and graduate students, more faculty members and athletic coaches. We also wanted the creation of an African-American cultural studies program, all things that eventually came, but sometimes with the swiftness of molasses falling in winter. Overtime, campus activists had a handful of allies from Black community and civil rights organizations in the surrounding town of State College, and later pressure from the federal government.

By the time I came to Penn State, news of the conditions on the campus for Black students, had already reached Washington, D.C. The U.S. Department of Health, Education, and Welfare, as it was known then, had also registered its dissatisfaction with the small percentage of Black students and faculty at Penn State. That agency, now called the

Department of Education, ordered the university administration to step up its efforts to increase Black enrollment by adding more Black recruiters, Affirmative Action coordinators, a minority affairs director, and a Black Scholars Program. Penn State's board of trustees responded by setting up its own committee on Affirmative Action. But progress was painfully slow in those days and by the mid-1980s, when I was graduating, the number of Blacks in attendance was only slightly higher than it had been a decade earlier.

That may have been why our recruiter, Cynthia, wanted to change our first-year script. Before dipping our freshmen toes in Happy Valley's expansive campus, she wanted us to get our start at one of the university's smallest branch locations. The chances for our success were greater there, she thought.

Away from the epicenter on Old Main would be the best place to learn the Penn State culture and to get a grip on living and learning as new undergraduates. But no matter where we landed, as Black students that year, we would be grossly underrepresented in the Penn State family. At first we balked and wondered why she would recommend that we start at a branch campus when we had been accepted at University Park, but Cynthia had already witnessed enough sad scenes in Happy Valley and the lethargy of her institution to usher in social and racial change. Fortunately for us, Cynthia was a part of that new wave, even if it was federally mandated. For her, recruitment that ended with commencement was the aim. But for some other university officials, who went in search of Black students, it was a numbers game.

Many Black students who came from across the Keystone State had been plucked out of the urban sprawl or even from the ghettos by Penn State recruiters. But many of them who were offered an invitation to come to the university weren't prepared for its academic rigors, its size, its Whiteness, or for the conservative, middle-class way of life in Happy Valley, which stood in stark, splendid contrast. So, those students came and they left.

Around 25 then, Cynthia wasn't that much older than her new recruits from South Hills High, but we trusted her like a mother. She had already pulled back the Penn State veil. As a new recruiter, she was privy to the statistics on race and attrition; she had already lived this college experience, and she knew that the Black students she brought in would be better off not knowing the things that she did, and that she could prepare them to avoid the pitfalls.

Penn State could be a tough, frustrating, and unwieldy place for African-American students trying to matriculate no matter how smart they were. Since there was only an estimated 19 full-time Black faculty members in 1979, Cynthia knew that the chances of us latching on to them or seeing them as role models in the classroom were slim because of their meager numbers. That's one of the reasons she had a plan in mind for our success as new college students, and in her way, wanted to protect us. Coupled with that was my own plan to be resilient like I had always been, especially here at school where I had no safety net. This was how I was going to survive.

A few years before we arrived at Penn State, Cynthia, the undergraduate, had bravely made her own way out of Pittsburgh's Black enclave known as the Hill District to the Nittany Mountains, and through Penn State's white hallowed halls. She studied education and psychology. Cynthia was willing to share with us the forces she'd harnessed along the way. While at the university, Cynthia saw few faces that looked like hers in the dining hall, or living with her in the dormitories, or sitting next to her at a reading table in the university library. As a Penn State freshman in 1970, she was among an estimated 1,300 Black students. That number was about the same when my two high school classmates and I arrived.

Our recruiter knew that reveling in the blue and white could be a really fun and bigger-than-life experience for neophytes like us. But for many Black students, feelings of isolation in the classroom and off campus could waylay us if we didn't stay focused and push forward. Cynthia also anticipated that if her South Hills High students started out on main campus, they could likely find themselves floundering or disconnected from their professors and from their purpose while in cavernous freshmen lecture halls that were brimming with students.

And she knew that they could be called out of their names by a "townie" or even another Penn Stater someday when their innocent brown legs and faces meandered down the quaint main streets of Happy Valley to window shop.

I began my Penn State years on the McKeesport campus. On the day that I arrived, a long winding driveway ushered me on to a stately campus blanketed in lush green grounds. When we arrived at Cynthia's alma mater, she was there to welcome us to the campus. This Penn State branch was sizeable, but it was less overwhelming than main campus. And although pleasant, the McKeesport campus was isolated. Students without cars pretty much had to stay put, study, and enjoy the student center.

Although we only found about 12 Black students among the 400 or so enrolled at McKeesport, we were determined to follow Cynthia's direction, which included planning our move to main campus in University Park when we were ready for all that it had in store. But as we got settled in, Cynthia had a few more things that she wanted us to do—study hard, earn good grades, stay out of trouble, and most of all, make it through freshman year without flunking out and being sent back home. That path, Cynthia knew, had been well worn by too many students who looked like us. I knew that I was going to make it here.

The dorm was stuffy, hot, and crowded with families bearing college-girl things. Confident that I had purchased most everything during the summer that I needed for school, the unpacking began. My corner of the room was taking shape. Like my clothes, my bedding was also color coordinated and accessorized, but I knew that it would take time to adjust again to living amid this many girls in a dorm space.

When classes began, I set out with notebooks and purpose, strutting across campus. I may have teetered a tiny bit in my stockings and low-heeled dress shoes cutting across the concrete paths, and may have even been a little unsure of myself as a new Penn State co-ed, but I looked sharp. That first week, I marked each class the same way. As I entered for the first time, I introduced myself to each professor before claiming a seat on the front row or near the front of their classroom. No one had given me a script or a hint about what to do or where to sit, but my instincts and determination just kicked in at the start of my college days. Those professors needed to know that I was Sharon, not another student ID number or worse, a Black student with failure waiting to happen at Penn State. It wasn't about the clothes — I knew my purpose for being in college — but on campus, I was fine with letting my wardrobe sometimes speak for me.

By the time I left high school, my teachers had convinced me that studying engineering should be my college pursuit. In freshman year, I had succumbed to the idea and did as they said. Being one of a handful of females and often the only Black in my chemical engineering courses, I needed to be taken seriously. My tailored look always included a jacket or sweater. I liked skirts, and most fell just below the knee, and some were matched up with Mandarin collar blouses.

Being a shopper wasn't a bad thing in my book. That adjective had described me to a "T" since I was about 14 and became like a willing apprentice under Grandma and later my foster aunt. It was nothing for me at the end of the month to spend all that I had earned from my $3.50- an-hour summer job on clothes. Even at 14, Saks Fifth Avenue wasn't off limits to me. I would make a day of shopping, leaving home on a Saturday to get to the store when it opened at 10 a.m. and leaving at dusk when it closed. My other favorite haunt was the bargain basement at Kaufmann's Department Store, where it was common to snag a $50 designer blouse for just $4. So, with about $80 which I could usually save up each month from my allowance and lunch money, I could go home happy with a shopping bag full of clothes from Kaufmann's.

And when I shopped with my foster aunt, she'd make sure that we had a new outfit for every event. She always kept her kids decked out. That early retail training made dressing during my college years effortless, even in a conservative college town. I knew what I liked, how to find it at a discount, and how to make an impression.

Financial aid and a scholarship from a Pittsburgh company covered my first-year tuition. Working in the campus cafeteria provided me with food and some spending money, but even then, I was an independent student who was just getting by on Pell Grants and, in my sophomore year, food stamps. Otherwise, I knew how to stretch my dollars until they cried out. The important thing was that I survived and managed well. I had to.

With my roommates or anyone on campus, I never talked about having been in foster care because, frankly, I didn't think that they would care. The story of youngsters like me who grew up in foster care was a matter of public fact, but here on campus, it was going to be my private reality. I was emancipated now and an adult. My life in foster care was behind me, and on campus, I just wanted to be as normal as everyone else. My freshman roommates were three nice but sometimes moody girls—two were Black and one was White—from homes that were traditional, intact, and included two parents. I was closest with my roommate Ginger whose home I visited on many occasions. Our lives, growing up, couldn't have been more different, but here in our dorm room, my roommates and I were just co-eds who knew how to play the spoiled princess from time to time, but we got along.

I listened and watched and learned about another life that young women my age, and who looked like me, embraced. They phoned home often, missed their mothers, and made the place where they grew up their destination during every holiday, school break, and even some weekends in between. But unlike Ginger, Janet, and Barb, I wasn't anticipating going home because I wasn't sure if it was still a place that I could call mine. What I did was just show up at the door; thinking if my aunt and uncle didn't put me out, then it was OK for me to be there. Sometimes I would be invited home with my roommate. Not wanting to be a burden, I limited my calls home to my aunt and uncle to once a month at most. Otherwise, I left them alone, not picking up the phone to call when there were things that I needed or when I got homesick, no matter what.

Once on campus, I realized that I didn't know where my forever home was anymore. McKeesport is where I laid my head at night, studied, and played, but South Hills was where my family was. They were my safety net. I didn't know if I could go back to join them when Thanksgiving, and Christmas, and summer break came around. Not knowing stifled and scared me. I kept those feelings undercover, thinking that no one here on campus could understand. No one ever told me yes, home was a place that would still be there for me as long as I needed it to be, even if I was emancipated. My last caseworker didn't cover that in his talk with me. And I never had that conversation with my aunt and uncle before we loaded up the car with all of my clothes, new comforter, twin sheet sets, books, and my violin piled high on the way to move-in day my first year at Penn State.

My foster family didn't owe me anything more; my aunt had made that clear. I was emancipated from the system and my aunt and uncle were no longer my caregivers or receiving the money they once did from child services to help raise me. That's why each time I wanted to leave campus and go home, I didn't ask permission. I would just show up back in South Hills at the front door. I was always too afraid of being refused and the uncertainty that accompanied each visit was like a time bomb. I never knew with each visit if it would be my last.

When I did go home, sometimes the air between my aunt and me was still cloudy, but each time I was just grateful to know that home was still there. I learned that while I was away at Penn State, my uncle had decided to enroll in college, too, earning his associates degree in Industrial Engineering Management from the Community College of Allegheny County. It was my influence and example this time, he said, that helped get him there.

At 17, as a newly emancipated college student who had the opportunity to study at one of the most well-known institutions in the nation, I knew that every decision that I made had to count. Failure wasn't an option, but the challenges that I faced as a result were real and seemed mighty big. I wanted so much to succeed and earn good grades, which I was used to in high school, but I seemed to be coming up short.

Studying physics and chemistry, and taking classes in strengths and materials and drafting, among others my first year, contributed to the spiraling pressure that seemed to engulf me. And even outside of the classroom, it was there when thoughts of my past became present and my 17 years didn't seem to give me enough maturity to manage campus life. I was alone and struggling academically in some classes. Math was still my favorite subject and where I continued to do well. I couldn't say the same for chemistry. I had to get help. My tutor turned out to be a cute Italian guy who graduated from Peabody High School back home. Most of the students who came out of Peabody were whizzes when it came to math and science.

Even working with him didn't help. I eased out of freshman year with a 2.5 GPA and with a transcript that had the one D grade—in a chemistry course—that I would receive during my college career. This wasn't good enough. My uncle had drilled into me that only the honor roll was acceptable. Now that I was in college, making the dean's list seemed far out of my reach. Among my friends and roommates, I was the only one with a technical major and carrying such a heavy course load. They did well, academically, their first year.

But thankfully, I was still in the game and gearing up to tackle my sophomore year. Year two would begin with an unexpected joy.

It Was Like Looking in a Mirror

There were days growing up when thoughts of my brother's well-being and whereabouts were all consuming. In those days, efforts to gather answers from the adults in my life were usually returned vacant or vague. But I'm convinced that God knew my concern and must have heard me. In my sophomore year, chance and a Penn State residence hall welcome party finally led me to my little brother.

The girl who my brother took to her junior prom was standing in front of me on the floor where I lived, asking if I had a brother named LaMont because she saw my last name on my bedroom door. Immediately, I said yes and latched on to her the remainder of the evening and showered her with questions: Do you have a picture of him? How did he dress on prom night? Do you have his address or telephone number?

The connection to my brother was right here; we were dorm mates. And thanks to her, I learned that LaMont was in Duquesne, Pa., about

45 minutes away by car. She wanted to help me and, on her own, made calls and found out where my brother was living. I tried not to be too eager and pester her. She even promised to bring one of her prom pictures posing with my brother so that I could see what he looked like, but she always seemed to forget it when she was home. That was OK; I had a feeling that she understood how important it was for me to see my brother and I knew that she would come through for me one day soon.

A few weeks went by and I tried not to appear eager when I'd see her on the floor, even if she was the only thing that stood between making a long-awaited reunion happen.

"I haven't forgotten you and I know where you can find your brother," she said smiling and waving a piece a paper as she headed to where I was sitting one afternoon in the dorm lobby. This slip of paper was my passport to the brother whose little face was still etched in my mind. The next time I'd see him, he would be a young man—I wondered how tall? The people in our family were short. I couldn't wait to see for myself.

That evening, I made plans to find my way to Duquesne, Pa. I would head there the next weekend. I took local transit; two buses would ferry me back to downtown Pittsburgh from McKeesport and from there, I'd transfer and go to Duquesne. Whatever it took, I was going to find my brother.

When I boarded the bus on that Saturday, it was without hesitation and with a slip of paper containing my brother's address. My destination was my brother. After riding for about two hours, I stepped off the bus, ready to find my way from there to my brother's address. I made up my mind that I would just keep asking around until I found out where he lived.

Standing with their backs to me, I walked just a few yards from the bus stop to where I saw a group of Black guys. They stood together on the sidewalk and I asked if any of them knew LaMont Toliver or where I could find him. I didn't have to look far. As I stood in their midst on that Friday, a rich voice, husky, but not too deep, piped up from among them and said, "I'm LaMont." That's when I realized that this face in the bunch belonged to my brother. He was a young boy the last time that I saw him, but staring back at me now was a stocky young man whose face now was wide and round and the color of nutmeg.

My excitement and anticipation for a reunion had propelled me like a gust of wind on my journey to that corner. I was on a mission and in the time that we had, I wanted to know everything about him—where he'd been those years after Aunt Inez took him from my dad? Did he have a good life growing up? Did he remember me?

Like gazing into a mirror, I saw my face in his. I told LaMont that I was his big sister and he was my little brother. Here we were, grown up. It was early fall and not yet chilly enough for the late afternoon air to drive us inside to one of the stores or fast-food places along the block. So, we walked slowly, unraveling nearly two decades of the travails of life and surviving. There were a few moments when we were even able to knit our stories together—about a young father and his drinking and pain, torn safety nets, a sister who was like a mother, dreams, school, and loss—with a little laughter. This was our reunion on a downtown sidewalk.

It was almost as if LaMont had been waiting for me, too. His experience growing up had been so different from my own in Pittsburgh. I had the benefit of caring kin and the familiarity of relatives surrounding me. That wasn't LaMont's experience. Though he stayed with kin, too, he had painful accounts of my father's visits to the house where he lived with Aunt Inez, my mother's oldest sister. Dad would come over just to spank him when Aunt Inez called to say that his baby boy was being "bad." She couldn't care for my brother after she took him away from his family. She didn't know best. I learned that Aunt Inez drank herself crazy and, on those days, her young nephew was forced to be the one who instead cared for her. When she died, LaMont landed first in foster care at age 7 instead of spending his early years infused with love. Most of his childhood was lived in group home after group home and later at the well-known Milton Hershey School, the private institution for orphaned, low-income, and other children and teens. He attended the school from the fifth through ninth grade.

When LaMont and I reconnected on that street corner, I was in college and 19 years old, and he was 18. He hadn't gotten a break. For years, no one saw to it that he went to school consistently or even learned to read. Using comic books, he told me that he taught himself to read. These were not the stories I wanted to hear that day and definitely not the scenes I had imagined when I thought of him growing up, I had at least hoped that my brother's life was a secure one. All of those years, I had dreamed of LaMont apart from my sister and me, being loved and adored, having found peace and place with a relative who was raising him as her own.

LaMont and I bonded that day. He looked just like me, and I like him, but the whirlwind of life had blown us apart. We had no relationship. My sister, my brother, and I were siblings; we belonged together. But to child services and on paper, we were merely identification numbers sequenced in case files that they had forgotten or refused to see as real lives that needed attention and family.

Out on that sidewalk with my brother, making up for nearly a lifetime only took about an hour. We said we would keep in touch. I had to get back on the bus and to my life on campus and my brother had to return to his spot on the corner.

Finding That Bridge

I hung in there as a chemical engineering major, at least for the first half of my sophomore year. Despite my fleeting thoughts of a career at Dow Chemical Co., where I would work on finding a cure for cancer or some dreaded disease, I was convinced that engineering wasn't for me. That scientific breakthrough at Dow would just have to wait for someone else to make it. My mind was made up, it was time to change course.

The strategic plan for transferring that Cynthia devised for her recruits was unfolding. I was ready to move on to Happy Valley for the start of my junior year. Switching majors at this point required some long hours of planning with my academic advisor. By now, I had amassed a good number of credit hours as a chemical engineering major, and fortunately, the university decided to count most of those courses as electives.

Working with my advisor, I wanted to be clear about the courses that were required for my major, and about the other general classes that I still needed to complete. But, most important, I wanted assurance that all of these credits and classes would get me to graduation at the end of my four years at Penn State.

Starting out as a chemical engineering major, I was challenged academically in ways that I never dreamed. Being compelled by others to study things that weren't in my heart and mind to do got me to this uncomfortable place. But the experience didn't break me. Instead, I made a plan to remove myself from behind the drafting tables and out of the chemistry laboratories, to put my sleek new Texas Instruments graphing calculator back in its case, and set myself on a path that would lead me to work with children. I would know their faces when I saw them and I would understand their stories when I heard them because they were mine.

But beyond those intangible things, I still needed to study and learn about their condition, what made some resilient and others crumble, or how they ended up in the clutches of juvenile justice or being wards of the state. As I took classes, I was confident that I would also find myself in the pages of some of those textbooks and in the academic discourse—shedding light on how the shifting forces of life and death and family landed me in the system and in the care of others who were like kin but not my relatives.

This area of study is where my college journey should have begun in the first place. But at least I had sense enough in my sophomore year to know that I had hit the wall and needed to pursue a new course. And despite it all, I remained motivated enough to keep moving forward with my education, my passion, and my life.

Settling on a bachelor's degree in social work would have been ideal, and it would have allowed me to explore the subject of children like me or at least read about them, but at the time, Penn State didn't offer a major. When I narrowed my search, I ended up choosing Administration of Justice, a major offered in the College of Human Development. Since I hadn't grown up a delinquent child, I wasn't familiar with some of the case studies that I read for my major, but I was able to transfer my own experiences of being in the system so that I could better understand the "why." I knew that there was a reason for a child's delinquent behavior and I wanted to be involved, working to find out why. Other courses I took, such as individuals and family studies, got me closer to understanding family dynamics, especially ones that were dysfunctional. There were also a number of sociology courses that I took, such as "Understanding Environment" and "Understanding People and Conditions" because I wanted to gain insight into those young lives. I wanted all of the courses that I chose to serve a purpose beyond satisfying a degree requirement. Together, I hoped that they would provide a bridge to the work that I wanted to do. When I graduated, I had earned enough credits in sociology to have a minor in the subject.

Sometimes Like Santa Claus

At the start of my junior year, my father came when I called. I needed him and that Saturday morning in mid-August when it was time to haul armsful of clothes on hangers, plastic crates with books, a box of shoes, household supplies, bedding, a few albums, and more clothes deposited neatly in a corner of my room at my foster aunt and uncle's house. Dad was present and ready. Still his quiet self, but visibly proud to be connected to his college girl and toting her things back to Penn State.

Years had stretched out like a river between my father and me. As they flowed, Dad didn't know the young woman that I was becoming because another family did the job of raising his daughter. He was here now. And it felt good.

Without hesitation, Dad became my driver and moved me from Pittsburgh to my new off-campus apartment in State College, Pa. We were together, but this wasn't a reunion; it was me being resourceful and doing what I needed to do to make my way and get through school. If I had asked my aunt and uncle to take me back to campus, I'm sure that they would have done it or found a way, but again, I was too fearful of being a burden to ask for any more favors. And it was rare that I called on Dad for anything.

Most of my things, mainly suitcases of clothes, had been packed and sitting near the door since the night before. I was moving off campus but not planning to cook much. I'd had enough of that when I lived with my aunt and uncle, but I did pack a few utensils and dishes that I could use to prepare some small meals. I wanted to be ready to load everything and head out as soon as my Dad arrived. He came on time just like he said he would and brought with him a small trailer hitched to the backside of a sizeable burgundy car that probably didn't belong to him.

"Hi Shannie," Dad said with a quick smile, before looking down, then over to the boxes, and books, and racks of clothes and shoes that were making the move.

"Hi ya doing, Dad? Thanks for coming over and for taking me back to school."

"You're welcome," he said quickly, again taking in all of my belongings that were sprawled neatly near the front door. "All of this stuff goes? I'm glad that I brought a trailer."

We both smiled for a minute before moving with purpose in and out of the morning sun, transferring boxes and bags from the house to the trailer. My things filled nearly every inch of available space before we climbed into the front seat.

The nearly three-hour ride to campus would have given me some long-awaited time to embark on a journey to explore days past with my dad but that journey wouldn't have been as pleasant as just sharing small talk or being content to just watch nature whiz by outside the car window. That morning, I could have taken my dad back five years, even a decade, if I had decided to ask "Where were you when I was in shelter? Or why did you let me slip away? Or simply, why weren't you there for me?" But I didn't. That day, I didn't see a monster behind the wheel driving me to school. It was Dad trying to find me again even if it was for just a few hours.

"You know, I've been telling everybody that my daughter is in college at Penn State," Dad said to my amazement.

Since we hadn't talked in years, I didn't know what he knew about my life or even what I was studying, but with some hesitation, he used the time to fill in the blanks. Dad wanted to know what Penn State was like, how was I doing in my classes, when was I graduating, and as he called it, "how was I getting along?" I shared just enough.

As we drove, we spun our words and they landed on talk about school and on sports, which we both loved; bands of silence were interspersed with more school news before we finally arrived at my new apartment. Entering the city limits, Dad made good time driving and we didn't lose our way. This squat man moved a little slower than I remembered since last seeing him, but here Dad was helping me unpack my belongings and chatting politely with my roommates. Then he was gone, a bit like Santa Claus. I could at least expect to see him again next year.

As it did for me at McKeesport, my new fall session began at Happy Valley with my game face on. I was here to learn and commence. I continued to dress the part on campus, putting the no-nonsense student that I had been since my freshman year on display. Even two days a week, when I had fewer classes, I dressed more casually, but it was never in jeans or sweat clothes. But the things that I did and that no one could see was how I tried to stay prayerful and self-motivated. All necessary things if I was going to keep the waves of pressure from spilling over.

This year, without math, physics, and chemistry weighing me down, I was eager to plunge into my new course work and major. Two of my classmates from freshman year also transferred to main campus; however, Ginger, Barbara, Janet, and me moved together to an off-campus apartment near downtown. Two of us were Black and the other two women were White. We lived peacefully together. But outside of our dwelling place, I learned that life in this college town could sometime be harsh. Twice it left me angered and bowed down after being called out of my name. All I did was walk down Beaver Avenue on the way home from campus. The first time the N-word was flung at me by one of the locals, I was too stunned and hurt to say a word. It compounded my feelings of isolation on large campus where few looked like me.

At this point, I'd had it.

My much-anticipated junior year in Happy Valley had become like riding a rollercoaster—slow steady ascents, pinnacles, deep plunges, and all. Academically, I was flying high and finally thriving in courses that I enjoyed, especially those where I could better understand the dynamics of children and families. And it hadn't taken me long to climb back to a familiar perch, now that I was making the dean's list every semester. I didn't work on campus during my junior year, but financially I was at least stable and had what I needed to pay my share of the rent, $125 each month. Financial aid I received as an independent student made those things possible. There was even enough in my small budget to help me stay outfitted with some new clothes. While at Penn State, I reconnected with my paternal grandmother. She was also looking out for me. During my senior year, she mailed me a monthly check for $110 to help with food and spending money

Yet, amid my highs in the classroom, worry and stress over home and safety nets were grounding me. Looking back, that plummet was what I now call a depression; and before long, free falling into what was likely a breakdown. Midway through my third year at Penn State, feelings of isolation, the fear of failing, uncertainty, and cultural trauma were bubbling up and colliding. I was afraid and didn't know how to tame them. I was on my own at Penn State and couldn't seem to find a refuge.

Perhaps the presence of the Christmas holidays compounded my problems. Everywhere I looked, what I thought of as normalcy swirled like eager December snowflakes in the wind—making plans for home, family, and happiness belonged to my roommates and friends. Through them I lived vicariously. I was the one without a family. The realization of having just one more year left on campus when I wasn't sure what my future held also pooled in my mind as did the continued pressure I put on myself to succeed and make it through Penn State. The thought of all of these things made my head feel like it was going to explode.

"What's wrong, Sharon?" My roommates begged to know. Sometimes no words came out of my mouth. I'd just cry.

"Are you OK? You seem different," they'd say. My poor roommates, lost for words to console me, would fall silent whenever I carried my grief into the same room with them. But I never unloaded it. I just took it to the streets, not telling my roommates where I was going; walking alone most days and for hours up the main drag—down Atherton Avenue or over to Beaver Avenue past the shops.

It took time and some trusted shoulders—a couple of girlfriends who didn't bother me with questions, but who comforted; and then there was an African boyfriend and confidante. By the spring, my mind and spirit started to feel renewed and hopeful. And with it, I took a leap. I threw myself into overhauling my body and getting in shape to compete in the 2nd Annual Miss Black Penn State Pageant sponsored by the Black fraternity Omega Psi Phi. Whether it was bolting up and down stairs or running religiously for seven miles a day to get me swimsuit ready, I did it in the weeks before the pageant. As a singer and dancer, I prepared two blended songs—Roberta Flack's hit "Killing Me Softly" and an African tune I can hear but can't remember the name. I danced to it and sang a cappella. The talent portion of the pageant should have clinched it for me, but instead in 1982, the title went to a graduating senior. That was the beginning and the end of my pageant days.

Making It After All

Although brief and periodic, the overseas calls that came from my sister were often comforting, like a balm. She kept me up on her life in Germany and I shared moments from my college journey. But I felt the distance. My sister got pregnant with my second niece while in Germany. She suffered during those early months of her pregnancy with debilitating morning sickness that left her dehydrated and often landed her in the hospital. Her condition was a constant worry for me and there were days when I wished that I could transport myself there, by her side. Calling was the next best thing. It was tough coming up with the money to make the international calls to my sister, but I did so whenever I could. She made it a point, though, to call me at least once a month until the baby came.

When her second daughter was born, she was injured during the delivery. The doctor's forceps had clamped her tiny ears. When I learned what happened to my new niece, I wanted more than ever for my sister to pack up and come home, but I knew that her place was there with her husband. Following the birth, and as I listened to my sister's voice, I already felt such love and compassion for her little one whose entry into the world was made rough. Today, while I am very close to both of my nieces, my sister's second child has become more like my daughter. In her I see snippets of myself in the way that she moves and handles herself, and in her drive and flair. She's grown up now. The day that she e-mailed to tell me that she was launching a business as a makeup artist, of course, I was thrilled with the news. She and I share this passion.

During most of my Penn State years, my sister and her family lived in Germany. When they returned to the States, my sister's family was stationed in Killeen, Texas, where they lived until returning to Pittsburgh in 1983, after I had graduated college.

Ending my third year at Penn State and heading into my final one at the university, I was filled with anticipation as I looked forward to an internship with the Allegheny County District Attorney's office. I hadn't yet begun that work, but already dread was creeping as I thought about where I was going to live when I returned. The months in between would go by quickly. I feared the future, because I knew what it was like to face homelessness. But at the same time, I was driven into action; I needed to find shelter. My roommate Ginger and I knew that we needed a flexible short-term living arrangement. We were graduating and interning and didn't want the hassle of trying to get free of a traditional year's lease that usually tripped up students. Our search for a flexible month-to-month lease began in the local newspaper classifieds — *lovely basement apartment available in the home of a local professor and his family*. This was the listing that caught my eye, or perhaps it was the word "family" that leapt off the page at me? It didn't take long for our search to end with an interview, and a signed lease with that family.

Kathy and Derrill were a vibrant young couple with open minds, big hearts, and room to spare for my roommate Ginger and me. I could leave State College that summer for my internship and return with peace of mind, knowing that I had found a home, and quite an elegant one for my final year at Penn State.

Kathy and Derrill were parents to three daughters. When we moved in with them, two of their girls still lived at home. Together they dwelled in an idyllic neighborhood, along a quiet street, just a block over from Atherton Avenue. It was a stunning place. Floor-to-ceiling windows stood in many rooms of the house, bringing the outdoors in, including sunlight that bounced off the gleaming hardwood floors. At the start of the fall trimester, I was eager to move in and proud to show off my new home when the young man I was dating drove me back to campus, his car brimming that day with all of my must-have college clothes, gear, and furnishings to fill my spacious new room in Kathy and Derrill's basement. It used to belong to their oldest daughter before she moved out to start her career as an actress. When Ginger and I showed up that first day, smiles and hugs greeted us at the front door. We were strangers then. But from that moment, I knew we would get along, they would become more than landlords and I would be more to them than their tenant.

My roommate arrived before me to move in, already claiming her side of the room along with ample space in the closet, but that was fine with me. I was used to Ginger's ways. I lived with her for four years while at Penn State, and had grown to love her. On that day, we were happy to see each other and to be rooming together, this one last time.

The entrance to our apartment was private and included its own laundry room facilities. I could come and go freely. There was so much to like and enjoy about this comfortable living space, but I soon realized that I was getting more than a homey picture-perfect rental. It didn't take long—within a week, it was clear that I would make this family my "forever" friends.

Kathy and Derrill and their children didn't look like Ginger and me. They were White and we were Black. Just months before, my worst encounter with racism at Penn State left my spirit bruised, and left me angry and wondering if life for Blacks in Happy Valley could ever truly be welcoming. Now, here I was living with a White family off campus in this prim college town where few reached across boundaries of the racial divide and where sameness and staunch tradition were the norm. But in Kathy and Derrill's home, there was room for real dialogue about race, about life, and so many things that mattered when we gathered regularly around the breakfast or dinner table, or relaxed together in the family room, or when I felt comfortable enough to venture upstairs from my apartment to her bedroom for a late evening chat, often about school and education. Being in their home was an opportunity to live and learn under the same roof with a family, not just have a series of White college roommates like those I had been used to while at Penn State. My roommate, Ginger, on the other hand, came from a strong close-knit family and had little interest in or time to befriend our land-lords. Ginger's goals were graduating early and planning her upcoming June wedding. There was little time left over for fun in this household, just school work for her.

The physical differences between the family and me were obvious. But in other ways, this family was much like me. Kathy and Derrill were outsiders, too in Happy Valley.

They came from Southern California where life was easy, the people laidback and diverse, and where the sun shined most of the time. For them, starting anew in State College was as jolting as its frigid winters, which came too soon and hung around too long. Derrill, a tall good-looking man with a crop of dark hair, taught geology at Penn State. He would tease and say that his grandma Mary asked him to promise her that he would grow up to become more than a California "beach bum." He made her happy and became a geologist. And his petite, blue-eyed, blonde-haired wife was every bit the sunny Southern California girl. But when it came to education, especially for her daughters, Kathy, a State College public school teacher, was stern and committed.

And as a runner, she was also fierce. One day she invited me along for one of her regular five-mile runs. I thought that I was a runner, too, before bounding on to the street behind her only to have my eager stride melt into a slow jog. It was tough keeping pace, but it didn't stop Kathy from inviting me along day after day. Running was something she did well, but I believed she used those brisk early morning hours to also get to know me better. It worked, and in time, our bond grew stronger and so did my stride.

By the time winter break rolled around in December, the family had woven me into their lives and they had become a fixture in mine. But I would be leaving them for nine weeks while I was an intern. I had an excellent experience working in the DA's office, but came away determined to someday do all that I could to keep those I loved out of the clutches of the criminal justice system. What I found when I interned there was a process of adjudication that was discriminatory, biased, and demoralizing. It was also confirmation that I needed to focus my efforts after graduation on working with "children of promise," those who just needed someone to believe in them as others had believed in me.

When I returned to campus and Happy Valley in February 1983, it would be my last semester as a student. The notion was bittersweet, but I was grateful to be on a solid course that would take me from the classroom to commencement. Then my thoughts turned to the family I had been living with and wished that I had only met them sooner. As I walked into the house where I was living, Kathy, Derrill, and the girls welcomed me back with a bouquet of balloons and a special dinner that evening. I couldn't have felt more special that day. In the morning, though, life here began again as it did everyday. Kathy and I set out for our morning run, afterward returning home to shower and change. She went off to school and I headed to classes on campus.

In those final weeks of school, the Penn State finish line was so close and in my sight. The weeks were also filled with angst and all-nighters. I struggled to maintain 17 credits during the trimester and pounded out paper after paper well into the early morning as I sat in the campus computer lab. The pace seemed relentless, especially when I didn't have a typewriter or computer of my own. Then relief came. Derrill offered to have his secretary type my final thesis. I exhaled.

After four years, which included summer school at the McKeesport campus, and with far more credits than I needed, I was graduating, accomplishing what I had set out to do. As I inched forward into that the "big new world" that most all commencement speakers talk about, my knees knocked and my spirit still quaked even after four years at Penn State and being away from my forever home. I was coming out of Penn State and still not sure where I would live and what I would do to sustain myself. But what I did know on that day is that I hadn't fallen through the many cracks that threatened to swallow and devour me. I had made it over and would do it again when I left University Park.

But for one afternoon, I put those weighty thoughts to rest and celebrated with my family and friends after the commencement.

The warm welcoming home where I had spent the past nine months during my senior year was transformed into a beauty in blue and white. Balloons adorned with "Go State" and matching streamers filled the backyard deck. Members of my many families (biological, foster and kin) were gathered in Happy Valley that day for a lavish feast and to send me forth in style and with love. Over the season I had spent with my State College family, I had become like a fourth daughter. And I loved them no less. Over time they supported my journey and helped racial wounds heal.

My family beheld a finished product—its first college graduate. I beheld my dad. This was the first time that he had attended one of my school graduations. This was the biggest one to date and Dad thought that he had arrived on time. He had actually shown up decades after the hard work of others—those who raised me—was done, but that didn't stop him that day from basking in glory that unfortunately didn't belong to him. I watched him, proud in his nice suit and tie, but kept those thoughts to myself. This was my day to celebrate and shine.

With my first full-time job as a new graduate close, but not confirmed, I headed back to my aunt and uncle's house in the South Hills where I waited and spent days interviewing for positions. All of my stuff from four years of college was here, and so was I. Less than 30 days after finishing school, the scant welcome mat that allowed me to return home from time to time while at Penn State was now threadbare on the doorstep of the place I called my forever home. This time, my aunt's tepid tolerance of me had worn out, too. She waited for the day that I told her I had found a job and was finally moving out of her house.

My aunt sniffed and taunted before her alarm went off. "I just can't take this mess anymore," she yelled, pointing at my heap. In that instance, something in me shifted and broke free—the voice that never quite made its way up from my throat and out of my mouth when I lived here for those years. Now, at 21, I was more sure and steady. The muzzle came off of me right then and there: "I'm grown and you're grown. If you want respect, you have to treat people with respect."

At first my aunt could only look at me as dumbfounded as I probably did on the day that I graduated from high school and she pulled me aside to inform me that there would be no more support because her work was done. If my aunt uttered a word after I spoke, it must have trailed off behind me as I marched upstairs and headed straight for the telephone.

Life for me in my forever home was over. I decided that day to move out. Dad was the only person that I thought to call. I had nowhere else to go.

"Dad, if I ever needed you, it's now. Can I come to stay with you for a little while until I get a job?" I poured out. This time he didn't check with anyone, he didn't put me on hold. Dad just said, "Okay." He was still with the same girlfriend who watched that summer morning as I was taken away to shelter when I was just 13, but their new home had to be my resting place for about a month.

As I grew tired of waiting to hear about a job that I was sure was going to make me an offer, I went instead with the one that did come through. The Hill House, a community service agency in the Hill District hired me as a case worker and my clients were the elderly, not children. While a means to an end financially, I worked hard and enjoyed my clients, knowing that my dream job was out there. My sights were on the Allegheny County Children and Youth Services, as the agency was known then, and it didn't matter how long it took me to get there, I made it my destination. For now, I was earning $12,500 a year and thinking that wealth had finally visited me. In about a month, I managed to squirrel away enough money while living with Dad to get my own apartment—$190 per month efficiency in Lawrenceville, a neighborhood not far from where I worked. I feathered my new nest with plants, some room dividers, and pieces of hand-me-down furniture from my sister and father. It was adorable, chic, and most important, it was mine. Still doting in her way, my sister offered to clean my place once a month. Signing that lease was one of the most exciting days of my life. It meant that I was responsible and didn't have to wonder where I would lay my head and where home was.

Yet, at times, loneliness had a way of eclipsing my exhilaration. I had a lot to learn about living on my own and finding contentment within these new four walls. Although the complex family dynamics that had defined my life for so long still left me wondering where I fit in, nonetheless, it was comforting to know that those I called kin were around for me.

Getting back and forth to work was an accomplishment that I proudly claimed. I was healthy and fit and willing to walk and hop buses to visit clients and get where I needed to go. With no car or driver's license during that first year on the job, I walked. The undulating terrain of Polish Hill took me pass framed row houses, detached bricks with front porches, and its cathedral on my way to the Hill District. At the end of the day, I would make the same trek. Home was a destination. It was the place where I usually nested in the evening, watched television, and spent time talking with my neighbor, Stephanie, another single woman living on her own. Like me, she didn't have a car. So, when we wanted to hang out after work or on the weekends, we walked to local shops and restaurants.

One day, though, I decided to take the plunge and learn to drive. I dipped into some of the graduation gift money that I had saved and took driving lessons. Each time I took the driving test, my father went with me. I did my test driving in a small compact from the driving school. On the second try, I did it. I passed the driving test and had my license in hand. The following year, I was able to afford my first car with the gift of a down payment from Kathy and Derrill. It was a used red Chevette that cost me $187.13 a month for four years, nearly as much as I spent for rent.

Not long on the job at the Hill House, I quickly learned how vulnerable the elderly could be; much like the children I would eventually serve. I handled Allegheny County's first elder abuse case after learning that a sweet but frail woman in her 80s was being beaten and swindled by her own adult granddaughter. Although three generations lived in that house, my client's daughter stood by, too afraid to protect her mother. It took about six months, but I worked with my supervisor to have my client, this grandmother, deemed incompetent, a move that enabled her to get out from her abuser and into a nursing facility where she would be cared for and safe. For most of my clients, I was their only lifeline and connection to the outside world. On the job, I unearthed crises in homes that my grandparents never would have known as they aged. While working at the Hill House from 1983 to 1985, there were even days when I saved lives by just ensuring that my seniors got food and nursing care.

I made good friends at the Hill House, too, and to my surprise, found a man and love there. Right away, my co-worker Emily and I clicked. She was bubbly, fun, and a bit older, but like me, Emily was a believer. Before long, she had introduced me to her church in East Liberty and to her Holiness Pentecostal faith. They were small in number, but the members knew how to have church and praise the Lord. They didn't hold back when the spirit took hold of them. Theirs was a free and spirited worship, not the reserved praise I had known growing up Baptist. It didn't take long to know that this church was for me. Before I knew it, church services were filling my nights at least three times a week.

When I didn't have a car, Emily drove me to church and back on Sundays, sometimes in exchange for babysitting her two girls. The congregation was warm and welcoming. I became fast friends with Brenda, one of Pastor Thomas' four children. Whether it was a holiday, special occasion, or just another weekend as a single girl, I was at home with Brenda and her family. In their house, they drew me close and treated me like another daughter. I knew then that it was time to go; to slip away from them before the members of this family slipped away from me. I had done it before. The closeness, the friendship, the safety I found with the Thomas' had been spotty and at times missing from the life I knew growing up in foster care. When I decided to disconnect, breaking from the relationship was quick. They didn't see it coming, but it hurt them when I left. After that, returning to my shell felt normal, but this family's loving ways stayed with me. It took several months before I could face Brenda and explain how lingering feelings of abandonment and connection had forced me away. But the Thomas' were people of God. They forgave me, tried to understand my struggle, and decided to accept me for me.

FIVE

Changing the Narrative

Walking Into My Destiny

Allegheny County's Office for Children and Youth, as it was called then, wasn't a welcoming place for my dad in the early 1960s. After losing his wife, he went in search of a way forward and thought that the child welfare office on the North Side could help him.

Twice Dad went there seeking assistance with getting basic necessities like food stamps or a sack of canned goods, medical care, or a few changes of clothes, maybe some tops and bottoms or cotton dresses for his two little girls. Twice Dad came in search of guidance and instruction that wasn't intuitive—how to take care of his motherless children and what to do with them when he had to get up, leave the house, and go to work every day. Twice he passed quickly through the agency's doors, exiting with little advice and empty hands. In those days, my dad was like most men when he accessed the child welfare system: a stranger in a strange land.

Mothers in need were commonplace and the agency understood what they wanted and why they came. Still, some 20 years later, the

Allegheny County Office of Children, Youth and Family Services, as it is now called, had been my destination in 1985, and working with children was my goal when I entered as a caseworker. In an odd twist of bureaucracy, though, it's almost as if once encountered, no matter how unkind the system was to my dad, my siblings, and I, we never completely left the system. Nearly 50 years after my father first sought help for his children and I first entered the system, a case file with my name on it still exists in the agency's archives. My new job was allowing me, once a product of the system, to become an insider, a civil servant determined to reach children in Pittsburgh who grew up like me—in search of a forever home, safety nets, and a family.

At 24 years old, in my crisp navy blue business suit with a bright white blouse underneath, and classic mid-heeled, patent leather pumps, I was marching into my destiny. It started to take shape while still in high school and as I was readying myself for one of the biggest journeys of my life—college. On the day that I began my new career in child welfare, I spotted Rick, the last caseworker that I had before aging out of the system.

"Rick, is that you? Remember me, I'm Sharon Toliver. You were my caseworker."

"Oh my goodness, Sharon. What are you doing here? Where are you these days?"

"I'll be working here at the agency. Today's my first day on the job. I'm on the way to my orientation. Oh, and I finished Penn State," came my response in one excited swoop.

"That is so great. I can't believe it's you, but I knew that you would do well," Rick said with a deep nod and big smile as he took in my accomplishments and the grown up and professional me that I had become. Rick and I met by chance that morning, in the lobby. He was emerging from an elevator and I was heading hurriedly onto it. That was how my first day on the job began. Before jumping into the elevator, I thanked my former caseworker and gave a quick hug to my new colleague.

As I sat through required job training that first week, I could have written the script. I knew the children that my instructors discussed each day because in many ways, when I was growing up, I was one of them. "You're talking about my life," I wanted to stand up and say. I couldn't wait to take on my first foster care case. But I soon learned that I was assigned to Child Protective Services (CPS), where almost every day was spent coping with a crisis, making critical on-the-spot decisions about whether a home should be declared unfit or unearthing evidence of child abuse and neglect. In Child Protective Services, I was on the frontlines of investigating those ugly cases. Those were the ones that some at the agency referred to as the "dirty houses, roaches, and sexual abuse cases." In many ways, the job that child protective services did was the most important of all in the child welfare system because it was the entry point of every child who came into the system. As a 24-year-old CPS worker, the responsibility for determining whether or not children would be removed from their homes was mine. But this wasn't the job I dreamed of doing when I came to the agency. Still, I was glad for the opportunity to be working with children. I knew that if they entered the system, they would need someone like me on their side.

Among my cases and investigations, it wasn't often that I recommended removing a child from their home. But when I did, believe me, the situation had to be egregious and even then, I'd rally support from inside the agency and strategize on ways to preserve that family while protecting the child. In one of my cases, it did make sense to remove the child and place him in a shelter, but it was done with the understanding that his parents would be supported and monitored and their son could return to them. There was a plan and exit strategy and a commitment to keep families connected.

And there were often times when I would encounter single mothers with multiple children, struggling to survive. As a young single caseworker, I often wondered how I could be instrumental in changing the conditions of the children and families whom I was called to serve. I did not want them to see their current condition as the sum total of their lives. I urged them to see and believe in a future of opportunities and possibilities, instead of in a life forever limited by their current challenges and constraints.

One of my cases involved a mother of 10 children, which included a set of twins. At age 28, this woman had been pregnant and conceived eight times. I was called to her home because of alleged physical abuse. What I found was neglect stemming from the impoverished conditions in which this mother and her children were forced to live in daily. And here I was. Only four years younger than her, what support and guidance could I offer? Then it became clear what I could do for her. I understood the importance families and the need for them to stay intact. I offered this struggling mother the opportunity to have her children remain in the family while she worked on securing a better life for herself and her children. In that instance, what came to mind was kinship care. Again, while it was not a stated policy practice during my years as a Child Protective Services caseworker, I was able to convince my supervisor that this young mother's plight was more about poverty than it was abuse. As a result of my position on the case, the 10 children, ranging in age from 10 years to infancy, were all placed with relatives who lived within the same housing project as the mother. That meant placing some of the siblings with their grandmother in a unit upstairs and others with their aunts who lived downstairs or across the courtyard in the housing complex. I believed that these children were happy, despite being plagued by poverty. And their mother, though struggling, wanted desperately to do more for her babies.

In some ways, my young life and that of this mother had been the same. Although I often went without food and stability, I did not equate my situation with being unloved. We were poor and, at the same time, my father was attempting to find his way without any intervention or support. I drew upon this background. So, when I presented the case of this mother before the court and shared with the judge why I took the actions that I did to help preserve the stability of this family, the judge seemed to understand my motivation and applauded my efforts. The outcome in this case and for the children is what I had hoped it would be. The judge classified the children adjudicated dependent, but as is often the case, they were not placed with strangers. Instead, the siblings were able to stay in their same community and housing complex, see each other and not be separated from their mother. Returning to this familiar place also meant that their lives would not be interrupted. They could play with their same friends and attend their same schools. This was the child welfare that I thought was important for children. While I did not have the political savvy or even the policy framework to call what was in my heart "kinship care," I just knew that it was the "right" thing for children in their situation.

But nearly three decades ago, few in child welfare were going to such lengths or making allies of parents and families, or looking for those who were like family to stand in the gap. Guiding my work was the belief that to protect and care for a child didn't have to mean permanently removing them from their families. Finding kin, those who were like family, also helped make permanency possible. Who knew better than I did about the benefits of being placed with kin when I couldn't live with my relatives? In dwelling with kin, I found the stability that my young life didn't know and the self-esteem that I needed. With people like Grandma and Gramps, their daughters, and extended family, I enjoyed a sense of belonging, identity, and culture. Much of it I experienced while gathered around Grandma's table for Sunday dinner, and before that it was time spent at her mother's house with fictive kin. My fictive kin weren't people who were related to me by blood or birth, but together we shared emotional ties and strong relationships—the important things that made us like family.

Memories of life with those caregivers served as a guiding force as I moved from case to case and made weighty decisions about removing a child. Finding a relative placement wasn't an agency practice or policy when I was there, although families could come forward, offering to care for a child. But few caseworkers sought out those family members, thinking that it was easier to just pack up a child and place him or her into an approved foster home or a shelter or group home. Searching for a responsible, caring family member or kin could be time consuming, especially in a crisis situation, but for me, it was a part of what I did on the job. It was what I did even when it meant sparring with judges in family court to keep children and parents together as a unit.

"We don't have to guess what Sharon is going to recommend in her case assessments. We already know," my supervisor would often intone during staff meetings. He was right. I was just grateful that my supervisor rarely questioned my judgment and backed my recommendations when it came to children and their families. This often meant that I consulted with social workers and other service providers to ensure that wrap-around care and services were in place to shore up families and protect their children. Leading by example is what I strived to do when I served as a caseworker. And in my heart and mind, I felt a bit like a rebel, full of zeal, as I rallied for relative placements.

Within four years at the agency, I was promoted to supervisor, becoming one of only two caseworkers in the unit to reach that level without an advanced degree. But at 27 years old, I was in pursuit of that degree, going back to McKeesport, Pa., where a new branch office had opened. It was during this time my new supervisor, and fellow Penn Stater, showed me the art of juggling new motherhood, graduate school, and professional responsibilities. My supervisor, Melrena, had been in the industry about 20 years. She was sharp and seasoned. Just by watching her, I learned to deal with difficult people; that team building was a powerful practice; and that wearing grace and carrying a ready smile could be my best resources when the going got tough. As a young professional on the rise and as a woman with purpose, I saw in her all that I wanted to be. She was phenomenal.

Families as Solutions

Child welfare, at its most basic, is defined as services, that promote the well-being of children by ensuring their safety, achieving permanency, and strengthening families so they can successfully care for their children. Federal, state, and local funding help fuel the system and its services and communities and neighborhood partnerships also play a supporting role in caring for those children who enter the system.

As a practitioner, I knew that child welfare was complex. It was tough to describe to those outside of its walls, especially families who have never found themselves on its rolls. In the early 1990s, when looking at who was on the agency's child welfare rolls, the snapshot was alarming. Most of those children and families entering Allegheny County's child welfare system were people who looked like me. Rates for Black female-headed families with children and Black children not living with two parents in the city and county in 1990 were the highest or nearly the highest in the nation. Employment and income levels for Blacks in the city and county during this same period were also the worst in the nation.

Although African Americans were about 25.7 percent of the population in Pittsburgh and 11 percent of the population in Allegheny County when I was growing up in the 1960s, African-American children were overrepresented in the child welfare system. Ethnic minorities were more likely to be brought to the attention of child welfare systems than any other group, and African-American children had the highest rate of cases referred to child welfare.

The prevailing thought in the field concluded that poverty was the consequence of personal and cultural behaviors. Social policy was fueled by the theory that much of Black life was a "tangle of pathology" that trapped African Americans at the bottom of society and became an unbreakable circle. It was also the reason, mainstream scholars claimed, why so many African Americans were tipping the scale. But it wasn't, some social scientists shot back. Poverty was a factor, but poverty couldn't explain away the disproportionate number of Allegheny African-Americans—mostly children who were male and young mothers—who were on its rolls. What had to be accounted for were social structures, which determined who got jobs, how much people were paid, where people lived, and which schools they could attend or gain access to.

Research tells us that a client's race and culture, and where they lived, were unfortunate factors when considering how certain families and children, and not others, came to be in need. Over time, systemic racial bias had woven a relentless, knotted web through the child welfare system. That same web snared many Black families, causing their children to linger in foster care, group homes, or shelters, usually with no timely exit strategy or a way back to their biological homes. At this time, those who provided these direct services for Allegheny County child welfare were overwhelmed. It was typical for White, large, and faith-based institutions, those with little historical or cultural connection to the children they served or with the communities where they lived, to be turned to in addressing the problems.

When I was 13, I lived for six months in Pittsburgh's McIntyre Shelter, until fictive kin provided a forever home and a way out of that institution. Being raised in foster care by fictive kin was the kind of placement that kept me connected to my biological father and some of my other blood relatives, to others who were like kin, and even to the community where I grew up. That home represented my final placement before I aged out of the system. The benefits that came with such a placement were what I needed. As I soon discovered, there were a few inside the Allegheny County child welfare system who were also pushing for such kinship care and saw it as promising. Thinking boldly, equitably, and outside of the norm, we envisioned plans for kinship care and exit strategies for non-relative placements that would land dependent children back with their blood relatives or with those who were like family. Getting the agency to a new way of thinking about the practice of kinship care was painful, until nearly two decades ago when institutional policy made such placements the norm and aggressively pursued in Allegheny County.

In the late 1980s, it was Marcia M. Sturdivant, Ph.D., who helped usher in that change. More than two decades ago, she began in the system as a regional director. After spending 15 years as deputy director of the nationally recognized Allegheny County Department of Human Services Office of Children, Youth and Families, Sturdivant moved on in May 2013, to head a Pittsburgh-based college access program and education philanthropy. But on the inside, in those days, is where she started pushing to transform the way the child welfare agency saw and treated families, especially the overwhelming number of female clients who looked like her. Sturdivant fast became a vocal warrior for Pittsburgh's African-American children and families. She worked by day in a White child welfare system where the problem of racial disproportionality, particularly the overrepresentation of African-American boys in foster care, was rampant. But home for her was in the Black community. She was a staunch believer that families not only mattered but also had what it took to protect and keep their children from harm. In time, Sturdivant helped change the narrative around child welfare's policies and practices in Allegheny County. But institutional change wasn't a battle she could fight alone. The concept of family wanting to take care of family was a tough one to sell, even in a place like Pittsburgh where family ties and the notion of blood being thicker than water was taken to heart. By and large, people here stay in the same communities where they were born and raised. And as a result, the neighborhoods where people grew up remained stable because they were the same places where strong family networks continued to take hold, flourish, and dwell. Somehow, though, that acknowledgment didn't seem to apply to those Black children and their mothers in the system who were looked upon as broken families without anchors and ties.

This was the kind of thinking that gave way to different treatment, if not racial bias, that festered from day to day in a system in need of change. Sturdivant was there. She saw it every day.

As a result of culturally irresponsive policies and practices of the child-serving systems of the past, including child welfare, it was clear that by the time Black families were turned over to the child welfare agency, determinations about their ability to care for their children had already been made by law enforcement or schools. And when these families were presented to child welfare, assigned a number and given a case file, those policies and practices pervaded every child welfare decision-making process. As it spun, that web of culturally biased policies and practices could begin with a substantiation of abuse and neglect, and could continue throughout the life of the case, which often included removal from the biological home. Such were the kinds of systematic policies, practices, and stereotypes that were working against the majority of families and children of color who were filling the county's system to overflowing during the late 1980s and early 1990s. In fact, the effect of that systemic racial bias was potent enough to undermine the strength of those families, deplete their resilience, and compromise their outcomes.

Family was at the heart of what I championed. But then, I found few believers. The prevailing thought was, when families break, they stay broken. And, compared to government-sanctioned institutions and placements for children, families just weren't important or viable solutions.

By 1992, the debate surrounding kinship care in Allegheny County was heating up as more children entered the child welfare system. The crack epidemic in the region grew more pervasive and catapulted many families into the system. While many in Pittsburgh enjoyed the benefits of residing in a place known then for being among "the most livable cities," urban despair often went ignored. Crack, which had already decimated the inner cities of Philadelphia several years prior, had now moved westward in Pennsylvania. The increasing explosion of babies born addicted to crack was among the most drastic results of the drug epidemic. Together, they represented a new and needy population of children that the county found itself ill prepared to care for and place.

One case in particular served to elevate the need for kinship care and helped position it as a credible child welfare policy and placement option for children in Allegheny County. As a result, family members, legal advocates, and community advocates began to pay attention to the workings of the child welfare system, and demanded that family become viable members of the dialogue and decision makers for their kin who came to the attention of the child welfare system. While Dr. Sturdivant and her child welfare colleagues were doing their internal networking and building political will, they advocated for change within the system to benefit all children, focusing specifically on the policies of racial inequity. At the same time, the external environment was forcing change.

As the then-lead foster care administrator, Mary Young and lead child welfare director, Mary Freeland, and Sturdivant, who was then a regional office director, joined forces and took deliberate steps to make kinship care a viable option for children in Allegheny County's child welfare system. While the external environment pushed the political process for this important family option, so did the 1989 Rivera Consent Decree brought against Allegheny County for discrimination practices against family members who wanted to become foster parents for their kin. In essence, the county agreed that any family member who wished to become a foster parent for their kin could not be discriminated against because they were blood relatives. This new posture in Allegheny County was consistent with the 1979 U.S. Supreme Court Ruling in *Miller vs. Youakim.*

By early 1993, the practice of kinship care was seen as relevant, as the demand for relative placements climbed. During this time, the business of child welfare was also coming under fire for what it lacked. When Black leaders in Pittsburgh looked closer at who made up the county's outsourced providers of services, they were outraged to know that there were no Blacks or other people of color operating private, non-profit foster care organizations, the group homes and shelters where so many Black and brown children were placed. And as that news smoldered, Blacks bristled, too, at being labeled unwilling to foster Black children—then a common problem in Allegheny County and in child welfare agencies elsewhere in the nation.

In the midst of change at the child welfare agency, I decided to make a move in 1993. I left the county child welfare agency to go to Pittsburgh's Three Rivers Adoption Council where I directed Black Adoption Services. I saw Three Rivers as a place where I could continue to support families and help children find the security of a permanent home. While at the council, I also wanted to learn what I needed to know about operating a non-profit. But it didn't take long before my views on family, kinship, and adoption, borne from working inside the child welfare system, clashed with others whose perception came instead from a traditional private adoption perspective. Typically, adoption was seen as a means to an end for those struggling with infertility issues. Child welfare adoptions were typically done by families who wanted to expand their families, but not necessarily because of issues of infertility, but rather, because such families saw a need to give back in some way to address this societal challenge. When I saw need and permanency for Black children, my colleagues saw the process as a privilege. For them, adoption was something that those with means did when they couldn't conceive and have a child of their own.

A Field Wide Open

The turning point for me at Three Rivers Adoption Coucil (TRAC) came when I heard the frequent and urgent calls from distraught grandparents. They demanded to know where their grandchildren were being taken and, most important, why they had been overlooked by the system in search of foster care placements. Something was awfully wrong in the child welfare system if the rights of these family members were being terminated and their relative children were about to exit the system for adoptive homes. This wasn't what these families and kin deserved and neither did the children in their lives.

By August 1993, about seven months after starting at Three Rivers, I set in motion, earnestly though quietly, my dream—launching my own non-profit. Crafting my plan after business hours and on weekends and sometimes well into the night, I vetted ideas and tossed around options for a fitting organizational name with a handful of confidents. And I even worked with an attorney to secure non-profit status. Research on the practice of kinship care was also a big part of moving forward, but in the late 1980s and early 1990s, there were few publications and little information to glean about a practice that families had done informally for centuries. Most readings, however, about early models for relatives taking care of family in need pointed me to the continent of Africa where often grandmothers were the kinship connections, the stabilizers, and family's "rock." And when I looked at the United States, I found similar scholarship and writing about Black families and kinship care. Despite generations of change and hardships that came with being Black in America, Black families held on to the practice of their pre-slavery African ancestors, when they cared for kin. And in many of those families, Grandma is the one who anchors and rescues her kin, something that still comes traditionally to most Black families.

At the start of the New Year, I saw a field that was ripe and wide open. The county was attempting to manage kinship families on its own. Working with a provisional license to service its kinship families, the agency was stumbling and being cited as the backlog of kin to be certified mounted and the complicated needs of these families went unmet. That's when Allegheny County responded to a 1989 judicial consent decree requiring that resources be provided to kinship foster parents. And that's when the county went in search of a private contractor who could deliver. Most providers in the pool were White and did not want to work with kin. When the county's requests for proposals went out, Sturdivant was among the agency's officials who sought traditional providers of care and took to the streets in search of qualified contenders of color who they could bring to the table. Whether it meant using proposal writing seminars to lure some to the competition, huddling over morning coffee, or organizing town hall meetings to help spread the word, they did what it took. But at the close of the competition, there weren't many providers, old or new, who were eager to compete for a chance to work with kin, thinking that they, unlike foster or adoptive families, had little chance of being approved as kinship caregivers or weren't willing to serve. During that same period, county officials reviewed and vetted proposals for traditional foster care because providers weren't interested in working with kin. That's when I decided to submit two proposals to the county—one to provide kinship foster care services and another for traditional foster care—with the hope that one would be funded.

As the county's problem lingered on servicing kinship care families, I knew before they did that a full-fledged program was needed. With my proposal, I saw an opportunity to meet the need and knew that I was competitive. I had more than 10 years of agency experience as a caseworker, supervisor, and director, and I decided to leverage it. Few could claim the experience that I had having placed so many children in kinship care and worked with kinship families. In fact, these were the people who raised me. Professionally, I was prepared to work successfully with traditional foster care clients as well as kin, but I knew in my heart that kinship care would be my aim as I pursued becoming a provider.

An aging IBM was the only computer that I owned. I claimed the computer, along with a ring and a watch, when Hilda, my grandmother, died. I used it to write the concept paper I submitted to the county on kinship care and my approach for achieving placement and family stability. It was well received by agency officials who knew me and I was asked to submit a formal proposal in February. But I wasn't supposed to be in the mix, murmured some in the established provider pool. And even as a child of the system, I felt the pressure of moving forward with a promising start-up called A Second Chance, Inc., which at the time, only existed on paper.

Ms. Young, the lead county foster care administrator and I vetted the name A Second Chance, Inc. I wanted "A" in front so that it would appear first in the telephone book when people were looking for resources. Gratified, confident, but scared, I learned in April 1994, that the county was going to take a chance on me, someone they knew and who understood kinship families. But there was no money available to fuel my contract. There were resources for others but not for me. It was coming. I didn't worry. In fact I felt at peace knowing that work with kinship families was my purpose, A Second Chance, Inc. was going to be the way to reach them, and God would take care of the rest. This was His plan for me.

The Burning Bush

"There the angel of the Lord appeared to him in flames of fire from within a bush. Moses saw that though the bush was on fire it did not burn up.... When the Lord saw that he had gone over to look, God called to him from within the bush, 'Moses! Moses!' And Moses said, 'Here I am.'" – Exodus 3:1-5

At 7 years old, going to church with Grandma was an adventure. We boarded the city bus in Oakland, a sprawling diverse community in the late 1960s, and rode the short way to reach Monumental Baptist, a gospel fortress and spiritual centerpiece of the nearly all-Black Hill District. I loved being in church as much as I did dressing up for the occasion in my Black crushed-velvet coat and white church gloves with the tiny pearl buttons at the wrist. But as big and sonorous as Monumental was, it wasn't here that I first heard God talking to me. No, I was in my bedroom at Grandma and Gramps' house when I first heard God's voice on the television, commissioning Moses from a burning bush and laying down the law for his people.

Every year around Easter time, I sat for nearly three hours uninterrupted by commercials in front of the TV, usually on a Saturday. It was my time to watch *The Ten Commandments*, my all-time favorite movie. I never grew tired of watching as Moses sprang from being a Hebrew baby set afloat by his mother in an ark of bulrushes to an adopted Egyptian prince on a mission from God, or seeing Moses' ashen face and wide eyes as God revealed Himself in a burning bush. Charlton Heston and Hollywood made this epic biblical story of God's miracles, the exodus of the Israelites out of Egypt, and a second chance for Moses, come alive. Moses' journey and obedience were staples of the preached Word and Sunday school lessons, too, but at least once a year, those signs and wonders were all there for me in living color.

I was only 12, much younger than Moses was, when God revealed himself to me. My fascination with Moses' story was all a part of God's plan, because when He came to me, I was not puzzled by my encounter with the divine. In fact, it seemed familiar. God came to me three times—twice in my bedroom when I lived with Grandma and Gramps and once in my aunt and uncle's basement. Each time, the message was the same: God wanted me to know that my attitude needed adjusting and the words from my mouth should be kinder and gentler, and not so caustic when I spoke to those who failed to understand or hear me.

I was always awake when He came. I wasn't dreaming.

At 12, anger over my mother's death and the realization that she was gone began seeping out and stirring up inside of me. I lashed out at my sister and anyone else who I thought was trying to step in and serve as my mother's surrogate. I dismissed them all and let them know, "You're not my mother!"

Then God told me that He was that Mother. He alone had been my protector. He alone had been carrying me when the woman who

My sister and I with our cousin, Lynn, near the Mall in
Washington, D.C.

A cherished baby picture of my dad.

My grandmother Hilda's high school picture. My great love for learning is inherited from her.

School Day memories! Me at 5 and my sister Rhonda at age 6.

My beautiful daughter Taylor at age 5.

A very special photograph: One of the very few of my mother, Joyce.

My father - living it up and always looking dapper!

My uncles Carl, on the left, and Don Allen.

My sister Rhonda and my brother-in-law Howard at church.

My brother's college graduation picture from Virginia Military Institute.

My brother LaMont with his wife, Lisa, and sons, Julian, Jordan, Tristan, and Jacquet.

Epiphany Church in Pittsburgh's Hill District where Ozanam Strings began.

The Ozanam Cultural Center, where I spent time with my violin.

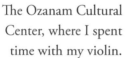

My grandmother Hilda's home in Washington, D.C.

Some of my love of fashion was influenced by Miss - looking stunning on the left.

At our "Dance for Life" cotillion in 2011. Standing with me is Peggy Harris, the CEO of Three Rivers Youth in Pittsburgh, PA.

My Aunt Marva and Uncle Carl.

Rhonda and me taking a minute to relax at the agency's Kennywood Park Day.

My sister and me dressed up for the A Second Chance, Inc. holiday party in 2004.

Rhonda's daughters, my nieces, Stacy (age 5) and Tanaill (age 8).

It was a true honor to receive the Angels in Adoption award in
Washington, D.C.

My friends and fellow Board members at Casey Family Programs. (From
left to right: Gary Severson, Joan Poliak, me, Marian Wright Edelman,
Dr. William Bell, and Gloria Regg)

Taylor, like her mom, loves fashion. Here we are at an ASCI end-of-year celebration in 2006.

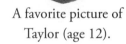

A favorite picture of Taylor (age 12).

Taylor and my grandson, Dontae.

The second office of A Second Chance, Inc. in the East Liberty section of Pittsburgh. Our first office was in a former church on Hawkins Avenue in North Braddock, Pa. Before that, we worked out of my home.

After 2005, we raised funds and held a capital campaign to add a wing to our current location in the Homewood section of Pittsburgh. Our building is a former public school.

gave birth to me no longer could. God let me know that He had been with me all the time.

On another occasion, I was steeped in anger. Fresh from spewing tears and hurling blame at Grandma and Gramps on that Friday night when my sister decided to run away from home and from me, I climbed into bed. Then with eyes wide open, I again saw a big ball of fire. And again, from it emerged the audible and piercing voice of God. Booming, like in stereo, His voice filled my room, but only I could hear it. Not long after God chastised me for being so angry, saying mean things, and showing out, something bad happened to me, just like He said that it would if I didn't change my ways. I was taken to McIntyre Shelter. I knew that I was going to end up there. But still I wasn't transformed.

Each time God showed up, I was stunned, but not frightened by his presence and voice. The thought of ever telling anyone about what I saw and heard, however, was out of the question. I feared that I wouldn't be believed or worse, called crazy and possibly taken away. But I wasn't hallucinating. My experiences with the Lord were real.

His ways were thoughtful and clever—God used the movie that I loved the most and the Exodus story to reach me. He had a purpose when He came. God wanted me to know Him and to make me obedient as He readied my life. While I didn't claim to receive a mighty commission like Moses did that day on Mount Horeb when God commanded him to lead His people to the Promised Land, but I felt even at a young age that something greater was destined for my life. And after meeting Him at 12, I've never doubted if there was a God in heaven or wondered who was the source of my crazy, unequivocal, undeniable faith.

Epilogue

The Bible teaches that there is a time and place and season for everything under the sun. With more than 47 years spent in the child welfare arena as both a product of kinship foster care and as a child welfare expert and kinship care provider, it is my time to write and share my story.

Since beginning this journey of discovery and storytelling in 2011, I've experienced major personal and professional life changes. When I first thought of beginning this book project about six years ago, I envisioned offering a story of hope for the many young people and older adults who continue to grapple with the complexities and challenges that come with living life in foster care. I emerged through such a life and have found solace and healing in telling and sharing my story. Too often, those of us who are products of foster care and kinship care wrestle with a whirlwind of emotions and suffer in silence because we have not found our voices or a refuge. Over the years, I have found a way to heal, resolve, and move forward with my life after kinship foster care and my hope is that something in these pages has both inspired and empowered you to do the same. In many ways, my caregivers — and those who were like kin — have enriched my life and taught me the meaning of family. My fictive kin chose to take care of me. These lives entwined with mine so many years ago, taught me values, shaped my thoughts, and influenced my life's work.

In the process of developing the book, I had to interview many people from my past and it was refreshing to hear about my life in the voices of those who remember me most. The interview with my sister was comforting and enlightening. Her spirit and the care that she had for me were evident as we began to share moments of memory and reflection. Further, our time in conversation allowed us to clear up unresolved feelings and emotions. When she felt isolated and didn't understand why she couldn't live with me, she knew I was having those same feelings about why we were not together under the same roof. The conversation with my uncle, my mother's only living sibling, was also refreshing, sad, and delightful. The interview gave me a glimpse into the world that my mother lived in and revealed the sacrifices that my family made just to survive day to day.

My mother's history is really a story about family resilience and how we celebrate this in the midst of the storms that often cloud our lives. The interview was sad because I realized, for the first time, the extreme poverty that my family had to endure. It reminded me of the early years in my life when we were often without and when my father reported that he was struggling to feed his children. My mother's story heightened my memories of the devastation of poverty and the despair that comes along with it, reminding me of why I work so hard for our clients who are faced with the same grim circumstances. The conversation with my uncle was delightful in that he seemed to be excited to be a part of the process and was happy to share recollections to help round out my narrative. A storyteller in his own right, he offered detail and filled in many of the blanks of my mother's young life.

The struggles that my father and mother encountered were painful. Through my father, I learned about pieces of my mother's life and death, and this book puts many of them together. He filled in a lot of the blanks and this writing process brought me closer to understanding all of the challenges that he had to endure and how he coped with the same. I, too, think that this process was healing for him as he got a chance to tell the story that perhaps he never thought I would want to know.

What has become the most important interview of this book was the interview with my brother. Who knew that 10 days following the interview my brother would suffer a massive heart attack and die at the young age of 48. So, when he talked to me about by the "grace of God and the kindness of strangers," I had no idea that these words would mean so much. We shared so many memories, but I was overcome with grief when I learned of his challenges with my maternal aunt and the tragedies of his young life. He grew up believing that his biological family did not love him and this brought sadness and pain in his life. For years, I struggled with why he and I could not turn back the hands of time and make things right as brother and sister. This is why I advocate for sibling relationships and ensure that the staff at A Second Chance, Inc. understand why sibling relationships are critically important for family well-being and stability. The dedication in this book honors my brother, his courage, and his life.

Here is an update on other significant family members and caregivers whom you met throughout the pages of this memoir.

My foster grandfather, whom I called Gramps, departed this earth about 10 years ago. Prior to his death, he had gout, which infected his limbs and resulted in him having a foot amputated, leaving him unable to walk for many years. He was bedridden for three years before he died, at 92, but he still had a wonderful sense of humor, was still smart as a whip, and continued to work his crossword puzzles. To see my grandfather dwindle away after being such a strong and tall pillar all of my young life began to make life real for me, especially the aging process and recognizing that life is so brief and so fragile. I loved my grandfather and the strong family man that he was. I forgave him for slapping me across the face in his fit of anger, as I know in my heart that that act hurt him much more than I could ever have imagined. I remain grateful to him for taking in a child not born to him, but choosing instead to provide a "safe place to land," a nurturing and loving environment, and a "place to call home." Thank you gramps, from the bottom of my heart.

When he passed, Gramps had a small service. He really didn't have many friends and most of his siblings had passed away. He was cremated. Gramps would always say that he did not want a whole bunch of money spent on a funeral and that he could be buried and/or have his ashes thrown in the backyard. The service was nice. He passed away in the fall. The leaves had already fallen and it was a brisk afternoon the he was laid to rest. Grandma was sad, but in my heart I know that she was relieved that she didn't have to see him continue to suffer. By the time he died, two of his children had already passed away before him. Death was not something that we talked about much when growing up with Gramps, but of course, because my sister and I attended so many funerals with my grandmother, we knew that it was indeed a part of life.

Grandma (fictive grandmother) passed away about six years ago. after suffering a stroke. On the day that she fell ill, Grandma met and had lunch with a young lady whom she had once taken care of. Their lunches, at least twice a year, had become a tradition. After Grandma died, I assisted in planning the funeral, but I did not attend the service, because I had a prepaid vacation scheduled that I could not get reimbursed for because Grandma was not my biological family member. I regret not going to the funeral; however, grandma and I would talk three to four times a year and we had a good relationship. I chose to see her as she was. I am sad that she, too, has passed on, but she taught me great lessons, including how to be a caretaker, friend, and mother. I will forever be grateful for her contribution in my life and for introducing me as a child to God. I thank you, Grandma for loving a child not born to you, yet taking the time to care. God bless you.

My biological grandmother passed away more than 20 years ago. I remember that it was during the summer. I was about 30 years old when Grandmother Hilda died at age 72. We learned from her doctors that she had developed a rare lung disease that caused her tissue to turn into a smooth mass, obscuring the surface of her lungs and impairing her breathing. It was a condition that she reportedly acquired as a result of asbestos exposure.

The news of her passing came suddenly one morning. I knew that I needed to get there. With my car in the shop for repairs, I reached out to my foster aunt that day and she was happy to let me borrow her car. It usually sat idle in her driveway in those days because she no longer felt comfortable driving. My foster aunt wanted to be with me as I made the drive to Washington, D.C. She comforted me and cared for my little girl as I drove.

Grandmother Hilda thrived in the nation's capital. In her eulogy, she was remembered as a lifelong learner and someone who was active in the community. At her home on the corner of Fourth and Taylor, she was a master gardener whose tidy yard, which wrapped around one side of her house, seemed always to have roses in bloom. I remember those roses as I spent many summers in a humid, steamy D.C. with my grandmother. Whenever I was there, grandmother always welcomed me with a hug that felt like being wrapped in a warm blanket. I'll be forever grateful for the support grandmother provided by sending me what money she could when I was at Penn State, and we kept in touch over the years. The summers with her were sweet. She was a model of integrity and sacrifice. Once, when I visited, she was at the University of the District of Columbia, completing her master's degree in English and making time to tutor young students.

A flood of such memories washed over me at her funeral as I sat with the family along the front pew of her Presbyterian church. At times, I got lost in the rituals, not knowing when to sit or stand, but as friends and family came forth to speak of her, Grandma Hilda's goodness remained in sharp focus. Lively strains of "I'll Fly Away" floated up from the church organ that day and filled an empty space.

My fictive aunt is still alive and we talk five or six times a year. We have redefined our relationship and many years ago she asked me to forgive her for the times when she was not emotionally present when I was growing up. We have a good and respectful relationship. She has repeatedly indicated how proud she is of my accomplishments and she plays a key role in ensuring that my half-brother and I stay in relationship with each other. She lives in Pittsburgh and is the manager of her senior citizen high-rise apartment complex.

My biological sister is very much a part of my life. She has indeed resumed her motherly role in my life. The book process was instrumental in helping to heal our relationship. My sister works at A Second Chance, Inc. and is our very talented Vice President of Employee Relations. My sister and I talk mostly every day. There have been many lessons learned about working with family and while we do it very well, there are times that there is a personal cost. She lives in Pittsburgh with her husband of 35 years, her daughters, and two grandchildren.

My fictive uncle is still alive and lives in the same home that I grew up in from the ninth grade until I graduated from college. We talk about twice a year, generally for his birthday and the holidays. He has always been very supportive and encouraged me to write this book. He lives in Pittsburgh and is enjoying retirement.

My biological father lives in Pittsburgh. We text every day and talk a couple of times a month. I just recently introduced him to his son, my half-brother. They needed the father and son relationship. It has been both therapeutic and a supportive relationship.

The loved one referred to as *Miss* passed away in February 2013. She had not been well physically. My half-brother was the one I turned to for updates about her health and progress.

My biological brother, my youngest sibling, passed away in February of 2012, just 10 days shy of his 49th birthday. This devastating blow to the family was a shock. I have a very close and supportive relationship with his son who lives in Pittsburgh.

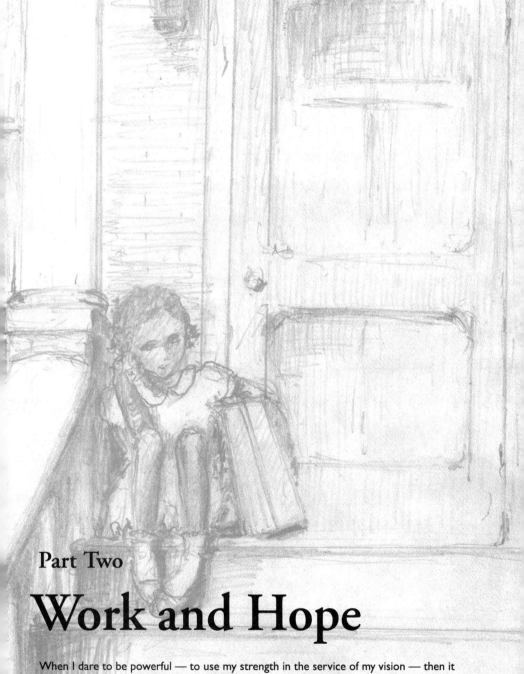

Part Two

Work and Hope

When I dare to be powerful — to use my strength in the service of my vision — then it becomes less and less important whether I am afraid.

— Audre Lorde

SIX
Finding Second Chances

Faith of a Mustard Seed

For me, faith has been a verb that influences, and molds, and changes everything that I do. Growing up hungry and without my mother, sometimes separated from my siblings, and living in shelter and foster kinship care, faith kept me from becoming a casualty. As I grew, so did my faith. And I continued to hear God's voice. It is ever present, not just caught up in a flickering bushel of flames. He speaks to me all of the time. Now, it's through the Holy Spirit.

He spoke to me in the summer of 1994, when I stepped out on faith, amid a universe of detractors who said that waiting families in the child welfare circle would never be approved as kinship care providers and that African-American families wouldn't be willing to step up and serve.

But I had a vision that included partnering with the child welfare system in Allegheny County so that it worked *for* children and families, not against them, when it came to placements and permanency.

By July 1994, I had become the county's newest child welfare provider, and only its second who was African American. And A Second Chance, Inc., my newly licensed foster care agency, had a $1.4 million contract with Allegheny County to service kinship care. The organization resided on paper—there was no brick and mortar place. I had my award letter from the county and the business plan for A Second Chance, Inc. To get started, I needed a loan. I found God's favor in a local bank. The loan officer—a churchgoing, African-American woman—saw value in what I delivered and approved my loan. Within seven days, I had a $100,000 line of unsecured credit and assurance that this, too, was a part of God's plan.

A Second Chance, Inc. was in business. God was right on time, because within 30 days of meeting the loan officer, other opportunities in Ohio had carried her away from the bank. If I had gone a month later would I have met someone with the same generous spirit? Who knows, but it was proof to me that all along God was ordering my steps.

A month after obtaining the loan, I opened for business. It was July and I was 31. By my side were eight staff and county administrators. We opened in a converted church rectory in rusted and worn North Braddock, Pa., a former steel town just east of downtown Pittsburgh. As we set up the agency, and in the midst of frenetic days, I couldn't help but be reminded of the space I was in—a former house of God. My many silent prayers went up to Him who was able to grant me what I needed most then—clarity, resolve, and fortitude to make building and operating a new agency a success. But from this once-sacred place, I knew kinship care could resurrect families in crisis. Strengthening and preserving healthy kinship families for children was our mission.

So, I set about renovating the rectory, preparing my staff, and moving forward to accept our first clients. It took about three months, but by early fall, we were ready for them.

From day one, there was drama. I opened with five caseworkers and a supervisor, a director, and an office manager who had to manage an onslaught of children and families who entered our doors in October. This represented some 70 cases. My young workers were a bouquet of diversity. Many of them were people who I knew. Some were fresh out of college, one had worked in the field with adoptive parents; they were

Black and White, male and female. One was my preacher's daughter. They all came to ASCI wanting to succeed. They embraced my vision and never complained. They had only two months of training before having to go right into the field. And, the cases kept coming. By December, we had serviced 350 kids.

Within the first three months that ASCI operated, we were aggressively licensing kinship caregivers to become foster parents for their kin; a process that many didn't believe was possible. Mounting our efforts, we concentrated on problems common to child welfare in the county and in agencies nationwide: licensing more African-American foster kinship families, thus, creating more strong and viable kinship resources for the children in need of emergency placement.

How did we manage? We meet weekly. Every Monday morning, we gathered around a table for review and to process the cases as a collective group. I used the time to coach. We'd also pray. It built trust among us.

We'd need that trust and more, because very quickly we had to rely on each other more than ever. Even with 2,000 square feet in use that first year, we outgrew the church space before its renovation was completed. As our client base and services grew, our staff mushroomed from nine to 60 people.

Toward the end of 1995, we had to move to the space that once housed the Pyramid, a popular venue for jazz. We were now in the urban core of East Liberty, a community that was once the third-largest shopping district in the state, but was now worn and neglected. By the time ASCI moved to the neighborhood, the agency had more than 100 employees. We filled a row of offices and became East Liberty's largest employer. ASCI provided a newfound energy on the streets and served as a root of the revitalization that was sparked around those families who still dwelled in a community that time and the city seemed content to let slumber. But even as we operated in double the space, the staff continued to grow rapidly, trying to keep pace with our caseload.

We were charged with developing a program second-to-none that would change the landscape of kinship care as we knew it. We were going to license families so that caregiving relatives could receive financial support from the federal, state, and local government, we were going to ensure that every child who we serviced was safe and had a way back home. And, if the child could not go back home, we were going to ensure that they had a permanent plan with the relative who was caring for them. We were going to make sure that the kinship triad—the birth parents, the child, and the kinship caregiver—had supportive services, and we were going to also make sure that the triad had an opportunity to move from despair to a life of repair and enjoyment.

In September 2001, we were on the move again. We purchased the old Larimer School in a neighborhood a few blocks away from where the Pyramid Club was located. After a short time, we had launched a capital campaign to fund renovations at that site, but the fundraising was interrupted by the turmoil of September 11. We never moved into Larimer, but instead sold the property around 2005. But ASCI was never without its base of operation and its work on behalf of families continued, no matter what. While we waited to build new work space, agency staff was split between the properties ASCI was renting at the time. As we grew, my goal was to bring agency operations together under one roof and have room for more on-site family activities. By 2005, our current Frankstown location became that site.

For two years, A Second Chance, Inc. was engaged in a rigorous capital campaign to raise much-needed money for the building. Meeting after meeting with foundation program officers would yield comments like, "you have a compelling vision," but no resources were brought to the table to assist in this effort. Again relying on my faith, I heard a voice from God saying, just continue to talk about the children and the work A Second Chance, Inc. has done to preserve families.

One day, the message finally hit the heartstrings of a person who looked like me. She was an African-American woman who was heading a local foundation with a focus on girls. Her colleagues urged her to take a risk on A Second Chance, Inc., and she did by issuing a challenge grant of $350,000. The goal was to match the set-aside funds for the capital building project. Since the agency had set aside $1 million in reserve funds that it had amassed over an eight-year period as a part of the A Second Chance, Inc. Charitable Foundation, we were able to match the funds.

And, as they say, the "rest is history."

I could have been embittered by the Pittsburgh-area foundation response to my capital campaign, but I was not. Our work ahead in support of children and families was too important for us to become debilitated by policies and practices that didn't appear to be inclusive or culturally and racially sensitive. But at the time, it was these kinds of insensitivities that permeated the philanthropic community. Rather, I focused on constructing our new facility so that we would be able to move forward with servicing families and making our process smoother, more streamlined, and more efficient.

As we were growing in brick and stone and community programming, we were also growing in the hearts and minds of local foundations and drawing their support. Once we made the connection, community philanthropy had been key to our development from the beginning, enabling A Second Chance, Inc. to plant the seeds of community change. As word of our emerging success with families spread, a bounty of groups embraced the mission of our fledging nonprofit, attaching themselves to various services and programs. We blossomed.

Over time, the face of the Pittsburgh foundation community changed, too. More African-American women were beginning to rise to roles of local leadership. They had a deep understanding of the parent-child issues we addressed and the community we were serving and generously supported our programs. Because of the presence of these women, the Pittsburgh Foundation gave us funding to develop our kinship support groups, visiting rooms and, later, the gifts to launch a mental wellness program with in-home clinical services for ASCI clients. The Eden Hall Foundation provided a matching gift to help kick start our capital campaign. The Heinz Endowments funded our afterschool educational component. In 2011, with the support of Eden Hall and Three Rivers Youth, our A Dance for Life Program began to focus on about 20 young girls aided by ASCI, giving them health, mental wellness, and etiquette training that culminated in an evening where the young women as debutantes presented their newfound skills in a formal dance. But for 10 years prior, our own A Second Chance, Inc. Charitable Foundation supported A Dance for Life, a 10-week program that for over a decade had helped more than 900 boys and girls boost their social skills and self-esteem. Also in 2011, The Jim Casey Youth Opportunities Initiative and Casey Family Services were among the philanthropies that generously supported the A Dance for Life event by purchasing tickets.

The Pittsburgh Child Guidance Foundation, a longtime advocate for the emotional health of children, has been a steady partner, too, giving us the tools and training to strengthen our outreach to the children of incarcerated parents. Other valuable funders included the U.S. Department of Human Services, the Children's Bureau, the Brookdale Foundation, the Allegheny County Department of Human Services, and the Philadelphia Department of Human Services.

ASCI had fostered a number of partner relationships with national and regional foundations, including the Annie E. Casey Foundation and the Casey Family Programs, two of the nation's chief philanthropies focused on the well-being of children; the Jim Casey Youth Opportunities Initiative; the Black Administrators in Child Welfare, the Children's Defense Fund; Generations United, ChildFocus; Pennsylvania Council of Children, Youth, and Family Services, the Pennsylvania Department of Public Welfare's Quality Assurance Committee Widener Law School, and the National Association of Black Social Workers, and Kinsolutions, a joint partnership between ChildFocus and A Second Chance, Inc., which were receptive to our innovative programs.

As a result of foundation support and partnerships, we were able to build capacity, strengthen our brand, and gain a national and regional reputation. This was important because over the years, the demand in Allegheny County for support services for children and kinship families continued to climb. Before we knew it, the agency, too, was experiencing exponential growth. It was fueled, in part, by demand among those families who were in need of services and supports and the presence of an agency, which sought to meet those needs. Organizationally, this rapid expansion wasn't without its challenges or its rewards. During the agency's first fiscal year, the budget leaped from $100,000 to close to $2 million.

Yes, we were growing, but by now ASCI was also learning how to thrive and plant its feet organizationally. I was the agency's CEO, but also a neophyte child welfare provider, muddling through the business side of providing kinship foster care services. A lot of this ground was new to me, but I knew that it was important to safeguard, and not lose, the core mission and values I put in place when A Second Chance, Inc. began. I instituted policies and practices that undergirded my beliefs and what I knew would work for these families. I hired people who brought passion, energy, and a willingness to reach out and touch the lives of children and families we served.

Before A Second Chance, Inc. reached 60 employees that first year, I conducted interviews with every new hire. Ours was a vigorous hiring process, but among the things I searched for in the words, spirits, and credentials of those I hired was their willingness to be open to the issues that our families and children bring to the table, and do it without being judgmental. Also in those early years, it was not unusual for the president and CEO to also be the driver, transportation aide, and janitor—I did whatever I had to do.

Having grown up in the child welfare system and in foster kinship care, my relationships and work with kinship families would always be special, but at A Second Chance, Inc. I couldn't touch them all. I relied on staff to carry my messages, my values, beliefs, and my hopes for a second chance for children and families.

"Treat every family with dignity and respect," is what I preached and wrote about and trained them to do. I hope each day that the motto is playing in their ears, especially when fragile families turn to A Second Chance, Inc.

Our mantra: "Every child touched by A Second Chance, Inc. has a right to be safe and must thrive," should be on their lips and on their minds. Beginning in the lobby of the agency, the words of our mantra are written on the wall there in gold letters. Like a bright bold banner,

I purposely placed it there and throughout the interior space for all to see. At A Second Chance, Inc., it's a part of our brand.

As the organization has matured over the years, so has its need to have stronger competencies to run ASCI. Over time, I shifted my focus from the organization's physical expansion to solidifying its framework and installing its corporate scaffolding. Doing these things is how I approached matters of technology, leadership, quality assurance, and more.

As a student of organizational behavior, I am keenly aware of the growth cycles of organizations and the pressures that come with them. That is why I have been working for nearly two decades on a plan for growing and honing leaders at A Second Chance, Inc.

A plan for succession has been evolving for the past 15 years. I never wanted an organization to be beholden to its founder forever, and I, therefore, moved to a consensus and team model of leadership and decision making. In this new model, each leader is responsible for making decisions and for being accountable. Recognizing that this is sometimes challenging for younger, emerging leaders, we developed a leadership academy and a training program that also benefits managers. The Academy is named for Mark A. Cleveland, a late ASCI staffer who exemplified leadership.

A leaders/staff mentoring initiative is also among ASCI's professional development opportunities. By twinning partnership and mentoring, members of the organization's leadership team are matched with a staff member on the frontline of client management. Together they work on what the frontline staff person identifies as areas in which they want to grow; it may include strategies for managing workload or identifying the skills needed to support promotion to the next level of management or staffing. ASCI believes in growing its own leaders and managers. Plans for doing so are modeled after successful corporate succession plans in place at The Boeing Co, and at Johnson & Johnson.

Because we also believe in providing opportunities for advancement for all at ASCI, not just at the senior level, succession plans are embedded throughout the organization. Those plans inform managers when a staffer is ready to move up and what it will take to get them there—additional education or certification, one-on-one meetings, or it could be opportunities to network outside of the office with other professionals in the field. At ASCI, these kinds of professional development activities are available as soon as a staffer completes the probation period. Access to training and leadership opportunities include my support as a CEO. At ASCI, it begins by having an open-door policy for staff.

As ASCI's founder and CEO, it is important for the agency's more than 180 staff to know that my "door is always open" and that I am accessible to them. When I worked in child welfare at the Allegheny County Department of Human Services, my experience with most senior administrators was not that way. As a staffer, when I had what I thought were some progressive ideas and strategies for improving how we did our work and served families, I found that many of my supervisors were not listening. But I found an advocate at the top when Marc Cherna came on board in February 1996 to head the county agency. Before then, I felt like I was just a number and not a name as I worked.

As a result, I never wanted any staff person at my agency to ever feel that they didn't have an outlet or an opportunity to share their ideas and concerns. That's why I created avenues for them to speak directly with me. I launched brown-bag luncheons, which are organized by the Employee Relations team. And in addition, I want to have a presence in matters of discipline and terminations—all such decisions are reviewed by my office. I am the last line of defense for the employee and I want to be assured that the organization is both fair in its dealings with employees and has also made a concerted effort to preserve, remediate, or allow the person to leave A Second Chance, Inc. with dignity. As a non-profit agency that is embedded and actively engaged in the community where it operates, I have a moral imperative to be both fair and supportive to members of the community who show up to work with ASCI, even when the staffing relationship is severed.

I value hearing from staff members at all levels of the organization. I learn from the perspectives of all employees, not just those on the executive team and I make sure that all staff members know that they are respected, and appreciated.

The kind of strong leadership that I have come to value at ASCI has helped propel the organization's business and technical side of kinship care delivery. ASCI now has reliable and optimal technology and cutting-edge fiscal management systems in place to support its work thanks largely to the leadership of one senior administrator and his team. Leveraging his business and accounting expertise, this senior administrator has been a great asset to the organization and its work. As he's consistently led the organization's operations for more than 18 years, we have learned what it takes to run a successful community-based organization. In the agency's earlier years, it was trial and error when it came to technology and operations. But today, we know that these two systems are crucial to ensure that data are in place to make both program and long-range fiscal decisions. Over the years, we have been able to fine tune what operating systems work best and have purchased various hardware and software to support our growing and complex internal systems.

Also important to ASCI's staff and leaders' training is learning the importance of hearing the voices of our clients and engaging them in problem solving. Because of our community focus, ASCI strives to understand the needs and challenges of the families it serves. For us, that means we meet families where they are. We tailor our services to meet the individual needs of each caregiver. Our service delivery model is not based on a "one size fits all" approach. For example, if Grandma cannot make the group certification training, we make sure that we take the service to her. We have a curriculum that has been created by ASCI to meet the specific and unique needs of the kinship triad: they include SARKS (Standards for Assessing and Recognizing Kinship Strengths), the country's first kinship-specific curriculum.

In addition, we use a strength-based approach in our work with caregivers. I always say that we "license" in, rather than create barriers for families attempting to meet all of the state licensing standards. Our staff understands the importance of trauma on children. That's why we would rather purchase such necessities as beds, food, and safety resources rather than place children in the care of strangers, causing further unnecessary trauma.

With more than 19 years of experience in child welfare, 15 of them with ASCI, the agency's senior executive vice president of Child and Family Services and Organizational Expansion has ushered in an array of services and programs to support clients. His focus has included external and internal oversight processes to assess and monitor program delivery and effectiveness. One such process is provided through ASCI's Continuous Quality Improvement Division (CQI). It offers the best opportunity for us to engage families so that we can gauge when we miss the mark and when we are on target and having an effect. We invite families to evaluate the services they receive; internal and external audits are a part of that process. There is also a dedicated feedback line for family members and other partners to phone in 24 hours a day, seven days a week to share their concerns and complaints. We listen and we respond to their messages. Also, through the CQI Division, a separate 24-hour, seven-day-a-week phone line is available to receive emergency calls from our clients. In addition, our focus on CQI has spawned several other internal supports that are allowing the agency to provide quality client care; one is a central filing system that ensures consistency in organizing case reports.

We have been deliberate about the organization's "right to improve our services for families and children." For a time, we are the caretakers and supports for these fragile lives. These are people who deserve our agency's excellence. As ASCI's CEO, it is the only acceptable standard that I can offer.

In addition, a code of ethics and being mindful of our mission, further serve as guiding forces of our work at A Second Chance, Inc. Our mission is to provide healthy kinship families for children. Peter Drucker, the great leader of American corporate management, said an organization's mission statement should be able to fit on the front of a T-shirt. This allows for clarity and brevity. Through its work with kinship caregivers, A Second Chance, Inc. ensures that each caregiver will fit the bill to provide healthy kinship care services to kin placed in their homes. We don't take for granted the relationship of the child to the caregiver; we want to always ensure that safety comes first. Therefore, our mission is indeed our driver.

The presence of a diverse group of board members and advisors was put in place to support our efforts moving forward. Since beginning A Second Chance, Inc., creating a diverse board membership has always been an imperative. Thinking broadly about diversity, my early vision for its composition included having members from the Pittsburgh community surrounding ASCI, along with representation from clients and families. That rich and interesting blend of people and voices reflects the diversity that I understand and want to bring to ASCI's work on kinship care. Our board of directors also reflects racial, ethnic, and cultural diversity as well as the expertise of those representing a variety of fields such as medicine, nursing, journalism, banking, and finance.

The diversity and experiences that each of these people brings to the agency and to the families it serves have informed and enriched the work that we are here to do.

The voices of those in the community, including clients, continue to be among ASCI's trusted advisors. While the ASCI Board of Directors governs the organization, an Advisory Board — made up of community members and our clients — is in place to offer advice about the agency's programs. The Advisory Board meets quarterly. A designated staff person serves as a liaison to the Advisory Board and is expected to report to the Board of Directors concerns and issues community and client representatives bring to the table. ASCI's Pittsburgh Advisory Board has operated for more than 12 years. There is also an Advisory Board that serves the ASCI's Philadelphia Regional Office. This board has been in existence for three years.

As an exclusive provider of kinship care services, A Second Chance, Inc. (ASCI) employs an integrated program delivery model for its programs and services to support the kinship triad—the birth parents, the child, and the kinship caregiver. We recognize that while children are the main focus in child welfare, we take a child-centered, family-focused approach as we work with the kinship triad. A Second Chance, Inc. was created to make life better for children and families involved in kinship care. ASCI's support services and programs span from in-take to permanency. Getting children and kinship families to permanency is the end goal. ASCI helps them chart a course for getting there. When a child leaves ASCI, we work to make sure that it is both to a permanent home and to a safe place. That desire reflects what we believe and what we practice—"Every child touched by A Second Chance, Inc. has a right to be safe and must thrive." It is our agency's mantra.

Efforts to ensure the safety of our children in their new placements include conducting multiple assessments for each member of the kinship triad. But our work doesn't end there. We want children to be more than just "OK." We want them to thrive. That's why we closely manage and monitor our children's safety and well-being even after they are in permanent homes. There are weekly and monthly home visits, and support with medical and mental health appointments, school visits, and more.

Nearly two decades later, I can look back and not only see that I made it, but also that ASCI is leading by example. But even today, the effect of the agency's swift ascent in the field and its organizational growth in those early years still reverberate for me. I've come to realize that while launching and running the then- start-up agency, and in the years since, much of the agency's strategic positioning has been built by effective and cooperative leadership and vision. "It's everybody."

The knowledge of kinship foster care that I brought to ASCI was born out of personal experience as an alumnus of care, and was informed by years of work in the field of child welfare, and by my scholarship.

A Time for Kinship Care

As A Second Chance, Inc. was building its reputation and steadily moving from being a pioneer provider in kinship care services to the must-watch national model that it is today, the practice and use of kinship care was fast becoming a viable placement option. Once the child welfare system's reluctant last resort for placing children, 20 years later in Allegheny County, kinship care is now the front door for placement. The county now places more than 60 percent of the children in foster care with kin and achieves permanence in 89 percent of its cases. Agency officials have credited A Second Chance, Inc. for hastening and influencing changes in the way that it now does business with children, families, and kin.

Still, I remained a relentless crusader for the product that I believed in and one that I knew worked. Kinship care — even without the data of our early days to quantify every effect of our work with children and kinship families—worked. I knew that there was something special about kin and all I needed to do was to take one hard look at myself. If it had not been for the grace of God and the kindness of kin, where would I have ended up? While we did not have the sophisticated IT systems to measure the data as we would have hoped early on, what we could see was a measurable effect of child safety, spiked reunifications, growth in a diversity of service offerings, positive consumer confidence, a flourishing community, and a positive public/private partnership. It certainly appeared that every life touched by A Second Chance, Inc. was indeed revived and given a second chance to thrive.

In just two years of beginning the organization, an estimated 1,400 of those children had already come through our doors. My faith and my experience told me that with a village made up of organizations like ours, and of course, kin, and community, the children we served could someday be college students. It happened to me. Or, they could be inspired to reach back into the child welfare system to lead and show others a new way forward. Or, they could be assured and employed. And having found comfort, kin, and safety nets for their own lives growing up, they would stand a better chance of creating safe, loving, and nurturing homes for their own children someday. For sure, there were success stories unfolding among them, but I knew that we had to be intentional about creating opportunities for these children to blossom despite their circumstances.

Since the organization's inception, we strived to find the balance of services that would enhance the lives of the triad. This included everything from conducting research regarding broader policy change, which would lead to federal legislation for subsidized guardianship for kin, to offering community specific, culturally sensitive initiatives, such as A Dance for Life, an etiquette training program for our youth.

Triad connections are paramount to maintaining healthy, unified families, so it is important here to highlight three programs connected with ASCI that emphasize how the kinship triad is supported and used to help young people, engage the caregivers and community, and professionals. First, there is FACT, or Family and Children Together; second, there is SWAN, or the Statewide Adoption Network; and third, there is Camp COPES, Children Optimizing Personal Experience through Sports.

The Family and Children Together (FACT) program was established in March 2000 to assist birthparents in attaining the goals needed to reunify with their children. It grew out of my doctoral work in applied learning as I noticed that adoption was an option for many of the children coming into our agency, but reunification with their birth parents was not. I wanted to change this. I wanted to give kids a continuum of care that would lead them back to their homes. To make that happen, our staff works in collaboration with the Point of Contact Casework Program and Allegheny County Children, Youth & Families Caseworkers to provide short-term, intensive services to birthparents and their children. A centerpiece of this is the family meetings, a plan to bring in family and extended family in a safe environment to talk about providing a safe and nurturing place for children. In this environment, families are empowered to share their exit planning, visitation, and, finally, reunification. This process is critical to understanding that the end-goal is to have the children returned home and have every stakeholder moving in the same direction. With this, we know that extended kinship is a resource, as the larger family network provides financial assistance, child care, and moral support.

During this intervention, realistic goals are developed as our staff and caregivers focus on concrete needs, kinship care/family dynamics issues, or strengthening concerns such as housing, educational, medical or vocational needs. Birthparents are expected to become empowered to problem-solve more independently over the project duration.

The clients who access the FACT program are selected from new referrals and receive 90 days of programming. Each client gets assigned a reunification specialist and a reunification supervisor. We believe if we can move toward reunification in three months, the less trauma and disruption to a child's well-being.

There were also innovations in our Philadelphia Regional Office to support the kinship triad.

In Philadelphia, finding permanent supportive homes for every child can be daunting, but trying to achieve permanency through adoption for children who've been languishing in care comes with a special set of challenges. Since 2006, ASCI's Philadelphia Regional Office has collaborated with state and county child welfare agencies, serving as kinship experts and a ready resource. And to families there, our agency has been a lifeline, especially as they prepare to step into new roles as permanent caregivers for kinship foster children. Many of them are in need of a forever home and are also in need of healing from abuse. Still, other youngsters have lived long term in out-of-home care within the child welfare system. And, Philadelphia's task doesn't stand alone: That's why ASCI has made preparing permanent families for these children paramount, because children are waiting in care and the numbers of youngsters needing homes continue to grow in Western Pennsylvania, too.

In an arrangement that highlights collaboration, ASCI's expertise in kinship care is making a difference in the lives of the kinship triad, while benefiting agencies. We provide case management and support to Pennsylvania's Department of Public Welfare's Statewide Adoption Network (SWAN), and Diakon Lutheran Social Ministries in partnership with Family Design Resources. And through consultation and training, parents and families get the help they need to build new, strong, permanent relationships with the children in their lives.

Since 2005, Camp COPES has used basketball as a vehicle to empower and educate our young people, while bringing them together with members of the community and with professionals concerned about reaching back. For three days during the summer, ASCI's outdoor basketball court and classrooms inside the building are transformed into nurturing, fun, and safe places where our children can learn and play. We also forged an extended village for our children through Camp COPES While the young people look forward to fun, games, and learning experiences, we know that the Camp is a source of prevention and protection from the violence that has crippled our streets, particularly urban communities and leaves our children with few safe outlets.

But even before we launched the FACT program, SWAN, and Camp COPES, in its early years, A Second Chance, Inc. was working to usher in change for foster care and kinship care. Efforts already underway inside the county child welfare agency to advance the cause for kinship care were churning and gaining traction. At the same time, we worked toward achieving permanency and renunciation for families and children.

When the county's new child welfare director was appointed in 1996, I found a kindred spirit. He, too, believed in the power of kinship care to mend families and keep children safe. In 1994, making kinship care the first consideration for county placements became the policy in the system the director was transforming. That policy told Allegheny County caseworkers to first search for a child's relatives or close family friends, godparents, or neighbors—those considered kin before placing them outside of their homes and communities and into foster care. It helped, too, that national recognition for kinship care and its benefits for children was now coming from the federal government, major child advocacy organizations, and philanthropies. Congress in 1996 passed the Personal Responsibility and Work Opportunity Reconciliation Act, directing states to give kin first priority for placement when abused and neglected children are removed from their parents. And that following year, passage of the federal Adoption and Safe Families Act pushed kinship care placements as a way to reduce the number of children in foster care.

Our partnership with Allegheny County Department of Human

Services led to more children being placed with kin and assisted in developing a network of services that led to complete wraparound support for the triad. All relatives, particularly those who were African American relatives and caring adults, were coming forward to care for their kin. A Second Chance, Inc. made sure that families were certified as licensed kinship foster care providers, and that they were supported in their effort to provide a safe, secure, nurturing, and if necessary, permanent environment, for their kin. As the only community-based agency in the country that focuses exclusively on the kinship triad, and that specializes in child-welfare involved kinship families, A Second Chance, Inc. has always beat the odds and the proven the "naysayers" wrong. Since its inception, A Second Chance, Inc. continues to have high licensure rates (between 93-96 percent) for its families, something that has allowed them to receive the same supports and services as their non-foster kin counterparts. We do this by what I call our ability to "license in," rather than "license out." While I have heard many other providers talk about how difficult it is to license a kinship caregiver, what I will tell anyone, if kin families are approached with a traditional model for placement and training, it will never work. We customize our services based on the needs of the kinship families. If Grandma is unable to come to the agency for her training (which we refer to as the Enrichment Workshop), then we will bring that service to her.

A Second Chance, Inc. understands the challenges that many urban kinship families face, and as a result, we are able to meet their vast and changing needs. This allows them the opportunity to go through the process with dignity, respect, honor, and love—four guiding principles that are couched in everything that we do with the triad.

In 1998, just four years after beginning A Second Chance, Inc., it didn't take long for the federal government to find me. Policy leaders and U.S. legislators wanted to put me on their national panels, share my recommendations with members of Congress, and present my models of success with kinship families to a kinship subcommittee called for in the Adoption and Safe Families Act of 1997.

They hear my voice. It belonged to a former foster child who at 17 years old emerged with determination and a flood of questions about a flawed child welfare system in Allegheny County. Even earlier, at age 9, my exasperated foster grandmother declared that my voice was too sassy for a girl growing up under her roof. In her world, my speaking out was seen as disobedient and there was no place for it. That's when she swiftly enrolled me in a Catholic school and put me in the good hands of no-nonsense nuns, in the hope of disciplining a young vibrant spirit and taming a voice that only wanted to be heard and understood, but sometimes didn't know where or how to direct frustration.

When the federal government invited me to the table, I was a 35-year-old provider, child advocate, and emerging expert in kinship care. I still carried that big voice and I owned it. I used it to engage policymakers, those in child welfare across Pennsylvania, and the nation in support of children in foster care. I told them all about my agency and how we were tailoring programs and services that would help repair young lives and work to keep families and children connected. A Second Chance, Inc. was steeped in cases and challenged to keep pace with referrals flooding in from a county child welfare system reeling from crisis. I told them we spoke to an unmet need. When we first got started, there was an overwhelming backlog of cases. In a two-month period, there were 350 referrals or about 700 children. The need has remained unrelenting. Since our inception, the agency has serviced more than 12,000 children, and by the time we got them, most were not in any stage of reunification: a third of them in foster care, most had been placed with strangers, and scores had been abused and shuttled from foster home to foster home until they "aged out" when they turned 18 or graduated from high school.

I told them about my agency's success. A Second Chance, Inc. went from servicing nearly 700 kinship families in 1995, just a year after our doors swung open for business, to about 1,600 in 1997. Permanency for our children then, like now, was a relentless pursuit, not a fledgling idea. And we were hitting the mark. During this time, 60 percent of our children were reuniting and living safely with their birth parents through the FACT (Family and Children Together Program). I told them that A Second Chance, Inc. was doing what it said it would do—knitting together the splintered families that most providers in the county had discounted. A Second Chance, Inc. was licensing kin usually within 60 days, using the same standards that traditional foster parents were required to meet.

Just a decade before, Allegheny County's child welfare system wasn't concerned about involving kin in foster care or making such arrangements feasible for low-income families. And there was little faith that these families and their homes could even be certified. Across the nation, there was a prevailing notion that most of these families were not worth salvaging. But because I believed in the spirit of redemption, I became that lone voice at the child welfare provider table. But this work, my calling, kept me steadfast and pressed into action.

And this is why in 1998, I went to Capitol Hill when the US Department of Health and Human Services called on me to inform its report to Congress on policy and practice regarding permanency in kinship foster care. I went willingly and carried with me the hopes and voices (many still silent) of hundreds of thousands of youngsters in foster care, many languishing. As I sat on the Department's National Advisory Kinship Panel, I did what I had been doing all of my professional life in child welfare—speaking up and pressing hard for permanency and placement for children because I was forever hopeful that a change would come. Hope was an everyday journey.

It's About the Children

The federal panel that invited me to speak and inform their next steps on kinship care represented the first of many national doors that would swing open to me.

The opportunity to inform Congress and influence child welfare policy was a humbling experience. And telling my story, although just one of many from foster care, was not intended to elicit pity, but to demonstrate the power of caring kin to influence a young dreamer, engender hope, and to rescue a life. The opportunity that day to speak resolutely about my passion and my life growing up was an honor and a privilege. The big wide rooms and white-columned buildings where I found myself addressing matters of kinship care and child welfare have never been opportunities and places for me to prop up ego. In fact, on that day in October 1998, when I strode with excitement and trepidation into the marbled halls of government to testify on Capitol Hill, I knew that I was there by the grace of God. As I sat solidly at the table, facing power and with a microphone in front of my face, I also understood that being there wasn't about me. Then, like now, wherever I go to speak up for the children, I know that they are the ones that A Second Chance, Inc. is working for and returning to safe homes.

My advocacy for kinship care began while I was a caseworker and supervisor in the Allegheny County system, I used kinship placements in my cases at a time when it was neither common practice nor mandated. I was motivated because I knew the value of keeping children with relatives or with those who knew them and who were like kin. This had been my experience and benefit growing up.

Working toward helping families form that "kinship triad" — the birth parents, the child, and the kinship caregiver—remains a rewarding aim. My mantra is to keep youth and families safe, work well with them, and see my theories of youth-centered services actually working. For this, some have called me a pioneer. While it did take a tenacious and entrepreneurial spirit to get me to this place in my life's work; I don't see myself as a pioneer. Rather, what has propelled me in this work is knowing that children placed in foster homes and not with kin were often not treated the same. It's not that the system wanted to treat these families differently, but rather they just didn't know how to do what was best within the social services infrastructure. What those in the county system did before making kinship placement the standard was blend services for kinship and foster families. But from personal and professional experience, this was something that I knew did not work. The needs of foster and kinship families remain different. It was this knowledge, coupled with my own life in foster-kinship care, which continues to make the difference in how kinship families are treated and serviced at A Second Chance, Inc.

Transitions

In the 1970s, as I came of age, permanency planning for children like me in foster kinship care was an incongruent notion. I was 12½ years old when my case worker rendered hopeless the notion of adoption or any other permanency option for me. In October 1973, that's what Miss Frances a social worker, concluded in her typed case notes for the little girl named Sharon who sported the *"Afro ... dark complexion and slightly chunky build ... [was] often somewhat disheveled."* All I wanted then was the forever home that filled my dreams, but Miss Frances, noted in my case file that since my foster grandparents were "somewhat limited financially," the best place for me was to remain in foster care.

That was nearly 40 years ago when long-term foster care, not permanency, was the prescription for the lives of so many deserving children. Foster care was meant to be a short-term fix for children in need of rescuing from unsafe homes and from families who couldn't care for them, not a long-term solution.

Decisions were made for me and my life. No one asked where I wanted to live or who I wanted to raise me, or did I want to be reunited with my birth father who placed me with kin. I remained in what I now call kinship foster care until I graduated from high school in 1979, and was deemed emancipated at age 17.

The following year, Congress passed the Adoption Assistance Act of 1980, which promoted permanency for those in foster care, but the law came too late for me. But it wasn't too late for other children to benefit and have a chance at permanency and reunification with their birth parents or other relatives. For them, I made myself an advocate. And through A Second Chance, Inc., we are providing kinship families with a way forward.

Any child, who is able to return home and live with their birth parents, should do so. In most cases it is the best place for them. But when that isn't possible, research tells us that kinship placements are the preferred choice for children. If there is no family available, which is hard to believe because there is always some family member some-where, a child should be a part of that family network, or placed with those who are like kin, and in a home where they can be safe, culturally connected, and can experience a sense of belonging.

But the reality for many youth was that legally there was no way for people who cared about the children to be a permanent part of their lives without adoption or without some way of building a permanent foster care relationship with them through the law. For families who had already solidified caring relationships with children, but who could not consider either of these options, children could be left adrift.

That's when I began to think about alternatives to adoption and a way that caregivers didn't have to relinquish their rights, but could pursue a path called subsidized legal guardianship, which created a legal long-term relationship between a child and caregiver with federally funded stipends for the caregiver to support that child. But subsidized guardianship wasn't a practice in place in every state, including Penn-sylvania, home to A Second Chance, Inc.

A couple of years later, I served as co-chair of the statewide kinship care committee and invited ASCI's corporate attorney Anthony Sosso Jr. to serve with me on a first-ever research report that explored subsidized guardianship for the state of Pennsylvania, which at the time, had no such legal status in its legislation. Closer to home, A Second Chance, Inc. was servicing about 50 percent of the children in out-of-home care who were placed with kin in Allegheny County.

The aim of the research was to inform state legislatures of alterna-tive options for kinship care givers if they did not want to adopt their kin. The practice often pitted parents against daughters and sons. It was unnatural and often went counter to the traditions of the African-American families served by ASCI. Clearly, there needed to be a way for kinship caregivers like able and loving grandmothers to receive federal financial assistance if they wanted to make a permanent commitment to being the legal guardians of their grandchildren and they should be able to receive the same financial resources, supports and services that non-family, licensed caregivers received.

But there was no such legal status in the legislation for kinship families in the state of Pennsylvania. Subsidized guardianship was in place for foster parents and served as a model for what needed to be systemic policy for kinship families as well.

My work on the project was informed by The Child Welfare League of America, which published findings in 1994 on kinship care that briefly addressed the need for guardianship. The research I did included visiting Hawaii, Massachusetts, Illinois, California, New York, and Nebraska. During our visits, we gleaned information about subsidized guardianship for kinship care families, where it was being practiced and in some states, yielding positive outcomes. Based on what we saw as best practices in Nebraska, I knew that such a model in Pennsylvania could yield positive results, cost-effective outcomes, and be culturally responsive for children and families.

The findings in our reports, "Subsidized Legal Guardianship: A Permanency Planning Option Study for Children Placed in Kinship Care" and "Subsidized Legal Guardianship Update," proved compelling enough to convince then-Pennsylvania Gov. Tom Ridge to put $1 million in his discretionary line item budget that year to move families to subsidized legal custodianship (as it was designated in Pennsylvania).

It didn't take long for the effect of our landmark work on subsidized legal guardianship for kinship families to migrate beyond the state of Pennsylvania and for the reports to serve as a platform for emerging and informed national conversations among key child welfare leaders and advocates.

Meeting the Needs

Specializing in child welfare-involved kinship families since 1994, A Second Chance, Inc. remains the only licensed foster care agency in the nation that exclusively meets the unique needs of kinship care families. Nobody has the specific focus of ASCI. For the past 19 years, our mission has been to support, care for, and reunite families and children. The agency is able to license 93 percent of its families so that they have access to needed financial support, while providing parents with services to help them regain custody of their children. And as we did this work, the comprehensive approach we took to servicing our children and kinship families has led to innovative models of care.

For ASCI, innovation has meant creating programs and services that benefit children and families, while giving them the dignity and respect that they need and deserve.

A few years ago while reading a request for proposals, I discovered that the federal government cited A Second Chance, Inc. among a handful of other kinship care services in the nation. The agency had the government's attention. But like any good organization, we regularly take our own pulse to see how ASCI is doing as a provider.

We care what our customers—our families—think when they respond to our written quality improvement surveys about the services that they are offered and even whether they are receiving their stipends on time. Those survey results from our programs and services, also tell us that our typical kinship care provider at ASCI is an African-American woman in her early to late 40s. And when caregivers are given the opportunity on the survey form to respond to open-ended questions about some aspect of their ASCI experienced, here is what two had to say: "We have been exceptionally happy with the overall care & treatment we have received from ASCI. The competency & caring of your staff is unusual for a Service Agency". And another client, in her written comment, simply stated, "Thank God that Mrs. McDaniel had a vision." If a relative or kin informs a caseworker or includes in a survey that they have a need that isn't being met, we respond by creating for them what's lacking.

About 10 years ago it meant outfitting for the prom a high school senior interning with A Second Chance, Inc. The student was living independently, when she turned to the agency for help buying a gown and getting ready for her special evening. From that one need, ASCI received similar requests from other young girls in foster care who also needed prom gowns and that motherly touch. It wasn't long before our efforts during prom season were recognized then absorbed by the Allegheny Department of Human Services, which launched the Prom Project in 2003, offering eligible high school students (male and female) the opportunity to choose from racks of free, donated, formal attire.

Sitting on the boards of some of the nation's most prestigious and well-respected foundations advocating for children, youth, and families has also been a source of hope for me. I was appointed to the Casey Family Programs Board of Trustees in 2005, the first Alumni of Care to do so. My work with the nation's largest foundation dedicated solely to providing and improving, and ultimately preventing, the need for foster care, has not only been historic but among my most satisfying and rewarding. As the Foundation's treasurer, I am the first African-American female to hold this post. In addition to my work on the Casey Family Programs Board, I also serve as a Trustee of the Jim Casey Youth Opportunity Initiative, which since 2001 has been one of the leading national voices in child welfare, particularly focused on supporting young people transitioning from foster care to adulthood. In many ways, my work on these national boards is all about hope. My work and participation with the two boards allows me to be a vehicle, ensuring that policies and practices that govern how children are supported remain a part of the conversation.

In July 2014, A Second Chance, Inc. will usher in its 20th year of providing services. The agency's growth during nearly two decades and its capacity to service children, families, and the communities in which they live, sprouted out of a culturally sensitive, profoundly personal, and strength-based vision of kinship care. For me, it's always been about family. ASCI's Kinship Institute for Program and Leadership Development honors my paternal grandmother Hilda R. Baker and bears her name. Like a compass, our programs and services guide and distinguish our mission while pointing to the work we do every day to build a village of care for children and families that includes comprehensive support for families, which begins when they walk through ASCI's doors. And our Point of Contact Program remains ASCI's foundation and its programs are what set us apart from other providers. We work to ensure that all of our families become certified and that the community of caregivers, including those outside of the child welfare system and other provider agencies, receive some of the same resources and even respite, through ASCI's Kinship Community Collaborative. In ASCI's Philadelphia Regional Office, families, children, and other relatives work together with staff on devising their own purpose-driven plan for building a strong support network that ultimately ensures that a child is cared for and safe. That program—Family Group Decision Making—is unique to our work in Philadelphia and again distinguishes ASCI from other national providers. Also in Philadelphia, families are offered specialized services leading to traditional foster care placements. And for families transitioning from kinship care to permanency through adoption, ASCI provides consultation and training.

The agency's work has been all that I hoped and knew that it would be. At the same time, though, my work in kinship care has not come with straightforward challenges. There was no tidy, compact beginning. It's just been about the families and about the children. Those watching our work want to give A Second Chance, Inc. and me the praise. But I recognize the hard work and difficult challenges that determined families face to stay together. I know this from personal experience. As ASCI has grown, there have been sacrifices in my own relationships. Early on, to meet the needs of my expanding agency, I was at work when the sun came up and I was there when the sun went down. It was important to be there and take care of some must-do-tasks, but there were intimate partner relationships that did not survive the jostle of building the agency.

I met Mr. J in 1984 on my first job as a caseworker at the Hill House agency. He was a building services worker and one of the most polite men I've known (he sweetly opened and closed the car doors for me). We dated for five years and were married in 1989, and 10 months later our daughter, Taylor, was born. As I bore down on ASCI business, my sister and other family and friends provided a safe space for my daughter, Taylor. Often, Taylor's precious family time was sacrificed when I had to take her with me on client visits, place her in a crib in the office while I worked, or forgo family dinners to eat on the run.

With my new family, I entered new territory. At home, in prayer, I asked for strength and direction. Thirty years ago, there were few instruction manuals on how to balance work/life responsibilities. I had no working mother to provide an example. I had no mentor. I had to figure it out on my own. At times I was the clean-up lady, sweeping floors and scrubbing toilets if I had to, and the part-time bookkeeper, sitting on the floor hand-writing a few hundred checks so my employees and vendors could be paid on time.

Through it all, Mr. J and I stayed married for 20 years, but the distance between us grew. It's sadly ironic that as I worked to strengthen the families of others, I could not fortify my own.

How does that happen? I often ponder the sacrifices that those of us in the human service professions make to help others. What is the divorce rate among doctors, firefighters, law enforcement officials, nurses? Why is it, I ask myself, that work/life balance eluded me?

I do believe in family, though. And, even if so-called traditional relationships aren't possible, people have to re-imagine family ties and know that we can remain in reciprocal relationships that are cordial and respectful and full of trust. Today, Mr. J and I are friendly and he works, along with our daughter, at A Second Chance, Inc.

If family matters weren't enough, my personal challenges certainly faced competition from the mountain of professional pressures I faced. As ASCI grew, there were certainly days — and across many fronts — that I felt as if our little agency was David up against a Goliath, a huge child welfare system that was being dragged toward a new century.

In the mid- to late 1990s, during our burst of expansion, there was tremendous public pressure, and organizational scrutiny. Across the nation, there were changing child welfare regulations; in Pennsylvania, there were class-action lawsuits regarding kinship care; and, more locally, there were professional jealousies with other providers of services who seemed suspicious of the new kid on the block —ASCI and its emphasis on reunification.

I felt especially vulnerable because of my race and gender and because I was doing something new. Up against such institutional scrutiny, there were moments of uncertainty. In some meetings, I felt invisible and unwanted. I felt targeted by institutional surveillance, as if the powers that be wanted me to fail. I wavered but held my own. In my heart, I knew my experiences mattered and could guide me to help others. As the organization's CEO, I had to face all of these issues with clarity, firmness, impeccable character, integrity, grace, perseverance, and great faith.

What this meant is from the beginning, ASCI was in survival mode. Failure was not an option. Though at times it seemed like it. I'd eventually have to be a wife and a mother and not just a CEO. My conflicting tasks tore me apart. I felt alone a lot. Who do I talk to? I was scared. Do I know what I'm doing? I pushed on.

Because I've endured such personal hardships, I completely understand what the families who access my agency are wrestling with and why their children are coming up short. Mothers and fathers are confronting and overcoming some of the worst of what life has to offer—violence that inflicts pain and poverty that cripples. For others, death has visited their home, leaving children motherless, and still some families who come to A Second Chance, Inc. feel like they've run out of options and can no longer safeguard the lives of their children. When faced with such seemingly insurmountable problems, even the strongest among us would probably just bend and break.

My two siblings and I were fortunate and blessed; we fared well considering our humble and unstable beginnings. We survived and made it because of the love and support of our caregivers—foster and kin alike. And today, through A Second Chance, Inc., we are proud to be able to provide the resources and create opportunities for families, to facilitate the process of reunification—healing and coming back together as a family and kin. Staff charged with ushering in these families and supporting them while in our care at ASCI must come with personal passion, yet not be faint hearted. This work is about what you value, not about looking forward to the next promotion and position. If you don't love families and kids, my advice to staff is "go somewhere else and sell shoes". Otherwise, welcome to work in child welfare and ASCI. I know what it means and what it takes to be on the frontline of providing the kind of services, support, and programs that our work in kinship care demands. I've been there. That's why a special night to celebrate and recognize ASCI staff exists.

A warm late summer's breeze greeted a busload of staff from the ASCI Philadelphia Regional Office when it pulled up to the Pittsburgh Children's Museum for the gala and as those from the Pittsburgh head-quarters drifted in, decked in pretty party dresses, suits, and formal wear. This was their night, a time of laughter and release, camaraderie, and acknowledging the contributions of individuals, teams, and departments who deliver every day for children and families against the odds.

The fixtures of a red-carpet event were all there, from the festive décor and strolling photographers assigned to capture each staffer and the moment, to the entertainment. After dinner, though, the elegant space filled with smartly dressed ASCI staff and executives erupted with the abandon of Steelers' fans on a winning Sunday. Cheers sprang up and fists pumped the air from tables around the room as I called names and awarded staff and departments that make ASCI and the lives of our families better because of the work that they do.

As I had said before Congress, and as I used my voice to share with my staff at the gala: Family will put your name in their prayers before their day ends and bid you rest until your day begins again. Family is where it all begins and ends.

NOTE: Appendix A contains a table that provides an overview of inte-grated service delivery for kinship care programming at A Second Chance, Inc. that is pertinent to this section.

Part Three

Making the Case

The greatness of a community is most accurately measured by the compassionate actions of its members ... a heart of grace and a soul generated by love.

— Coretta Scott King

SEVEN
Winds of Change

A Snapshot of Kinship Care in America

Across time, race, ethnicity, and culture, extended family members have cared full time for children when, for various reasons, biological parents have not been able to provide care. It's a tradition that spans generations. In the United States, there are millions of grandparents, godparents, adult siblings, aunts, uncles and close family friends who are raising 2.7 million children in a time-honored tradition known as kinship care. The practice of kinship care is growing. During the past decade, almost 18 percent more Americans were caring for the children of family members, according to "Stepping Up for Kids," a 2012 policy report released by the Annie E. Casey Foundation.

Much of the care is delivered informally, where various layers of legal and private arrangements to assist children are made without the involvement of state or municipal agencies. But that is changing. Now statistics show that 104,000 children are in formal kinship care, meaning that they are part of a state-supervised foster care system. The children in kinship care make up about 25 percent of all the children who have been removed from their homes and are in the public child welfare system or state custody, according to the Annie E. Casey Foundation report.

Today, there are approximately 400,000 children who intersect with the child welfare system, but who get "diverted" to relatives and kin to raise them and thus avoid any legal connection or custody with the system. But those data are changing, as more families seek legal kinship and, as research shows, a large number of children will spend months living in kinship care. One in five Black children is likely to spend time in kinship care, a figure more than double that of the overall U.S. population.

Children get separated from their parents for many reasons, most of which are traumatic for the child: parental substance abuse, mental illness, child abuse and neglect, abandonment, illness or death, incarceration, and violence.

What research shows is that living with kin reduces the stress of such trauma because it enables children to more quickly adjust to new environments, and possibly prevent behavioral and psychosocial disorders. According to U.S. Census data, kinship caregivers face challenging socioeconomic conditions and need help: they are families who are most likely to be poor, single, older, less educated, and unemployed than families in which at least one parent is present.

This section of On My Way Home is designed to trace the legislative evolution that helped to create support for growing levels of kinship care. It offers case studies from A Second Chance Inc. that represents how policy, philanthropy, advocacy, and innovation can make a difference in the lives of children. In addition, this section showcases the "voices" of thought leaders, offers recommendations for a 21st century child welfare system, and finally, points to the direction in which the system is progressing in response to the needs of young people who emerged from kinship-foster care.

For three decades now, the numbers show that the phenomenon of kinship care is becoming a significant element of federal, state, and local foster care policy and practice, according to Urban Institute researcher and author Rob Geen.

It wasn't always so. In the 1960s it was prevalent to think that children in the child welfare system needed rescuing from their parents. If a child was to be removed, it was a standard philosophy that "an apple doesn't fall far from the tree." In other words, if the parent was dealing with social disorder, most likely the family had the same level of social dysfunction. There was no redemption. To improve the outcome for children, caseworkers and child welfare systems believed it was best to remove the children and seek institutional placement or foster care. In the African-American community, the stereotype or bias was perhaps more rampant and pervasive — guided by the theory that Black lives were a "tangle of pathology."

But in 1972, Robert Hill, Ph.D., a Black sociologist, stepped forward with a fresh view and a different reality when he wrote about the strengths that were inherent in many Black families, even among low-income ones headed by single mothers. At the time, Hill was director of research for the National Urban League when he wrote the landmark book *The Strengths of Black Families*, which described the seldom-noticed strengths in Black American families. His scholarship was among the first to identify and portray five of those strengths, chief among them, strong kinship bonds. As many in the child welfare arena have long focused a lens on the Black family's failures, the role and existence of their kinship networks have been challenged and discounted. Hill also counted these as strengths of the Black family: "A strong work orientation, adaptability of family roles, a response to economic necessities on the part of Black, low-income families; high achievement orientation, and religious orientation."

He also concluded that many poor Black families were no different from those cultivated by some White families. That was forty years ago, and still some in the child welfare arena are not convinced. In 1972, Hill offered a way forward when he asserted that an examination of Black family strengths is what's needed to understand their weaknesses, and to ultimately develop targeted aid and well-suited programs.

But because assumptions and factors about families in the system were perceived as anything but strong, non-kin or foster care placement was considered the best practice. If family or kinship caregivers stepped in, it was considered that they were doing so because of cultural tradition, moral obligation, and familial responsibility. This kind of thinking influenced legislative policy and the idea that government had a limited role in supporting these kinds of family arrangements.

Over time, that began to change. And as Hill suggests, the strengths of poor Black families, especially its kinship bonds, can be bolstered by policy, innovation, philanthropy, and advocacy. As more agencies began to turn toward kinship care as a way to act as foster parents for abused or neglected children, child advocates pushed for legislation and policies that would address the changes.

- In 1979, the U.S. Supreme Court in *Miller vs. Youakim* was about the high court indicating that kin could not be discriminated against by the child welfare system if they met the same licensing standards as non-kin because of their blood relationship.

- In 1980 came the federal Adoption Assistance and Child Welfare Act. A number of child welfare experts became concerned about the numbers of children floating through multiple foster placements and lacking permanent outcomes. The goal of the legislation was to halt unnecessary separation from families, to encourage adoption, and to seek reunification of families when feasible, among other goals.

- In 1997, the Adoption and Safe Families Act clarified the importance of safety, permanency and well-being for children who come to the attention of the child welfare system. The act also called for kin or non-relative caregivers to meet the same regulations as non-relatives to qualify for federal funding. And the Adoption and Safe Families Act helped increase accountability among the child welfare system — the U.S. government established new measures to monitor states' performance. In another provision, limits for permanency hearings—no later than 12 months after entering foster care—were put in place.

- Fostering Connections to Success and Increasing Adoptions Act (Fostering Connections). Passage of Fostering Connections in 2008 is considered by many in the field to be the most significant child welfare law in more than a decade. Among its many provisions, all states were given the option to use funds through Federal Title IV-E to finance subsidized guardianship or funds to enable children in the care of relatives to exit foster care into permanent homes.

- Passage of Subsidized Guardianship. Subsidized guardianship or financial provisions to support caregivers who legally assume guardianship of a child in an out-of-home placement, was first established in Massachusetts in 1983. While most states offer subsidized guardianship, after nearly three decades, not all families stepping in to raise children in need have the support.

These series of pivotal laws have encouraged and advanced the capacities of kin to care for children related by blood or emotional connections. But policies and practices differ by states. This means that efforts to identify and recruit kinship caregivers can vary between states and can be hindered if good relations do not exists between parent and the kin caregiver. States also determine their own licensing standards, which means the link between payment and licensure and uneven development of licensing policies and practices can complicate efforts to provide fair compensation to kinship caregivers. Also, across states, kinship caregivers receive less supervision and fewer services that non-kin caregivers and as a result the best care and support to protect children can fall through the cracks. Finally, another quagmire for the states is how kinship placement blurs the lines of permanency — leaving caregivers unsure about adoption or seeking legal guardianship of children.

Without a doubt, more states and the child welfare agencies are finding ways to respond to the growth of kinship caregivers. Through a look at three case studies, it is possible to see locally and regionally how A Second Chance Inc. has supported kinship care families. But what happens there also serves as a model of what is possible when community partnerships are formed, and when frontline workers and leaders are compelled to think outside the box and champion new policy and practices. In this next section, the following case studies provide a look at how A Second Chance, Inc. has gone about its work, supporting the needs of the kinship triad through policy, philanthropy, and practice.

A CASE STUDY ON POLICY

From the Philadelphia Regional Office of A Second Chance, Inc.

The early morning call had awakened Mrs. Arnold. On the other end of the line, the firm voice of a caller from the child welfare agency indicated that Mrs. Arnold's niece and great nephew were in the agency's custody and that she had been identified as a potential kinship resource.

The call came at 2 a.m. on a blistering cold winter morning, and Mrs. Arnold *(not her real name)* was not prepared to become the full-time caregiver of her kin, but she knew in her heart that her failure to act could result in her not seeing her family members for a very long time. So without much hesitation, she agreed for the child welfare agency to explore the possibility of placing the children in her home.

Within three hours, the children, a 15-year-old and a 1-month-old infant, were now full-fledged members of her home. This placement was a clear sign that the responsive and family focused policies of the Department of Human Services (DHS) were clear and operational. There is an understood policy and practice model that kinship care is the first placement option for children needing out-of-home care in Allegheny County (Pittsburgh). In fact, the policies of DHS create a wealth of placement options for children needing out-of-home care. In order for children to be placed outside of a kinship environment, the casework staff must obtain approval from the deputy director, and this comes only after the deputy director has engaged the caseworker and supervisor in a structured conversation where they are required to explain their attempts to find kin.

In the case of Mrs. Arnold, within four days of placement, she was referred to A Second Chance, Inc. so that the licensing kinship foster care process could begin. Mrs. Arnold, now divorced, had two children of her own, a 20-year-old and a 22-year-old living with her. She did not understand the foster care process. All she wanted to do was to take care of her "kin folk" without a lot of hassle. Mrs. Arnold was an educated and successful businesswoman. None of that mattered when it came to this process, she thought. In her early 50s, she was questioning if she had the skills and the patience to go through the requirements of foster care. Also, she worried about how this new role would affect her ability to continue to do the things that she enjoyed (playing bridge and swimming).

Once assigned to an ASCI case manager, Mrs. Arnold received a call indicating that the organization was required to come to the home to complete a 24-hour Safety Assessment. Of course, Mrs. Arnold had no idea what this entailed, but she had heard about how ASCI supported families by some members of her church community. However, she never expected to be a client and now she had to pay particular attention to the details.

Much to her surprise, when the worker arrived to her home, the worker had food vouchers and an application for Mrs. Arnold to complete to receive emergency assistance of $150 per child. She was unaware that she could obtain emergency funds and was grateful that the organization was sensitive to the emergency situation that the 2 a.m. phone call left her in. The visit also entailed a lot of paperwork. Having worked in government in the past, Mrs. Arnold knew of the paperwork of government; however, she never expected that she would have to complete so many documents. But she said at the outset, "I will do my very best for my family...they need me and I want to be there for them."

From the beginning, Mrs. Arnold had a very cooperative and collaborative disposition. She complied with and excelled at all that was required of her. She participated in all of the enrichment workshops required for certification, in a timely manner completed all of her paperwork, and was an active participant in the once-a-week required visits from the ASCI caseworker, and the child welfare worker.

Throughout the 60-day certification process, Mrs. Arnold never wavered in her decision to care for her niece and great-nephew; she just wanted to be a support to her kin as much as possible.

Once the family had completed the certification process, the family worked toward reuniting with the birth mom. Unfortunately, this attempt failed over and over again. In addition, as Mrs. Arnold's niece became more comfortable with the living arrangements, she began to leave the home unannounced and would often leave the baby with Mrs. Arnold. About a year after placement with Mrs. Arnold, it was clear that her niece was not responsible enough to care for her infant without parental support. Because an infant of a minor child in care is not automatically adjudicated dependent, the infant was able to live with the minor mother and caregiver without court involvement of the infant, although the judge always asked how the baby was doing.

One summer day, after nearly three years in the home of their aunt, Mrs. Arnold had just about had enough of her almost 18-year-old niece, who was rarely parenting her now-toddler. Mrs. Arnold informed the caseworker that she would be willing to adopt her great-nephew if her niece could not get herself together. With her niece now turning 18 and not wanting to live in her home or sign a waiver for continuous care, but, more important not being prepared to take care of her toddler, the family made arrangements for the great-nephew to be adopted by Mrs. Arnold. Because of the family agreement, the excellent care of the great-nephew and the consent of the now 18-year-old birthparents, the courts agreed to have Mrs. Arnold adopt her great-nephew. This is indeed an open adoption. Birthmother and other family members have liberal visitation rights and have a very positive relationship with one another. While Mrs. Arnold's life changed one morning at 2 a.m., she has been blessed by the experience and her great-nephew has been a joy.

Like the maternal aunt in this case study, millions of relatives—mothers, uncles, grandparents, and godparents—have stepped up to care for the children who are part of their extended families. Increasingly, these families are being connected by emotional bonds and not just linked by blood relations. In looking more closely at the positive actions that allowed the maternal aunt to care for her niece and great nephew, it is possible to see how the process from kinship care to adoption was seamless because of the system that is in place on all levels in Allegheny County.

First, you have a Department of Human Services that unequivocally supports kinship care and has done so for more than 20 years.

Second, you have a community-based organization that has the fluid structure to be adaptable to meet the immediate needs of family and does not have a bureaucratic structure that impedes the certification process.

Third, you have a family court system that has embraced family as a viable placement option and supports children with family first.

With the aforementioned in place, more than 12,000 children have been serviced by ASCI's system of care that we call kinship care between 1994 and 2013. What happened to Mrs. Arnold is just one example of how good policy resulted in good outcomes. Our efforts to achieve permanency and safe placements are exemplified in policies that employ 24-hour Safety Assessments, provide emergency cash assistance, and offer support in beginning the licensing process for becoming a kinship care provider.

In addition, there are here are numerous "voices" of how policy can and should 1) affect the work of local agencies, 2) suggest what needs to happen on the municipal and national level and 3) influence budget decisions. Here are a few of the voices from across the industry who weigh in on emerging trends and philosophies of how policy can make a difference.

The Voices of Thought Leaders: On Policy

In Pittsburgh in 1996, Marc Cherna, then the newly appointed head of the Allegheny County Department of Human Services, came into what was considered a "national disgrace."

Case work was out of control and — with most workers being responsible for at least 30 families — also out of compliance with state regulations. In Allegheny County, there were 3,318 kids in placement, roughly .3 percent of the county's population (there are 1.2 million people in Allegheny County), only a quarter of which were in kinship care. Today, there are 1,443 kids in placement and about 66 percent are in kinship care.

To turn matters around, Cherna instituted new policy: he told case-workers that if a child has to go in foster care, they should first try to find relatives. Cherna also allowed resources to follow his philosophy. Kinship care, he said, is something "I also strongly believed in from day one." Kinship foster parents, he says, "should get the same rate, the same money, and the same resources as relative foster parents and non-relative foster parents."

Cherna's decisions were important, because when we look to history, we know policy matters. Beginning in 1965, more than a decade of policy was shaped by research that concluded Black lives were a tangle of pathology and that "the apple didn't fall far from the tree" — meaning that if Mom was addicted, wasn't it Grandma's fault? So, why send the grandchild to live with grandma? It was this kind of bias that determined it was best if children were placed outside of their families. Cherna was influenced by different scholarship and his own perceptions of family. His policy was undergirded by a belief that "it's so much less traumatic for children to go with people that they have a relationship with."

At times, the policy has to come from the top. As it did in 1979 when the Supreme Court ruled — in *Miller vs. Youakim* — that relatives raising other family members' children were entitled to federal aid to support them. That's why in Pittsburgh, when a family meets the licensing standards set forth by the state regarding kinship care, it gets offered the same benefits foster families would. It should also be noted that the family is in control of whether they want to be licensed or not. Families can provide for kin through the court process and do not have to go through the licensing process. Licensing is necessary to obtain federal funding for foster care. If they are eligible, families with children under age 18 can receive assistance through the federally funded Temporary Assistance for Needy Families (TANF) or they may receive social security if their children are eligible as well.

A couple of years ago, it was federal legislation — based on the testimony of young people — that gave birth to a policy allowing brothers and sisters to stay in touch with their siblings. For a child, one of life's most painful experiences is to lose a parent, and siblings often felt twice victimized when losing touch with each other.

In 2008, there was more sweeping change in the policy community that, according to Jennifer Miller, of ChildFocus, a consulting firm specializing in policy advocacy, strategic planning, organizational development, and government relations in child and family issues, went a long way toward helping children find their way to safe and stable kinship placement. Again, this change was initiated on the federal level and applied locally.

Known as the Fostering Connections Act, the 2008 law aims to improve outcomes for children in foster care through policy changes in six key areas: 1) support for kinship care and family connections; 2) support for older youth; 3) coordinated health services; 4) improved educational stability and opportunities; 5) incentives and assistance for adoption; and 6) direct access to federal resources for Native American communities. The new law means that agencies need to make sure that children in foster care have the opportunity to stay in their schools and that financial assistance be provided to relatives who become guardians for children leaving foster care. Both are issues that A Second Chance, Inc. has been advocating for over the years.

For Miller, more local institutions should help children stay connected to their fathers and the paternal side of the family. But, generally, placements have been matrilineal, following the mother's side of the family. Miller said: "Fathers and their families are overlooked. Some jurisdictions do a better job with this." She suggested that there should be explicit policy to identify fathers and a father's family when considering kinship care.

In practical terms, one way to get more agencies to this level of novel practice is through hiring. Caseworkers are a frontline defense for families and children and having the right worker can make all the difference in appropriate responses to meeting the needs of families. "If you hire people whose standards are in line with what is needed to protect children and preserve families," said Miller, "it can help ensure their needs will be met."

Hiring people who share your values can also help agencies steer away from a judgmental workforce and avoid frontline workers who act based on misperceptions about poverty and stereotype about low-income families. When workforce barriers are removed, Miller said, then you can foster innovations in how you work with families. This includes, for instance, ensuring families have access to mental health services, support to raise adolescents, and information to access basic needs, such as food stamps, she added.

While the policy movement to help fathers is slow, there are social changes that could influence decisions that enable more fathers/males to enter the kinship care arena. For instance, the growth of more stay-at-home dads is positively altering the perception of men as caregivers, said Robert Watt, a trustee with Casey Family Programs, the nation's largest foundation focused entirely on foster care and improving the child welfare system. Furthermore, there is movement to recognize the model that gay men raise children successfully and to recognize that low-income or no-income males can provide in other ways for their children and make similar contributions that low-income or no-income single women would. To not tap into these fathers, said Watt, is to deprive a community of 50 percent of its kinship care potential. In terms of policy, said Watt, some states have begun to overlook minor drug offenses for adult males, but more work needs to be done on the whole issue. It's a critical one for the African-American community because 38 percent of Black males are in jail on minor drug offenses.

With such high levels of incarceration, it is a "ridiculous thing to exclude that many people," said Watt. "If we took every child in America away from a house where there was an adult who smoked marijuana, we would have a real crisis on our hands." There is more work to do to develop more policy that engages fathers, he said.

But tapping into federal resources is a tough sell in an economy with such a stubborn recession. The situation is compounded by the stubborn attitude of some lawmakers who believe that caring for family members is solely a moral responsibility and can and should be done without government assistance.

On the other hand, family and child advocates also remind policy-makers that unemployed fathers, overburdened grandparents, and all kinds of families need help. Bottom line, say child welfare experts, when you make the early investment — such as with subsidized guardianship, which in some states, provides stipends to relative caregivers raising relatives' children—it improves a child's chance at permanency and saves government dollars in the long run.

David C. Mills, a member of Casey Family Programs Board of Trustees, agrees that the flexibility Title IV-E waivers offer some states in using federal child welfare funding represents a significant support, but the addition of "comprehensive child welfare financing reform" is where even greater gains for families could be made. Such reform, Mills suggests, "will bring with it the resources to take kinship care placement support to the next level. The success of the waiver program and resulting success in reducing the number of children in out-of-home care speaks volumes about the effectiveness of contemporary strategies and will make it possible to secure the needed resources even in a recovering economy.

"Without reform, however, I do not see a continued growth in the number of children placed in kinship settings."

In addition to making funding for kin and families a centerpiece of child welfare reform, Mills says those in the field should also be concerned about the challenges to kinship care posed by immigration debates and issues of citizenship, which are thorny realities for many families.

"One thing that stands out as an impediment to accelerating the rate of kinship care placements is the need for comprehensive immigration reform which would provide certainty to families that currently have any undocumented immigrant members among even the very extended family. And, it's that "fear of government involvement through the licensing and placement processes opens the perceived (and perhaps very real) risk of family members being exposed, serving as a major impediment to kinship efforts to accept a formal placement."

But to really affect policy, decision makers need to not only understand the degree to which aunts, uncles, older siblings, grandparents have played a role in raising a relative, but also the current complexities they face. "Kinship care touches everybody's life," said Mary Bissell, a founding partner with ChildFocus. From a policy perspective, argued Bissell, if you can bring lawmakers back to understanding that kinship care is "a true American archetype and a fundamental value ... then when it comes to [creating] effective policy, leaders can really tap that into the strength of family."

And what better way to affect those lawmakers and strive to influence policy than to hear directly from kin, adds Mills, who believes in the power of those stories to encourage and spur other relatives into caring for their kin. For example, putting "A greater focus on presenting positive outcomes for kin caregivers and families could encourage more families to open their homes to children of relatives." The move, Mills says, "isn't intended to detract from publicizing the positive outcomes for children, but rather to also emphasize the wonderful effect on kin families that often results."

In Allegheny County, Cherna counts judges among child welfare's allies and influencers. He makes sure that they are among those at the table, too. Judges are at the table, too. They are the ones who are responsible for making placements and issuing court orders that determine when a child enters or leaves foster care have become willing partners with the county's child welfare system.

Cherna remembers when the bridge between the courts and the child welfare system was at best a tenuous gulf despite their shared goal of doing what was best to meet the needs of vulnerable children and families. Judges and courts, Cherna underscores, are important links in the cast of partners and advocates the system needs to help human service agencies secure the safety and well-being of children and families. It's the judicial partners who are responsible for ensuring that foster care rolls don't swell with children placed there unnecessarily or don't get clogged with those youngsters lingering longer than necessary.

Keeping children safely in the home whenever possible is the foundation for Allegheny County's child welfare philosophy. Cherna frequently espouses its tenets: "Treat people the way that you want to be treated; try to keep kids in the home whenever possible; and involve the community, create opportunities for partnerships."

He counts provider agencies among those community partners. They too can be a family's best advocate. But Cherna isn't swayed by foster-care providers claiming to know and understand the needs of kinship families. He knows that few do. But in 1996, when Cherna was appointed to lead the system, there was a new provider in Allegheny County with that kinship care expertise—Sharon McDaniel of A Second Chance, Inc. Cherna took note.

"What I like about what Sharon was doing is something that I had never seen before," says Cherna of the county's sole kinship care provider. The agency, which Cherna points to as a model, blends "that expertise and that sensitivity, with cultural sensitivity, and everything else that is important to families" who are largely Black. McDaniel's role as an advocate and provider is deeply rooted in experience, having lived her life in foster-kinship care. McDaniel is involved in discussion, setting directions for the Department of Human Services child welfare work, too, lending the expert voice of one who now serves and one who has been on the receiving end of care in the system.

More and more, those who have experiences within foster-kinship care, plus the voices of youth still in the system are wafting up. They are emerging as some of the most compelling tools for educating systems and providers about what needs fixing in child welfare and prompting of widespread policy change, contend both Cherna and Annie E. Casey's McCarthy.

There is also learning underway. When the Annie E. Casey Foundation trustees asked McDaniel to tell her personal story to those funders advocating for kinship care, it moved the issue from remote to real and personal. And, most important to move it to a plan of action and advocacy.

"The board loved hearing directly from someone doing this work" and who had emerged from a system of care, recalls McCarthy. Likewise at the Annie E. Casey Foundation, young voices in foster care are informing how they will experience one of the biggest transitions in their lives, aging out of the system. Most states require foster youth to emancipate at age 18. For more than a decade, the total number of youth in foster care has eased downward, but when the Jim Casey Youth Opportunities Initiative, a national foundation, began tracking the numbers in 2001, it found that those youth aging out of the system was on the rise. Between 2000 and 2010, more than 260,000 young people transitioned from foster care without having permanent connections to a family. Also, each year, nearly 30,000 young people leave the system without ever being placed in a permanent home with a family. But before they go out on their own, most systems and caseworkers consider the classes offered on such things as resume writing and tips on balancing a checkbook as preparation enough for foster youth transitioning into adulthood. And many foster youth poised to leave the system wonder, is this all that there is for them? The Jim Casey Youth Opportunities Initiative, supported in part by the Annie

E. Casey Foundation, is partnering with states and asking youth about what they need most to prepare for their journey, make their transition smooth, and enhance life after foster care.

And in a region like Allegheny County, the power of those youth voices and stories are present and repeated.

When Cherna listens he, too, hears "youth currently and formerly in the system with perspective that can't be gleaned from research. Real-life experience makes a much greater impact on the public, the providers of service, and policymakers. They tell a story better than anybody. It's powerful when you've been there."

ChildFocus founders Mary Bissell and Jennifer Miller agree that "partnerships, working across "silos", and honoring the contributions of others," when it comes to children and families in kinship and foster care, is essential and is occurring. The consulting firm ChildFocus specializes in policy advocacy, strategic planning, and organizational development and government relations in child and family issues.

Bissell and Miller point to the critical role of foundations as change-agents. It's what happened when a well-respected philanthropy known for its work on aging issues recognized the contributions of grandparents and older relative caregivers took up the cause of these kinship families.

The New York-based Brookdale Foundation Group became one of the rigorous and early supporters of the grandparents and senior kin, who became surrogates for grandchildren, say Bissell and Miller. The Brookdale Foundation, which works to advance the fields of geriatrics and gerontology and to improve the lives of senior citizens, opened the door for those caring seniors when it launched the Relatives as Parents Program in 1996. RAPP, as it is widely known, has funded hundreds of seed grants to state and local initiatives that encourage and promote the creation or expansion of services for relatives raising children outside of the formal child welfare system.

So, whether for grandparents, teens, fathers, or other populations, when foundations, agencies, and diverse community partners advocate and come together, benefits for families and children can sprout across race, class, gender and all kinds of barriers.

A CASE STUDY ON PHILANTHROPY & ADVOCACY

A Dance for Life Program

At A Second Chance, Inc. almost from day one, a multitude of local and national philanthropies has boosted the nonprofit's innovations and policies that strengthen family, children, even staff. Here is the case of one specific initiative among many that discusses a program that meets the unique needs of teen girls of color in kinship-foster care, overall it provides an example of how one event can be transformative. And, in doing so, it serves to showcase how institutional collaboration, the power of advocacy, and the largesse of national and community-based foundations can bring together cultural- and gender-specific care, intervention, and response to nurture progressive, positive change for families and youth.

In 2011, A Second Chance, Inc. (ASCI) made it possible for 20 teens in foster care and kinship care to spread their wings and shine. On the evening of November 5, young ladies recruited by ASCI caseworkers glided into a glittering hotel ballroom wearing elegant white satin and tulle, ready to waltz, slide, and celebrate having entered a world of possibilities that most had never dreamed of. They were participants in A Dance for Life, the agency's decade-old signature program.

The 10-week, rite of passage program culminates in a cotillion or formal dance. For the first time in the program's eight-year history, A Dance for Life in 2011 included a pregnancy prevention component along with community-based events, social functions, and classes that reflected the changing time and culture in which the agency's young girls of color lived.

The philanthropy of well-respected and established Pittsburgh-based child welfare partners including Three Rivers Youth, a private non-profit that provides residential and in-home programs and services for youth in crisis, and The Eden Hall Foundation, a private foundation supporting social welfare, education, health, and the arts and culture—became a lever of advocacy. Together these philanthropies and community-based partners also linked arms with A Second Chance, Inc. so that the girls had a support system to help them feel like they belonged—despite the family circumstances that landed them in the system, despite where they lived, and despite who was raising them. Three Black women in Pittsburgh — all influential nonprofit trailblazers who understood how the intersections of race, class, and gender can play out in the inner city — came together with a common mission: to see to it that these teens had a chance to climb society's ladder and were motivated enough to dream big.

In a region still struggling with racial diversity, these Pittsburgh CEOs and philanthropists—Sylvia Fields of the Eden Hall Foundation, Peggy B. Harris of Three Rivers Youth, and Sharon McDaniel of A Second Chance, Inc.— offered lessons that were culturally sensitive and authentic when it came to sharing with the girls what it means to be female and Black.

As a practice, ASCI represents the ways in which neighbors and family and community must partner in the work that it does for those who are in its care. Their participation in A Dance for Life was no exception. Those who attended the formal affair also represented the circle of life for the young ladies. There were birth mothers and grandmothers, uncles, friends and neighbors, local government leaders, teachers and preachers, brothers and sisters who waited eagerly in that ballroom to welcome the teens back from the journey they spent 10 weeks completing. And before they were presented, those who mentored them watched as beaming teens in tiaras moved with grace and with a gloved arm linked to their escorts. The mentors knew that some of the things that they taught their mentees during those weeks in the program—be respectful and ask for the same, persevere on the way to success, stay in school, it's okay to say no and mean it, text and Tweet responsibly, always act like a lady, and speak up and clearly—were too important to leave to chance.

Caseworkers, mentors, and other staff of ASCI, were part of their circle of life that evening, including ASCI Founder and CEO Sharon McDaniel whose vision gave birth to the A Dance for Life program. Sticking close and feeling proud, ASCI mentors and staff—members of the village—moved quietly about checking on hair and makeup, gently squeezed a trembling hand, tucking in a bra strap, whispering words of encouragement, and trying not to cry. For Dr. McDaniel, a breath of empowerment, a gift of voice, came with each good wish she delivered to the teens. For her, the night was a celebration, but it was also personal.

That's why those at ASCI who had a hand in nurturing and teaching those in A Dance for Life wanted each young girl to know that they were special, beautiful, and strong, and never had to be afraid to speak out. They would have allies to support them. A Second Chance, Inc. is using advocacy and the gifts of foundations to help them find their way.

Changing the tide in these young lives touched by A Second Chance, Inc. has meant harnessing the power and support of philanthropies, child advocacy organizations, providers, and other partners. The following thought leaders share trends on the effect of these emerging collaborations, what lessons they see working, and what's on the horizon.

The Voices of Thought Leaders: On Philanthropy & Advocacy

Whether he's talking about kin and extended family members across the nation who have stepped up to care for more than 2.7 million children through informal arrangements or those who have formally become surrogate parents for an estimated 104,000 children nationally, Patrick McCarthy, president of the Annie E. Casey Foundation, says service systems and provider agencies should improve supports for these families and children.

In April 2012, the Annie E. Casey Foundation laid out a blueprint to do just that, with the publication of the policy report, "Stepping Up for Kids: What Government and Communities Should Do to Support Kinship Families." The report called attention to kinship families and the need for policy makers and child welfare practitioners to do a better job of supporting them. Outcome research continues to confirm the ability of relative caregivers—extended families members and kin to "ensure that children are kept safe and healthy and are able to achieve their full potential," he says. Most of those kinship families provide care for grand-children and other youth without the kinds of supports, both financial and psychological, that they need to cope with such a big transition.

"And even in instances where the placement is made formally by the child welfare system, we hear from kin and families that they are not able to take full advantage of the supports that they are often not able to take care of the kids," McCarthy says these are missed opportunities for those grandparents, other relatives, and close family who share unique needs as caregivers.

"I think that A Second Chance, Inc. is an example of the kind of formal and informal supports that kin families need to thrive in those kinds of placement situations," he says. "We've got to recognize that extended family taking care of children, often have unique needs. As ("Stepping Up for Kids") states, they are often lower income, their health is often not as strong as those in foster families, and they have other barriers or challenges."

Those providing direct service and support to families and who know them best may also be one of their best advocates, McCarthy underscores. When guided by a philosophy of reaching out to caring community partners to provide critical services, lives can be changed. As one such agency, A Second Chance, Inc. offers in its arsenal, pro-grams and services for kinship families that are tailor-made, informed by foundation research, the community, and what families and kin say that they need.

By partnering with A Second Chance, Inc., the public child welfare system in Allegheny County, which includes Pittsburgh, has understood that one size doesn't fit all when it comes to meeting the needs of kinship families. Partnerships, along with the advocacy and philanthropy of foundations like Annie E. Casey, can provide "essential resources for such change in care and support," says McCarthy.

Reaching a greater number of children and families is a part of the Foundation's "forward look," he adds. And in fact, Annie E. Casey Foundation has already embarked on that work and is enlisting the support of like-minded philanthropies and other partners as it moves forward to bring about that change. "We are looking at what we can contribute, in partnership with others, in figuring out how to take these programs of promise to a scale where they are not just best pr=actices but common practices."

Such partnerships, for example, are proving necessary to the Annie E. Casey Foundation's work with states, helping to reduce their reliance on the use of group, institutional, and foster care placements for children and youth. Creating these needed changes in policy and practice will also take time and a large financial investment. The Annie E. Casey's philanthropy, says McCarthy, will be aimed at "the improvement of frontline practice across a variety of areas, including child welfare. And frontline practice, as it relates to supporting kin, will be a part of that."

Those are some of the reasons that in Allegheny County, Cherna, director of the Allegheny County Department of Human Services, makes sure that foundations are at the system's table. If you're talking about creating change, foundations and philanthropic organizations are among the partners that are already there, he says resolutely.

Cherna, who's credited with overhauling the county's once-troubled child welfare system, which today is hailed as a national model, recognizes the ability of philanthropies like Casey Family Programs, the Annie E. Casey Foundation, and the Jim Casey Youth Opportunities Initiative, to advocate for change, highlight cutting-edge research, and fuel promising programs and practices that improve outcomes for children and the lives of foster-kinship families. Practically speaking, "Foundations are extremely important because they can invest in new programs that the government may not be able to fund," Cherna says. And during tough economic times, they can be among the system's best allies. Foundations can also leverage scarce dollars with their support. They also help with private sector and community support for child welfare."

But even as philanthropies consider making socially responsible investments, including those that improve the lives of families and children, there will always be on "the bottom line," contends David C. Mills, a Casey Family Programs Trustee and retired executive director and chief executive officer of the State of Wisconsin Investment Board.

"Whether one is trying to influence policy makers (i.e., the funding sources) or whether one is trying to encourage families and communities to invest in their own growth and positive change, what motivates more than anything is helping them to see the incredible cost to individuals, families, communities and society that can be avoided by their own investment in that growth and positive change," Mills explains. "I definitely think we can and should advocate more for this, and I think Casey Family Programs is beginning to do that with our Communities of Hope Initiative. We are promoting the replication of these community-based efforts by helping others see the wonderful outcomes that can result."

A CASE STUDY ON INNOVATION & PRACTICE
The Staff and Family Health and Wellness Programs

This section focuses on two innovations in health and wellness. One example showcases how ASCI looks inward, designing opportunities to address the physical, emotional, and overall health and wellness of staff. The other wellness initiative is directed outward, at clients, seeking fundamental ways to share information among caregivers, mental health counselors and other stakeholders so that children's physical and emotional needs are optimized.

We begin with what's happening for staff. It's 3 p.m., and a small group of staff at ASCI has gathered in one of the downstairs meeting rooms. The tables are pushed aside and staffers are warming up their voices. It's karaoke time. The musical break happens for one-and-a-half hours every two weeks and is facilitated by a staff member who sings like an angel and wants to share the joy of live music. It's also one of the programs that ASCI has brought into the building in an effort to reduce stress in an industry where burn-out among workers can derail continuity and threaten client outcomes. Staff wellness has always been a part of how business is done at A Second Chance, Inc.

This program focus grew out of my doctoral dissertation. As I considered approaches for supporting ASCI staff, I was also guided by a fundamental belief that healthy workers produce more positive outcomes for families and children. The process began by assessing the level of stress among ASCI staff. The results told us that workers were affected on many levels, sometimes experiencing an overall loss of perspective, which affected their ability to assess safety and risk, caused distrust among colleagues and supervisors, increased absenteeism and attrition, and decreased motivation. We further examined unexcused staff absences, such as unscheduled "call offs" that may have been for sick leave. In addition, we chose to examine departures from the organization, knowing that high rates of staff turnover are common in our field. At the same time, this transient nature creates challenges in an agency where the continuity of care and services for families is paramount.

In the early days, staff had time to pamper themselves with manicures, haircuts, and the agency even offered staff services such as babysitting. More recently, we have included a movie afternoon (complete with pop-corn and candy); there is high-energy Zumba, and a full-service gym. In ASCI's Philadelphia Regional Office, there is art therapy and because the facility is so close to a park, there is a walking club. Across the two ASCI sites there is a day off for cancer screening, and birthday time off for staff.

ASCI is aiming to reduce staff turnover and to have less stress-related illnesses and absences, said the director of employee relations and the manager of the de-stress activities. The enhanced programs are fairly new and, to draw participation, she reaches out to staff through e-mail, staff meetings, and personal invitation. She wants to continue to change the culture of what's expected in taking care of staff and, to get their buy-in, she encourages staff to design their own fun. From early feedback, there is talk of starting a card game competition.

The employee relations effort comes out of what I recognized all those years ago. ASCI's growth was swift and steady and before long, the daily challenges of work in the child welfare environment also began to grip the staff. Supporting kinship families demanded a healthy workforce that was ready and able to take on the rigors, but over the years, my experience taught me that this is a stressed system where staff stress, client stress, and management stress intermingle.

Organizational stability goes hand-in-hand with positive child welfare outcomes. In addition, as a caring organization, and as the CEO, it was essential that staff be clear that there was conviction about the changing work environment and an understanding of the added stress that they were encountering daily on the job. The result, a few years after we began, was a robust wellness initiative developed to address these prevailing issues. At the time, ASCI was a pioneer in the child welfare field when it offered its employees a comprehensive wellness program that addressed the physical and mental health demands that come with the job. Our innovative program model included informal child care, allowing a parent on staff to bring a sick child to the workplace when needed. ASCI also became a welcoming place and refuge for the children of staff when school or daycare closed, or when new parents needed to work through separation issues from their child.

ASCI also offers the Employee Assistance Program, an onsite counseling initiative for staff. Other wellness activities also include: a workout site at each office and department, salon/barber services, movies, and a variety of other activities and services that bring relief, personal care, and relaxation during the workday. Since these employee wellness initiatives were put in place, the results have been tremendous, with positive effects on things like staff morale, absenteeism, and reduced rates of turnover. This wellness program, now a hallmark at ASCI, is one of the perks that staff returning to the organization anticipate most. And compared to other organizations where they've been, those staff members report that ASCI's innovative employee wellness program is in a league of its own.

In 2014, we plan to scale up the wellness amenities for both our kin families and our staff so that the services will include programs that will examine the risk factors associated with poor health outcomes for children and families of African-American descent. While those expanded supports will be open to all families, special emphasis will be placed on this underserved community around health domains. For instance, I am beginning "Say Yes to Life," a new suicide prevention program designed to both educate caregivers on the signs of suicide, and train staff working directly with youth. For adolescents and teens growing up in kinship foster care, the already turbulent process of coming of age is compounded. Many grapple with feelings of abandonment and loss, and for them, life can be a struggle. In 2012, one of our young people took his life. One life lost was too many. I knew that it was time to act and do more to keep our children alive and well.

But a new program that's designed to keep families well is the Mental Health Roundtable. This clinical service taps into a village model of mental health care, calling "all of the players to the table who are responsible for the rehabilitation of the child," said ASCI's vice president of Child & Family Services. That table may grow full at times, not only with those who comprise the kinship care triad—kinship caregivers, the child, and the birth parents—but a teacher, sports coach, counselor, clergy, or a psychologist may be there, too. Together they represent "the key people who provide support and serve as resources and mentors in a child's life," said the vice president of the Roundtable's hallmark: a coordinated treatment plan and approach.

Getting all of those people to the table, while essential to the child's care, can be challenging, but an ASCI facilitator trained in social work and mental health, provides the careful orchestration. That work also includes scheduling the initial meeting and the program's three supervised, follow-up sessions.

Referrals to the Mental Health Roundtable began in 2013. The agency begins the healing with a frontline network of experienced case workers, clinicians, and other caring professionals who understand things like the bonding and attachment challenges of kinship placements. Building the treatment plan begins in the home. It's the place to see up close the interaction between the child and the kinship caregiver. When they go in, ASCI clinicians and counselors look for such things as signs and symptoms of stress, a growing concern as the number of adolescents being cared for by aging and elderly caregivers rises. Many of those kinship families are struggling alone to cope and communicate in the midst of a generation divide.

The Roundtable doesn't just focus on the needs and well-being of the child; the well-being of the kinship caregiver is also a part of the plan. For example, their skills as caregivers are assessed and addressed. Once a coordinated treatment plan is made, the caregiver and the child are asked to take ownership of the goals that have been set for them then take the next step when they agree to the plan and sign off on it. Participation in this comprehensive mental health program is a part of ASCI's treatment protocol when counselors here spot "red flags" signaling a child's severe emotional distress and a review of their case file prompts immediate intervention. Before referrals to the program are made, screenings further help to determine whether the Mental Health Roundtable is the treatment choice. In these and other instances, a referral is made to the Roundtable, the vice president said: if a child is suicidal, is suffering from severe depression, has had multiple home placements because of aggressive and other behavior problems, or is cycling through the criminal justice system and is on probation.

Research shows that the earlier children's emotional trauma gets treated, the more stabilized they become and the less likely they are to face unstable placement, homelessness, drug abuse, early pregnancy, or gang involvement. About 80 percent of youth transitioning in and out of foster care are in need of some type of therapeutic support compared to 25 percent of those in the general population, but their mental health needs often go unmet in the system.

At ASCI, mental health interventions and supports are innovative and available to ensure the well-being of the child and the caregiver. But the demand for clinical intervention is high. With about 1,300 children a year coming through our agency's door, we provide mental health services for about 100 at a time. With the launch of the Mental Health Roundtable, an extension of our current in-home therapeutic support services, we expect to provide care and intervention for an additional 100 children.

The agency's mental health supports for families were once offered off-site. In 2005, ASCI developed the Mental Health Wellness Unit, a treatment service that includes psychiatric education and assessment; medication monitoring; and individual family cognitive and behavioral therapy, to bring that care to children and families where they lived.

This pioneering program, along with the Mental Health Roundtable, is addressing trauma and other unmet mental health needs of children in kinship foster care, guided by research and experience.

The Voices of Thought Leaders: On Innovation & Practice

Patrick McCarthy, president at the Annie E. Casey Foundation, believes a 21st century child welfare system will require new ideas and new ways of responding to families and child issues. No longer, he said, does "a one-size-fits-all approach work." Not all family problems require full investigations or ongoing supervision. Instead, some families can be helped with services on a voluntary basis, especially material services. It's important today to understand the connection among concerns about neglect, family homelessness, the housing crisis, and how the binding of these two factors impact a child's entry into the welfare system."

Child welfare agencies need innovations that both protect children and help their families find a path out of poverty. "Neglect is the most common threat to children," McCarthy adds. "Despite the overriding misperception that kids come to the child welfare system because of physical abuse, more than three-fourths are victims of neglect, which is directly tied to a lack of family income that in turn creates the family crisis."

A starting point for innovation is to think of the family holistically. Systems and agencies and workers can then begin to think differently, transforming attitudes and practices. "We should not remove a child from the home because the family doesn't have housing. Nor should we ignore these problems. The combination of poverty and other situations need a range of support, not just child placement. That is the new frontier," says McCarthy.

Another example of a fundamental shift is recognizing that older youth don't always need to be placed in group homes. They can do well in kinship care homes. But this shift requires a willingness to do things differently, including a belief that older youth can find permanence. Far too many kids, said McCarthy, age out of the system and are put on a road alone, without any lasting connections to permanent family. From Sharon McDaniel's own experience, she was assisted with financial help to emancipate but no one talked to her about fostering relational permanency with her caregivers once she turned 18. What's needed, he continues, is support for older youth in care that moves them beyond just learning how to write a check. Finding a lifelong family must be encouraged earlier so that youth are connected emotionally and socially. This permanent connection is the bedrock for helping youth transition, complete their education, employment, and housing, and move on to healthy adult relationships.

But such new attitudes must also be accompanied by innovative practice. A Second Chance, Inc. earns applause from Marc Cherna, the leader of Allegheny County Department of Human Services, because it is an agency that boldly wanted to address kinship care issues by developing a grassroots expertise to help families. The work there, said Cherna, went against the grain that the government had to be the problem-solver.

A Second Chance, Inc. specializes in keeping family and children connected. In the agency's Pittsburgh office, there is a focus on intervention and kinship care placements, and when the agency became involved in Philadelphia, it entered a fractured Human Services Department—and worked with an innovative national strategy known as Family Group Decision Making (FGDM) that gives families a voice and a place for safety. The Philadelphia involvement was critical, said Cherna, because "a bunch of kids were dying" in unsafe placements.

The innovations in both Pittsburgh and Philadelphia are being fueled by a "huge sea change in attitudes toward kinship care," said Cherna. Much of it is aided, Cherna added, by philanthropic foundations and their reports that educate by documenting new research, that issue policy recommendations, and that help to push trends to keep kids in their own homes.

Of course, any innovative child welfare practice needs to be preceded by a mindset that caring for children and families can be done differently. That difference is what first got Julia Danzy, the former Deputy Secretary of the Office of Children, Youth and Families and Director of the Division of Social Services for the City of Philadelphia, excited about what ASCI was bringing to kinship care and families in Philadelphia. A Second Chance, Inc. came in treating families with respect and offering them a chance to do something they hadn't been asked before—to be active partners with providers and with DHS, instead of the strangers they were perceived to be. The system needed them to be "our eyes and ears," offers Danzy of the families that were relegated to the margins.

"These (families) are the people who best know these kids," she says. Galvanizing them while providing services was new, different, and a part of ASCI's holistic approach. She adds that this was also why the agency was able to positively affect how services were delivered to children and families and why A Second Chance, Inc. continues to thrive.

For Jennifer Miller, with ChildFocus, that is one of the most impressive characteristics of the work being done at A Second Chance, Inc. In Miller's observation, the Pittsburgh kinship agency uses a passionate leadership that builds pioneering practices to help families because the staff and employees there are people who dare to dream differently.

In her work around the nation with ChildFocus, one of the most important elements that Miller uses to evaluate agencies is trying to listen for passion; this sense that caseworkers are doing what they do because it matters to children and families and not just because legislation is passed that mandates certain action. Miller says in her work with ChildFocus they try to listen for a philosophy that says: "We value families." If that is present, believes Miller, the innovations to help families create stability, emotional connections, and culturally sensitive outcomes will follow. "Children belong to people they know and deserve to be connected at the earliest point possible with their own family network. From a cultural perspective, it's the right thing to do. For the perspective of trauma and being removed from their parents, it's the right thing to do. And, in terms of the long-term outcomes and the ability to create stability, it's the right thing to do," said Miller. Because this is the philosophy that drives the work and the innovation at ASCI and its partnership with the county, it shows up in what the agency does for kinship families and children, Miller said.

In practical terms, one way to get more agencies to this level of novel practice is through hiring. Caseworkers are a frontline defense for families and children, and having the right worker can make the difference in appropriate social responses. The key is be innovative in hiring, said Miller, "hire people whose standards are in line with what [you] want to do to protect children and also preserve families."

When there's innovative hiring, most of the time agencies can steer away from a judgmental workforce, especially in bringing on frontline employees who have the kind of authority that can remove children based on misperceptions of poverty, stereotypes and bias. When those kinds of barriers are removed, said Miller, then you can foster innovations such as mental health units, support for grandparents raising adolescent grandchildren and even supporting the broader population of different kinds of families who care for children by navigating families to food stamps and other support services.

Increasingly, child welfare leaders are recognizing that innovations aren't always agency-based. Science sometimes leads. In recent years, there has been neuroscience research suggesting that infants form emotional and psychosocial attachments to their biological parents and early caregivers. Being separated can cause trauma to the children's brain patterns, which later in life can cause social disruptions that can disadvantage children. The research shows that some of that damage to children can show up as poor impulse control, as lack of empathy, an unwillingness to live within the rules. "When you get that combination," said Bob Watt, a Casey Family Programs Trustee, "by the time a child is a teenager, they are a target for gang involvement, they are set up for doing bad stuff at school, for behavior outbursts that are uncontrolled and feeling like they are misunderstood by the adults around them… and they end up in jail."

The Casey Family Programs is engaging with neuroscientists and leading the charge to halt such negative progression by helping to share such research with Departments of Human Services across the nation. This innovative partnership and research crosses policy, services, and practices as it suggests that caseworkers must try harder to leave children attached to kin and familiar environments. For too long, said Watt, the trauma of separation has been misunderstood, understated, and disregarded, but the cutting-edge research helps the child welfare system to understand its significance. Furthermore, the research underscores that the "whole" child must be considered — a development that intersects the psychological, the physical and the social. In other words, said Watt, caseworkers need to understand that a household that doesn't look good from a lot of perspectives can still do a great job raising children with a little help. And that keeping kids with their biological parents might be better for a kid's "developing brain than a separation, which can produce brain damage."

One practice that matters is understanding that the child welfare system can't just "snatch" kids away—place them in foster care or institutions—because parents and the whole family are viewed as evil. The question that must be asked is "Why aren't we helping moms with medical issues get the treatment they need to be good moms. I think that people are asking that question more and more. And as a result, we are beginning to break down that old thinking—this whole family is completely screwed up and there's no way that anyone in that family can do any good by this child," Watt said.

With this research, there is recognition that out-of-kin or out-of-home placement can be traumatic for a child. That perhaps the separations can cause post-traumatic stress. But it also opens the door because an innovative response is that systems, agencies, and caseworkers can begin to think of their work as being preventative. There is now discussion about how to "fix" parental depression, substance abuse, and other issues to keep a healthy connection between family and child, said Watt. By many accounts, it's increasingly seen as being better to keep a child out of the system, which is a way of thinking and practice that didn't exist about a decade ago.

But even as the practice of kinship care placements enjoys greater acceptance and its benefits are more widely touted by those in the system and in the federal government, still, "we have to come to grips with at least three different potentially conflicting opinions about its present and its future, contends Mark Testa, the Sandra Reeves Spears and John B. Turner Distinguished Professor at the University of North Carolina at Chapel Hill, School of Social Work. One is "the positive side—kinship care is good and everyone recognizes that it's better to place a child with a relative than a stranger; two, recognizing that the apple doesn't fall too far from the tree does not generalize to all parents and relatives of parents with children in the child welfare system; and three, we have to recognize that our notions of family and duty and obligation may have worked well 200 years ago on the farm, but it doesn't work as well today when relatives themselves are struggling to make ends meet," explains Testa. He knows that if relative caregivers are going to continue undergirding "the biggest substitute care system in the nation" and if the growing needs of children living apart from parents with relatives are to be met, the nation, just those in the child welfare system, must adopt a "new attitude" about kinship care and "begin to accept the fact that we should be supporting relatives as generously as we support non-relatives."

Borrowing two pages from the history books, Testa points to the passage of the Social Security Act of 1935 and to the eventual adoption of Subsidized Guardianship, an idea first floated by the Children's Bureau in 1940s and 1950s. These landmark family support models took time and major shifts in attitudes about caregivers and dependent relatives before they could be realized. And in 2012, Testa says, it's time to make a similar transition for dependent children and kinship care. The days of relying solely on family to care for children are over, he maintains. "It must be a community responsibility. Once we make that leap, the same way that we changed our attitudes toward the care of the elderly and reframe our attitudes towards the care of dependent relatives, I think we'll be in a better place."

In some regions, those promising practices and new attitudes are emerging or are already in place. And like many other experts in the field, Testa points to Allegheny County's child welfare system, the leadership of Marc Cherna, and to Pittsburgh's A Second Chance Inc., as shining examples of what's possible when those sentiments change and unique kinship supportive services are in place for children and those who raise them.

But as scholars, advocates, and providers like Testa look to the future of kinship care and call for transition, these are difficult times for change with an economy in decline and the availability of government resources shrinking. For Testa, changing attitudes and perceptions about kinship care and relative caregivers represents just one part of what it means to "make the transition." Fostering the well-being of dependent children also demands the nation's focus, society's support, and government resources.

"Certainly care and the provision of care needs to be recognized as just as important as other values like health," he adds. "Somehow we have to recognize that a healthy life can only flourish" if dependent children are afforded safe and stable care that begins in infancy. Researcher are already providing a glimpse of the role that neuroscience is playing in helping to understand what's needed to provide a safe and stable home to a child who can grow up to be a productive member of society. "That is the foundation upon which we understand now as well-being."

Kinship care remains child welfare's "biggest backup, substitute care system" and it is working, concluded Annie E. Casey Foundation kinship care policy report "Stepping Up for Kids." According to 2010 census data, about 5.8 million children, or nearly 8 percent of all U.S. children, live with grandparents identified as the head of household. However, many of those children have one or both of their parents in the household, as well as grandparents. The Annie E. Casey Foundation kinship care policy report, "Stepping Up for Kids," focuses on the estimated 2.7 million children being raised in the absence of their parents by grandparents, other relatives or close family friends. The report says this category of children — whose parents might be dead, incarcerated, implicated in child abuse or struggling with addiction — increased 18 percent between 2000 and 2010. The majority of such living arrangements are established informally, but as of 2010 there also were 104,000 children formally placed in kinship care as part of the state-supervised foster care system.

But imagine what would happen if "the biggest backup, substitute care system" crumbled. With some trepidation, Testa has already begun to look down that road. There are signs of erosion as the majority of relative caregivers—women—shoulder the burden. Not only has the economy weakened their capacity to provide good care, but the demands of these caregivers have become so much greater. "Now they have to balance multiple roles.

"The sandwich generation, the caregivers who are wedged between fulfilling obligations for their older relatives at the same time that they are fulfilling obligations for their younger dependent relatives, has put a lot of caregivers in a very difficult place," says Testa. And when relative care providers, that first line of defense against child neglect and child maltreatment that the nation has relied on for so long, erodes, "the number of kids who would come into our foster care system would overwhelm the entire court system, child welfare system, and child protective system."

With such a potentially bleak picture on the horizon, there is good news and help on the way to keep relative caregivers from floundering and kinship care from crumbling.

McDaniel and A Second Chance, Inc. heard the needs of its caregivers and responded with such supports as respite care and even spa days to help rejuvenate those who were weary and stressed. Testa says caregiver support groups are another intervention that is low cost but offers tremendous payoffs for families.

At the end of the day, what makes researchers like Testa hopeful, is knowing that the practice of kinship care and its study is slowly emerging from the place its been for too long: "in the shadows." Long considered a curious relic of the past with no place in the modern family, the formal study of kinship care slowly became a focus in the 1990s, Testa says, with both child welfare and those in the aging arena investigating it merits and practice.

"My hope is that we can produce more scientifically based research," says Testa. "We understand that children who are in need or who have been neglected are better off placed with relatives, but solid, scientifically based research is needed to ground those observations and to identify the reasons that kinship care works."

Thought Leaders' Recommendations for Progressive Change

More children and families than ever are accessing kinship care. Practitioners, philanthropies, researchers, and policy administrators are re-imagining how a 21st century child welfare system might look and how it can best serve families. It is based on a philosophy that families have strengths, and children thrive when they can grow up in their home and with family or kin.

To offer well-being to families and children across the nation, here are selected recommendations across the spectrum of practices, policy, and philanthropy that thought leaders believe are necessary for progression. In addition to the voices of these thought leaders, I consider these same key areas in the final chapter with recommendations of my own for the perfecting of the system.

PRACTICES

The practices recommended here are for the industry overall, but the list includes specific thoughts on how to improve practices that must consider the whole kinship triad, families dealing with the incarceration of parents, and actions designed to protect the most vulnerable in the kinship triad, the child.

To make a difference, it is recommended that the industry continues:

To understand the effect of maltreatment on brain development: The development of a child's brain architecture depends on early, healthy family relationships. The development can be disrupted by separation and stress, which can then negatively affect the brain's ability to control and focus attention; inhibit impulsive behaviors; and disrupt the ability to hold and incorporate new information in decision-making.

To understand that typical programs for youth yield poor outcomes: Across tutoring, mentoring, life skills and case management, studies show these programs have little significance on high school completion, pregnancy rates, homelessness, and employment matters.

To understand that maltreatment of children impacts relationships throughout life: The maltreatment shows up in poor peer relationships, impaired coping skills, psychological distress, and dysfunction in adult/peer relations.

To understand that an integrated framework shapes children's well-being: From infancy to adulthood, an integrated set of factors shapes healthy children. These factors include environmental supports such as family income and social supports; personal characteristics, cognitive development, and social functioning.

To use functional assessments: It is important that children's well-being be assessed with holistic evaluations and not just with a point-in-time diagnosis, which could cause a misinformed intervention. It is important to evaluate kids across an array of assessments on social-emotional well-being.

To use vehicles that promote social and emotional well-being: These include implementing discretionary funding, which can cut across and provide for various needs such as trauma and mental health screening, assessment and treatment; educational stability, youth services, and child welfare and supportive housing. But it also means examining opportunities for initiating regional partnership grants, placing high priority goals on trauma, and using psychotropic medication with proper oversight and monitoring.

To understand that achieving family permanency will require well-equipped and educated frontline child welfare workers: Providing frontline child welfare workers with the training, with the time, with the resources, with up-to-date information systems, and with the mechanisms for shared decision making, is a critical element of working to achieve family permanency.

To routinely listen to and hear the voices of families and children being served in the process of delivering real family permanency: The evidence is now abundant that the common-sense truth of children and families about their needs and interest can inform child welfare practice, policy, and spending.

21ˢᵗ CENTURY BEST PRACTICES MUST CONSIDER
THE KINSHIP TRIAD

Longtime kinship care experts and scholars have researched the changing family dynamics involved in kinship care. Their efforts have focused largely on relations among members of the "triad" or the relative caregiver, birth parent, and the birth parent's child. Changes in the triad's family dynamics can be both assets and challenges for the kinship family. Some of these changes include loyalty, pre-existing attachments and bonds, guilt, loss, hope, denial, changes in parental roles, authority and responsibilities. These are things that must be considered in strategies that emphasize training and social services practices.

Such plans ask the industry:

To know that it is essential that service providers be aware of these changing family dynamics: These family shifts can affect the relative caregiver's ability to provide safety, protection, and permanency for the child in kinship families. Equally important is that providers offer the services, supports, training and skills to caregivers necessary to manage and cope with these family dynamics and changes.

To have providers understand the similarities and differences between relative (kinship) and non-relative foster care, adoptions and placements: Kinship care researchers and advocates know that an important first step in understanding the differences will assist providers in developing assessments and intervention strategies, support services, training programs (for relative caregivers and professionals), case planning and decision-making models that are more effective with kinship families.

To train caseworkers to understand and to work effectively within the triad—parents, children, and kinship caregivers: The training should include assessing a family's strengths, using family-centered practices that meet the needs of child and family; locating and accessing the services and resources available to kinship caregivers.

To support kinship caregivers: Understand that this support should be informed by cultural competence, and guided by sensitivity to the kinship triad. All support should be guided toward making a home safe for a child and helping to achieve permanency.

To inform the kinship caregiver: All relevant information on a child's care, regarding medical, psychological, and educational history, should be disclosed. Educate the caregiver on the options, benefits and levels of care possible; inform caregivers about the role of the court or caregiver in any possible court proceedings.

BEST PRACTICES WHEN CONSIDERING INCARCERATED PARENTS

The growing rates of incarcerated parents, especially women who are being sent to prison, mean families and children are challenged by high levels of poverty, substance abuse, poverty and unemployment, reunification, and grandparents raising their grandchildren.

As a way to address the phenomena, the industry is asked:

To create a task force of state agencies that will partner and advise correctional organizations: The task force should draw personnel from prison, parole, and probation offices, but also from education, mental health, the courts, child welfare, mental health, and other services that touch children's lives. A major focus should be the common problems associated with visiting (distance, facility culture, decorum, waiting time, alternative modes of visiting such as tele-visiting, etc.).

Another focus should be the integration of services across agencies throughout a parent's movement through the criminal justice system, including kinship services providers. The task force should address the service-provider implications of parenting arrangements that tend to be intergenerational and vary considerably in complexity and severity.

To publish and develop an incarcerated parent kinship care toolkit. The toolkit is a protocol to help practitioners and systems such as jails engage children when their parents are incarcerated. It is also used to help educate these systems about the needs of children.

To develop an assessment, screening, and supportive services program: These programs connect children, parents, and kinship caregivers in a co-parenting approach. They also include mental health professionals in the development and implementation of this program.

To involve kinship programs in planning for non-foster care children of incarcerated parents placed with relatives: This should include implementing post-subsidized guardianship services. For instance, caregivers of children of incarcerated parents almost invariably face most of the special challenges of kinship care, and need special help, including respite care as well as subsidized child care and wraparound services, and case management assistance for relatives having to deal with surrogate parenting issues on limited income without the assistance to which the children would be entitled if they were in the foster care system (i.e., education, delinquency, drug abuse, etc.).

To increase outreach to incarcerated parents: This can be accomplished through collaboration between kinship care programs and criminal justice, child welfare, and social service agencies, as well as community-based organizations specializing in serving children of incarcerated parents or serving kinship families.

To engage judges and court administrators: This improves parental access to judicial proceedings and mediation, and ensures the consideration of children in sentencing, as well as during probation and parole hearings.

To recognize that children of incarcerated parents face issues of loss/ bereavement as well as stigma and isolation from being involved with the criminal justice system.

To recognize that grandparents raising the sons and daughters of their incarcerated children face an array of special emotional, financial, and other challenges.

To consider co-parenting, where the caregiver shares duties with the incarcerated parent: This can be facilitated by supportive visiting programs and other methods that involve the incarcerated parent.

ALWAYS, CONSIDER THE CHILDREN

Vulnerable children, especially those in kinship and foster care, deserve a Community of Hope, contend scholars, researchers, and those on child welfare's frontline. And when philanthropies and communities intervene and are counted among child welfare's partners, a Community of Hope can exist for those children and youth. The following are recommendations that diverse partners—communities, businesses, philanthropies, faith-based organizations, and others—can work to instill, restore, and sustain hope in the lives of vulnerable children and youth.

It is suggested that the industry make efforts:

To adopt family-centered approaches to serving vulnerable children: The practice has often been to blame families as the source of problems rather than enabling them to be part of the solution; and to view children's interests and parents' interests as antagonistic. Working toward family-centered approaches is not without its challenges, especially during tenuous economic times, but there are viable funding and governmental strategies and supports to consider, including: redirecting and using public funding streams and grant requirements to reward work with families or that allow for investments that support, strengthen, and sustain lifelong families for children.

To develop integrated approaches and form partnerships to restore hope for vulnerable children and youth: The needs of vulnerable children are linked to the issues their families and peers are facing and to the conditions in their communities. Research has shown that where a child lives can be a major factor in determining his or her life's direction.

To always anchor the well-being of children in and around a strong network of support: Child welfare systems are well positioned to build public will and engage the community, public and private agencies, faith-based groups, social organizations, educational institutions in new strategies to create communities of hope. Building communities of hope means demonstrating and implementing effective practices that can be replicated.

POLICY

Policy is critical. Since the mid-1960s and the introduction and interpretations of the Moynihan report, Black families, for years, have been viewed as a tangle of pathology. The industry, accepting many of Moynihan's conclusions, designed systems to attack the so-called pathology, often creating programs that kept families apart and made reunification difficult. Policy today must be more culturally aware and designed to support families. Most often, the children who land in child welfare or the juvenile justice system come from families who are disproportionately minority, economically fragile, and otherwise disadvantaged. Clinical and other research and child welfare experts and advocates contend that fragile and vulnerable children's health, mental health, behavioral, identity, or esteem issues can't be addressed unless the industry understands, engages, and addresses the child's family and family networks.

However, the landscape for vulnerable children can change when efforts to achieve permanency for children, strategies for family economic success, and policies aimed at reducing poverty become central to the work of child advocates, philanthropies, states, the government, child advocates, and those on the frontline of child welfare.

The following policy recommendations are for moving those issues to the forefront of their work and budgets.

To be able to do that, governments and agencies must be able:

To ensure consistent and increased funding for kinship programs.

To address specific policies that pose barriers to access for kinship families: These policies help ensure that children can stay with families while going through the foster care process; allowing an exception for mandatory document policies; provide an administrative procedure for kin to seek approval as foster parents, enhance access to housing.

To mandate family-finding services for all local social services districts.

To ensure that every district has a kinship liaison and a working agreement with its kinship service providers to facilitate enrollment of kin in non-parent grants.

To translate knowledge about family permanence in children's lives into action and practice: For two decades permanence has been the official child welfare policy, but the unhappy truth is, only rarely has it been the predominant child welfare practice. Well-proven and replicable family preservation interventions and supports are available, as are qualified relatives who can be considered appropriate caretakers or permanent guardians.

To ensure permanent family connections for 18-year-old youths when they leave the system to live independently: Asking older youth who exit the system to live successfully without the support of family and other resources has been a counterproductive pattern and practice. What's needed is an authentic and effective commitment to restoring families for every child who enters and leaves the system. At a minimum, this means vastly increasing the quantity and quality of supports for these young adults.

To consider flexible funding: Of course, the bedrock of most change is sustainable funding, which drives the intent and purpose of effective reform and programming. In recent years, there have been calls for Congress to set the standard of progress with proper child welfare financing. Fully funded reform can support innovation, allowing for funding flexibility to align with the aims of keeping children safe.

To change the current federal funding policy to expand the allowable usage of Title IV-E funds, which are designated for foster care and adoption support, including a percentage of foster care maintenance costs paid to foster parents to care for eligible children. Reform would give all jurisdictions the ability to invest existing federal funds in different ways to address the specific needs of the individual children and families they serve, a critical component to keeping children safe and slowing down out-of-home care.

To restore the Department of Health and Human Services' (HHS) capacity to grant Title IV-E waivers so that more states can participate in flexible funding demonstration waivers while collective agreement is being reached on the components of comprehensive federal finance reform: Title IV-E waivers allow for evaluation of new reform strategies to comprehensive finance reform. The potential of IV-E waivers to spur system reform — in partnership with strong leadership, agency collaborations — has been demonstrated.

To ensure that federal financing reform supports an effective array of foster care, shorten lengths of stay, and increase exits to a safe and permanent home: Bringing funding policy into alignment with U.S. legislation that supports the ideals of strong families opens the door for permanency through kinship, adoption, and reaches diverse populations of children.

PHILANTHROPY

Nationally, projects such as The Annie E. Casey's "Stepping Up for Kids" report and Casey Family Programs' Communities of Hope initiative show the power of philanthropies to make a difference in the lives of children and their caregivers. In Pittsburgh, Pa., the Eden Hall Foundation, with its support of ASCI's A Dance for Life program, highlights the ability of foundations to change lives for children in kinship foster care and who are otherwise vulnerable.

With this in mind, philanthropy must continue to play a critical and significant role in bringing about systems change that empowers and uplifts vulnerable populations. Philanthropy has the ability and flexibility to take risks, transform systems, serve as a change agent, encourage innovation, and to take a high-level view of challenges, problems, gaps, and opportunities, which makes it a highly valued partner. Through philanthropic dollars, real change can be achieved in advancing the needs of kinship and other vulnerable children and families. Responding to societal ills is not just the work of one philanthropic, government, or community-based organization; rather it requires a collective response from the intervention of many.

In fact, charitable giving is at its best when it works to build knowledge that is shared among stakeholders, fosters collaborations between and among others in the field, seeks creative ways to leverage funding, and works to broadly disseminate that knowledge. But for philanthropy to have the greatest effect in the lives of society's neediest children and families in a way that is directed and sustained, it must be mindful that the social ills that strike at the heart of this population stem from cultural, environmental and social challenges that compromise health, education, and employment outcomes. These challenges are among the social factors that determine a community's well-being, and whether children and families will thrive. Probably chief among these social determinants is poverty and economic status, but they also include, housing, culture, age, and religion. The U.S. Census Bureau data supports the research—kinship caregivers, like other vulnerable families, are more likely to be poor, single, less educated and unemployed than families in which at least one parent is present.

To that end, philanthropy is an integral part of creating environments where children and families are not only less vulnerable, but thrive. To be truly effective, philanthropy should first recognize that many of our systems (education, health, social services, etc.) are often flawed and broken, and, second, that the social determinants of health should form the basis of changing those systems. For example, it may be surprising to learn that our zip code, where we live, can determine how long we live. While just one of the elements of the social determinants of health can effect the lives of those most in need, any one of the factors can provide a needed lens for philanthropy to use and embrace as they consider supporting the needs of kinship and other vulnerable families and communities.

To insure a progressive system, it is recommended that philanthropies:

Create and fund an integrated system model using the social determinants of health. Often, the very systems that are in place to support vulnerable children and families are themselves flawed, disjointed, and in need of fixing. It is not feasible to think that these flawed systems can be dismantled or totally overhauled if political and cultural will, resources, and a long-term plan are not in place. However, these systems can be disrupted in a favorable and positive way. If we begin to address poverty at the root and as the major public health issue that it is, we would be able to create systems that are integrated in their response to addressing children and families holistically.

There are many studies and articles that discuss how poverty and poor health are intertwined and how a myriad of issues affect poverty and social services. They point to children who are most affected by poverty. Kinship and other vulnerable families whose baseline status is not good often live on the edge of society, but they are not hidden away.

Like poverty, a host of factors can ensnare the lives of these families—lack of access to educational, economic opportunities, health care services, community-based resources, public safety, social support, and exposure to crime—but they are also ones that philanthropy can fund and target, working through an integrated system.

Seek opportunities to fund or support small non-profits and see them as valuable resources and partners. There are opportunities to fund and support small non-profits while embracing them as a valued resource and partner. Funders tend not to support these non-profit organizations because some lack plans for sustainability beyond the funding cycle. But often small non-profits have emerging innovations, are close to the populations they serve, and are trusted community networks. As they approach their work with families, funders can influence new models for also engaging these non-profits that emphasize collaboration and partnership.

Build collaborations to meet children and families where they are. Consider collaborations that offer innovation. School-based health clinics are among the best examples. Although the primary purpose of schools is education, not providing social services, there are ways in which to provide support for staffing, nurses and social workers to interact more directly (one-on-one) with students and their families. The research, especially those framed by the social determinants of health, concludes that good health is a prerequisite for a strong, stable family. This can begin in the schools where opportunities abound to build wellness and to create a culture of health care access. Together, such collaborations and funding can make a difference and create opportunities to reach children and their caregivers where they are. When done well, the research points to students and families who emerge healthier and less vulnerable.

Fund research, communicate best practices, and promote discussion that spur action and encourage collaboration. While foundations are well suited to support projects that conduct research, measure progress and communicate best practices on vulnerable children and families, little data and research exist. More research and lessons learned about the needs of our most vulnerable are warranted. This approach will take leadership and innovative thinking. Influencing policies to affect systemic barriers, incentivizing the adoption for change, knowledge sharing, and designing strategies to inform and influence individuals and communities to act, is well within our purview. Advancing the agenda of kinship and vulnerable families can be supported through the continued funding of research, creation of new evidence-based practices and guidelines, and the exploration of model approaches and by translating research to practice.

Invest directly, pull an entire family (generation) out of poverty and make it whole. This is not a new concept. Over a decade ago, Oprah Winfrey courageously tried to tackle poverty single-handedly by moving families out of public housing. The time is right to strengthen our efforts to help families thrive. Moving families and generations up and out of poverty represents a much-needed innovation, and an opportunity to rethink how philanthropy influences and sees change, as well as offers solutions to breaking the cycle. This should be the end goal. It's imperative that we create new positive realities and make dreams come true for children and families. It is not difficult to do, but it requires a retooling and rethinking of what it means to make children, families, and communities whole. This large-scale process could begin with a direct investment in these families, followed by ongoing monitoring and tracking of their results. For these families, once identified, the work would focus on removing the social barriers that keep them from being healthy and whole. It is then that they can begin to realize what it means to thrive. Nearly two decades ago, ASCI did just that for kinship foster families. When ASCI opened its doors in 1994, it ushered in an innovative and needed approach to providing kinship foster care in Pittsburgh and in Allegheny County. The agency remains the only provider in the country that specializes in child welfare-involved kinship families.

About the Sources: In addition to my own, the recommendations included in this section were culled from the selected reports, presentations, papers, and addresses from the following thought leaders: ***Yvonne C. Cook, MPM*** *(with special thanks to Christina L. Wilds, Ph.D. for her insight on this subject),* ***Joseph Crumbley****,* DSW; ***William C. Bell****,* Ph.D.; ***Marva Hammon***, ***Douglas W. Nelson***, and ***Bryan Samuels****.*

EIGHT
Work in Progress

My Recommendations

My life and work has been and continues to be shaped by my professional experiences and personal encounters as a child and young adult in the system. I have observed a system that didn't know quite how to respond to single fathers, one that stumbled over race and class issues, and one that saw birth-parent families as problems, not solutions. It has been my goal as an alumnus of care, a practitioner, agency CEO, and an emerging national voice of change to always push kinship forward, to respond to needs, and find solutions. Here, then, are my recommendations and offerings for the field.

With urgency, we must:

- Understand kinship in the context of race, culture, and community. Various racial groups practice kinship care from diverse socio-economic and historical contexts. For example, it is considered a cultural norm among some racial groups to care for their own without the intervention of the child welfare system. Taking such factors into consideration means that one size does not fit all. At the same time, we should guard against making kinship care look like a traditional foster care model. It is not. The uniqueness and strengths of kinship care should be celebrated by and taught across the child welfare system at large.

- Create an ongoing federal Commission on Kinship to not only address ongoing policy changes in the kinship care arena but to also keep those changes in the forefront of federal policy and practice.

- Engage in real conversations about racial bias and its role in decision-making, which should begin at the "front door" of the child welfare system. Child welfare systems routinely place its most inexperienced workers in Child Protective Services, often the entry point for families most traumatized when they come into the system. Although well intentioned, these child welfare staffers are often uniformed and untested about such critical issues as racial differences, structural bias, community engagement, and family system dynamics.

- Keep these important questions in mind, when working with children and families: What if it were me? How would I want to be treated? Child welfare can be fraught with bureaucracy and complexities. In 2008, Congress enacted laws for child welfare systems to address the need for sibling visits for children in the child welfare system. If we truly valued family and relationships, there wouldn't be a need, for example, to mandate sibling visits. Visits would be routine, a part of a practice model. In child welfare, policy makers tend to focus on some of the more complex issues (i.e., trauma), but at the same time, those in the field tend to exacerbate that trauma, and things like levels of stress on families, children, and caregivers. Much of this could be alleviated by keeping the "standard of oneself" at the forefront of the work being done in support of families and the decisions being made about the placement of children.

- Determine whether there is a need for more "community-based organizations of promise." People often respond better to those who can identify with their plight. Guided by this understanding, there is a need to shift greater funding to community-based organizations with promising practices to work with kinship families in their own communities across the country.

- Understand and know there is a need to create a research agenda that examines formal and informal kinship care. Because many children are being diverted from the system without supports, no one knows how they are faring at any level. It is incumbent upon those of us in child welfare to not only be concerned about those children entering kinship care, but also to ensure the well-being of those youngsters who are formally enrolled in the child welfare system as well as those who are diverted. In addition, the overall well-being of the family must be a consideration given the age of kinship caregivers. Other questions and concerns should include how kinship care can provide a protective factor to mitigate the adverse effect that occurs when child welfare removes children from their homes. Asking the right questions as well as understanding the trauma that comes with removal are things that can help inform kinship care policy and practice.

- Understand the interplay between poverty and risk and the placement of children, particularly children of color and how systemic child welfare policies and perceptions about poverty perpetuate placement removals. Such practices continue to be cause for concern as they culminate in the disparate treatment between kinship care placements and traditional care placements when such decisions are made.

- Allocate resources to county and state contracts with community-based organizations to support the move to evidence-based models. Most community-based organizations are focused on doing the work and improving their practices, but very few resources are earmarked for data collection so that these organizations can sufficiently determine what's working and shape best practices.

- Understand the intersection between serving systems for children and how those systems can improve outcomes for kinship children, as such systems are serving the same children and yet the outcomes remain poor (i.e., well-being, mental health, behavior and mental health, and more).

- Retool the system because it is not designed to work with young adults. The former system was focused on safety and protection and not on the life continuum. It was a model of protection that is there for those ages 0 to 18, but it needs to be redesigned to give young adults a voice in helping to design the plan for their life. At issue is that jurisdictions can work with young adults until 21, yet systems are struggling with how to do that. The paradigm for young adults needs to be one of empowerment, not simply protection. If we want to ensure that they can live independently, we need to give them the tools and the strategy to do so. This includes no longer calling them foster children. Responses are emerging, but the need for best practices are essential.

- Vigilantly pursue permanency for kinship children at the beginning of our engagement with them. The notion that children are with family and kinship bonds are intact is true. However, birth parents have a right to resume parental responsibility, relatives have a right to continue on with their lives, and most importantly, the children have a right to understand what the future will look for them. With that said, the family must be given the right to decide the permanency option that is best for them once the permanency goal of reunification has been ruled out. This decision must include the voice of the youth. Adoption and Subsidized Guardianship, as alternative permanency arrangements, must be discussed early in the life of the case. Aging out or APPLA is not to be considered a permanency option for kinship young people of promise.

- Consider that Interstate Compact agreements must use collaboration, technology and common sense when arranging relative care for children across state lines and other jurisdictions. Placement should always be guided by what's best for the child. States must work with court systems, school systems and other agencies to place children with approved caregivers in another state and make sure that school and health records, services and resources be available in a timely manner so that children and families can thrive.

- Identify, consider, and employ effective child welfare leaders. These leaders and professionals should be:

  ➤ Selfless individuals who understand that they are in the child welfare field to be servant leaders, not those who view their positions solely as a career. Our work is a ministry and a high calling.

  ➤ Committed and have a heart for the work; not see the position as a stepping stone to yet another political position. Children and families deserve the best leaders in child welfare. Leaders who want to make child welfare their career should be in these stressful and difficult positions, not someone just passing by.

- Collaborative and must have an ego that is healthy and intact. Child Welfare does not belong to one organization, rather it belongs to multiple systems coming together as one on behalf of the children that we jointly serve; therefore, a healthy spirit of collaboration is a must.

- Innovative. If the work we perform is business as usual, we do children an injustice and perpetuate problems.

- Knowledgeable of how the system works at all levels of government no matter if county administered or state.

- An awesome leader of people. Child welfare professionals are often underpaid and labor hard and long. That is why child welfare leaders need to be progressive in creating healthy environments that encourage and support the well-being of staff so that they can thrive. Our children and families need the support of staff who are healthy, satisfied, and able to bring their best to helping them succeed.

- Fiscally and technologically proficient or at least knowledgeable of the power of data and fiscal management. These systems make a difference in the work that child welfare does on a daily basis.

- Culturally aware, engaging, relevant, and viable. These characteristics are essential for staff working in a community-based organization and setting such as ASCI. They must be able to relate on all these levels to clients and to other staff members who come from the community that we serve.

- Willing to recognize the value and expertise that clients represent. Clients should have the largest voice on committees and should be employed by the child welfare serving systems, as they can be the biggest advocates for systems change and family/ client engagement.

Reflections on the Profession

In the 20 years since I started working with kin, it is clear that this new practice model in child welfare is here to stay, but it remains in constant change and flux. With emerging research, kinship care is becoming more widely known and accepted, but we have long understood the emotional benefits that strong and healthy families have on children. My notion of approaching families with dignity, respect, conviction, and honesty comes from the heart and a place of "truth."

Families need to understand both the challenges and opportunities before them. They, too, need to understand how these systems work. More important, the child welfare system needs to respect and understand the value that kin bring to the process of caring for children and ensuring their safety. In many ways, kinship care has "saved" the child welfare system both financially and as a resource. With a dwindling number of traditional foster care providers, agency officials have sought out kin to care for their own. Child welfare systems in many jurisdictions are benefiting from kinship care. But there are still other jurisdictions where kinship care remains a challenge and policies of the past still exclude a group of potential caregivers.

There will always be a need for some level of traditional foster care and group home placements, however, with child welfare leaders becoming more intentional regarding the need to address the system from an early intervention/prevention lens, more children will be able to be serviced in their own homes. Attention will need to be given to how to create stronger communities where children and families live, work, and play. National foundations are exploring how they leverage more resources for communities. This is where change can happen. The policy level has its place, as does the practice level; I would submit that real change in communities happens on the ground with the people who live in those communities. Building a collective impact where the voices of community members are heard and listened to in policy, practice, and funding will be key to community success and kinship care.

More work must be done to build community-based organizations of promise. There are many well-intentioned community leaders who have the "right answer for the wrong problem." We must go back to where advocacy and education starts: "at the grassroots level." We must stop believing that the academics, politicians, educators, administrators, law enforcements have all the answers. We must know that real answers are ever-present in those who struggle with the challenges every day. It is imperative that we change the paradigm and become the listeners and allow the folks on the ground to become the doers. They might surprise those of us in child welfare if we become bold enough to give new and emerging community-based organizations of promise a chance to serve their own without the shadow of skepticism.

I have the great privilege and honor to serve on various boards throughout the country. Most of my work is at the national level; however, I stay grounded in the work of A Second Chance, Inc. Anyone who encounters me knows that I am an advocate of kinship care. I have found myself shifting the conversation about why kinship care works, to showing the results so that one can examine the results; I do this, rather than trying to convince the unconvinced that kinship care can work if policies and practices support this placement and family option. It is a moral imperative that I continue to seek to improve on how we collect data to, become an evidence-based program, one that will validate the promise of the practice that we test out each day. I continue to serve as a voice not only in the foundations that I am associated with, but to members of Congress, and other political think tanks. I lend my voice to help shape policy and practice at the national, state, and local levels wherever and whenever I can.

The practice of kinship care in America is much better off than it was almost two decades ago when I founded A Second Chance, Inc. We have seen national, state, and local policy and practice changes that support kinship. In fact, some jurisdictions like Pennsylvania exceed the standards set in the Child and Family Services Review baseline set by the federal government for kinship care. Yet, others pale in comparison. These jurisdictions that are still grappling with the "apple doesn't fall far from the tree" syndrome; but what they need to understand is that the "apple has fallen and has now become apple juice, which for the children is nutritious and deemed a good source of daily sustenance." Children want to be with family. In fact, we know that in child welfare, when children reach the age of majority, even when adopted, they seek to understand "who is family." The family bond is strong and child welfare jurisdictions that still have the "rescue mentality" need to move from this failed practice model and join in with those that have seen their system transform as a result of their openness to include kin in the conversation and decision-making process. Until this occurs, some families and children in this country will continue to fall victim to failed policies and practices that have never worked and are not very family friendly. Real change will only begin with a personal inventory, as a leader must examine ones biases and unwillingness to move forward.

Moreover, there is much that can be learned by listening to today's foster care youth. Children in care today are still grappling with a system where bureaucratic structures inhibit and impede real change. Young adults are now informing legislatures, social workers, and administrators on the challenges of foster care. However, universities and schools of social work have not used these same young people to come and educate their budding potential child welfare professionals. I have heard of individual instructors using alumni of care to come in to talk to their students from time-to-time, but every school of social work should mandate that those students, who are receiving the federal educational program dollars for budding child welfare professionals, be required to receive one-on-one training with an alumni and a current child welfare mentor. These young students come out college believing that they are purposed to save the world and in the wake of saving the world, they unintentionally destroy families.

In addition, lead administrators in child welfare organizations need to have a strategic partner or mentor who can help them negotiate the system and ensure their effectiveness. The average tenure of a child welfare administrator is 18 months. This is entirely too much turnover as each administrator brings in new ideas and creates inconsistency in the work place and services to children. We must examine new ways to recruit leaders and particularly leaders of color. There are very few leaders of color in top-tiered leadership positions. While the vast majority of the children in the system are Black and brown children, the child welfare leaders do not reflect the same. While some foundations are supporting the emerging leaders in child welfare work, more must be done to work with organizations to help recruit and train Black and brown administrators who would be child welfare leaders.

Every child touched by the child welfare system has a right to a kinship care experience!

RESOURCES

The following is a list of selected national and regional organizations and resources for those concerned about issues of kinship care, foster care, adoption, and overall child welfare and safety. These and other entries will also be included on the book's website

ADOPTION

Adoption Assistance for Children Adopted from Foster Care

Adoption Assistance's fact sheet describes how adoption assistance, in the form of subsidies, may help make adoption possible for families considering adopting a child from foster care.
Child Welfare Information Gateway | Children's Bureau/ACYF
1250 Maryland Ave., SW, 8th Fl. | Washington, DC 20024 | (800) 394-3366
www.childwelfare.gov/pubs/f_subsid.cfm
www.wednesdayschild.adopt.org/

Center for Adoption Support and Education

Post-adoption counseling and educational services to families, educators, child welfare staff, and mental health providers in Maryland, Northern Virginia, and Washington, DC
4000 Blackburn Ln., Ste. 260 | Burtonsville, MD 20866 | (301) 476-8525
www.adoptionsupport.org/

The Congressional Coalition on Adoption Institute
Works to raise awareness about the needs of children without families. Its programs bring together policymakers and individuals with direct foster care or adoption experience.
311 Massachusetts Ave., NE | Washington, DC 20002 | (202) 544-8500
www.ccainstitute.org/

Council on Foster Care, Adoption, & Kinship Care, The American Academy of Pediatrics
Dedicated to improving the health and well-being of children and youth in foster care, kinship care, and those who have been adopted.
National Headquarters | 141 Northwest Point Blvd. | Elk Grove Village, IL 60007-1098
(800) 433-9016 | www.aap.org/sections/adoption/index.html

The Evan B. Donaldson Adoption Institute
A national not-for-profit devoted to improving adoption policy and practice.
525 Broadway, 6th Fl. | New York, NY 10012 | (212) 925-4089
www.adoptioninstitute.org/whowe/contact.html

CHILD ADVOCACY

The Center for Children & Youth Justice
Works to shape better lives for youth involved in Washington State's foster care and juvenile justice systems.
615 Second Ave., Ste. 275 | Seattle, WA 98104 | (206) 696-7503 | www.ccyj.org/

Child Welfare Information Gateway
A service of the Children's Bureau, promotes safety, permanency, and well-being.
(800) 394-3366 | www.childwelfare.gov/outofhome/kinship/

Children First Advocacy
A family organization offering support and information about the interaction with governmental agencies related to children in the state of Massachusetts.
(978) 798-1368 | www.childrenfirstadvocacy.com

Children & Youth Advocacy Clinic, University of Washington School of Law

A multidisciplinary program of the schools of law, social work and medicine focusing on child advocacy and holistic legal programs for children and youth.

Child and Youth Advocacy Clinic | University of Washington School of Law

William H. Gates Hall, Ste. 265 | PO Box 85110 | Seattle, WA 98145-1110

(206) 543-4550

Children's Law Center

Advocates for a child from the day they are removed from their parent's home until they are safely and permanently reunited with her birth parents, living permanently with relatives or in new adoptive family.

616 H St., NW, Ste. 300 | Washington, DC 20001 | (202) 467-4900

www.childrenslawcenter.org

Children's Rights

A national advocacy group, fights for the nation's abused and neglected children.

(888) 283-2210 | www.childrensrights.org

Lawyers for Children

Provides critically needed, top-quality legal representation and social work services children in foster care.

110 Lafayette St. | New York, NY 10013 | (800) 244-2540

www.lawyersforchildren.org

Legal Advocates for Children & Youth

Advances the legal rights of children and youth, empowering them to lead healthy and productive lives.

Legal Advocates for Children & Youth at the Law Foundation of Silicon Valley

152 North Third St., 3rd Fl. | San Jose, CA 95112 | (408) 293-4790

www.lawfoundation.org/lacy.asp

National Youth Advocate Program

Provides community-based services and support to children, youth and families.

1801 Watermark Dr., Ste. 200 | Columbus, OH 43215| (888) 202-2965 www.nyap.org

The Child Welfare Initiative
Implements programs and practices that produce measurable improvements in the lives of children and families involved in child welfare systems.
5757 Wilshire Blvd., Ste. 448 | Los Angeles, CA 90036 | (323) 549-3400 | www.cwinitiative.org/

The Tennessee Commission on Children and Youth
An independent agency, advocates for improving the quality of life for children and families.
610 Mainstream Dr. | Nashville, TN 37243-0800 | (615) 741-2633 | www.tn.gov/tccy/

CHILD WELFARE & EDUCATION

BACW – Black Administrators in Child Welfare, Inc.
An advocacy, membership, research, training and technical assistance organization. to respond to the need for culturally appropriate services to the overrepresented African American children and families, and to provide a support network for individuals serving as executives managing child welfare and other human service agencies.
7625 Wisconsin Ave. Ste. 300 | Bethesda, MD 20814 | (240) 482-4968
www.blackadministrators.org

Child Trends Data Bank
A one-stop source for over 100 key indicators of child and youth well-being.
(240) 223-9200 | www.childtrends.org/databank/

National Association for the Education of Young Children
A membership group for those working with and on behalf of children from birth - 8.
1509 16th Street NW | Washington, DC 20036 | (202) 232-8777 | www.naeyc.org

National Black Child Development Institute
Dedicated exclusively to the success and well-being of Black children.
1313 L St., NW, Ste. 110 | Washington, DC 20005-4110 | (800)556-2234 | www.nbcdi.org

Portal for Federal Child Welfare Resources
childwelfare.gov/

FOSTER AND ADOPTED YOUTH: EDUCATIONAL OPPORTUNITIES (ONLINE)

ASPIRE (Access to Student assistance Programs in Reach of Everyone)
Oregon's official mentoring program on post high school education and training.
www.oregonstudentaid.gov/aspire.aspx

College Goal Oregon
Supports Oregon college-bound students and their families with the financial aid application process.
www.collegegoaloregon.org/faqs.html

College Possible
Resources for Oregon residents thinking of returning to college or enrolling for the first time.
www.collegepossible.org/portland

DREAM Scholarship for Foster Youth
A scholarship for youth who were in a child welfare system, who were adopted between the ages of 14 ½ and 16, did not receive Chafee funds before age 21, or are over the age of 23.
www.collegexpress.com/scholarships/dream-scholarship-for-foster-youth/2017089/

Chafee Education and Training Grant
A grant for youth who were in foster care (DHS or one of the federally recognized tribes) and dismissed from care at age 16 or older with 180 days of foster care placement services.
www.oregonstudentaid.gov/chafeeetv.aspx

Federal Pell Grant
Foster youth are eligible for this grant if their status is "independent."
www.fafsa.ed.gov

Federal Supplemental Educational Opportunity Grant (FSEOG)
Foster youth are eligible for this grant as they have "exceptional financial need."
www.fafsa.ed.gov

Fostering a Future
Scholarships benefits youth adopted from foster care after age 13.
www.childrensactionnetwork.org/scholarship.htm

Free Application for Federal Student Aid (FAFSA)
The document used by every college and university to determine eligibility for federal aid.
www.fafsa.ed.gov/

Get College Funds
Oregon's official website for student financial aid, grants, and scholarship opportunities.
www.getcollegefunds.org/

Guardian Scholars Program
Helps former foster youth gain a university, community college or trade school education. There are now partner schools throughout California and in several other states.
www.orangewoodfoundation.org/programs_scholars.asp

National Foster Parent Association Scholarships
A website offering lists of scholarships available at the University of Phoenix.
www.nfpaonline.org/youthscholarship

National Council on Black American Affairs: The National Council on Black American
Promotes academic success through its Foster Youth Alumni Success Initiative.
www.ncbaa-national.org/

Orphan Foundation of America Scholarship Program
America's College Fund for Foster Youth - The foundation offers scholarships, including the Casey Family Scholarships.
www.fc2success.org/programs/scholarships-and-grants/

Oregon Opportunity Grant
An education grant for foster youth in Oregon with financial need.
www.getcollegefunds.org/ong.html

Oregon Student Assistance Commission
Listing of scholarships available through the Oregon Student Assistance Commission.
www.oregonstudentaid.gov/

Point Foundation – The National LGBTQ Scholarship Fund
Empowers promising LGBTQ students to achieve their full academic and leadership potential. The foundation also offers mentorships.
www.pointfoundation.org

FOSTER CARE

Children First Advocacy
Support and information about governmental agencies related to children in the state of MA .
(978) 798-1368 | www.childrenfirstadvocacy.com

Child Welfare Information Gateway
A service of the Children's Bureau, promotes safety, permanency, and well-being.
(800) 394-3366 | www.childwelfare.gov/outofhome/kinship/

Foundation for Foster Children
Enriches the lives of children placed in foster care due to abuse and/or neglect.
2265 Lee Rd., Ste. 203 | Winter Park, FL 32789 | (407) 422-4615
www.foundationforfosterchildren.org

Foster Care & Adoptive Community
Online resource for training, workshops, and materials for caregivers, families, and professionals.
http://www.fosterparents.com/

Foster Care Alumni of America
The term "alumni" describes those who have been in foster care during their childhood/youth. Its mission is to connect the alumni community, transform foster care policy and practice, and ensure opportunity for people in and from foster care.
(888) ALUMNI-0 | www.fostercarealumni.org/home.htm

Foster Care Central
An online resource for youth in foster care, families, and professional.
www.fostercarecentral.org

Foster Parent Advocacy Foundation, Inc.
Assists foster parents and children in foster care through advocacy, education, and workshops.
(888) 692-9471 | www.fpafoundation.org/index.html

FosterParentCollege.com
Interactive online courses for foster, adoptive, and kinship parents.
Northwest Media, Inc. | 326 West 12th Ave. | Eugene, OR 97401 | (800) 777-6636
www.fosterparentcollege.com

Living Advantage, Inc.
Works to reduce the disconnect between services to foster care and homeless youth.
7095 Hollywood Blvd., #726 | Hollywood, CA 90028 | (323) 731-6471
www.livingadvantageinc.org

National Resource Center for Permanency and Family Connections
Offers training, technical assistance, and information services to help strengthen the capacity of state, local Tribal, and other publicly administered or supported child welfare agencies.
2810 Third Ave., 7th Fl., | New York, NY 10035 | (212) 396-7640 | www.nrcpfc.org

Pennsylvania State Resource Family Association
The Association serves adoptive, kinship, and foster families.
PO Box 60216 | Harrisburg, PA 17106 | (800) 951-5151 | www.psrfa.org/

SHIELDS for Families
Award-winning programs and services that address the spectrum of human needs.
PO Box 59129 | Los Angeles, CA 90059 | (800) 735-2922 | www.shieldsforfamilies.org

The Bazelon Center for Mental Health Law
Protects and advance the rights of adults and children who have mental disabilities.
1101 15th St., NW, Ste. 1212 | Washington, DC 20005 | (202) 467.5730 | www.bazelon.org

United Friends of the Children
Offers housing and education programs that support foster youth in becoming successful adults.
1055 Wilshire Blvd., Ste. 1955 | Los Angeles, CA 90017 | (213) 580-1850 | www.unitedfriends.org

GRANDPARENTS AND FAMILIES

A Second Chance, Inc.
Established by this book's author, in 1994. The agency p=rovides a safe, secure, and nurturing environment for children who are being cared for by relatives or close family friends.
Corporate Office | 8350 Frankstown Ave. | Pittsburgh, PA 15221 | (412) 342-0600
Philadelphia Regional Office | 1341 N. Delaware Ave., Ste. 101 | Philadelphia, PA 19125
(215) 564-0790 | www.asecondchance-kinship.com/home.html

Generations United
Offers resources for improving the lives of children, youth and older adults through intergenerational collaboration, public policies, and programs.
1331 H St. NW, Ste. 900 | Washington, DC 20005 | (202) 289-3979 | www.gu.org/

Generations United National Center on Grandfamilies
Enact policies and promote programs to help kinship caregivers address their specific needs and challenges.
www.gu.org/OURWORK/Grandfamilies.aspx

GrandFacts from AARP: State Facts for Grandparents and other Relatives Raising Children
Online resource offers state fact sheets on benefits eligibility, budgeting, foster care information, and other resources for kinship families.
www.aarp.org/relationships/friends-family/grandfacts-sheets/

Grandfamilies of America
A national organization devoted to supporting kinship caregivers.
6525 Fish Hatchery Rd. | Thurmont, MD 21788 | (301) 358-3911 |
www.grandfamiliesofamerica.com/

Grandfamilies State Law and Policy Research Center
A national legal resource supporting Grandfamilies within and outside the child welfare system.
www.grandfamilies.org

GrandsPlace: For Grandparents and Special Others Parenting Children
A Fact Sheet on Kinship Care Resources in Pennsylvania
www.grandsplace.org/gp8/pa.html

National Family Preservation Network
A voice for the preservation of families through preservation and reunification services.
3771 North 1400 East | Buhl, ID 83316 | (888) 498-9047 | www.nfpn.org/

National Fatherhood Initiative
Works to increase the proportion of children growing up with involved and committed fathers.
20410 Observation Dr., Ste. 107 | Germantown, MD 20876 | (301) 948-0599
www.fatherhood.org

National Foster Parent Association
A champion and resource for those families that open their homes to children in out-of-home placements.
2021 E. Hennepin Ave., #320 | Minneapolis, MN 55413-1769 | (800) 557-5238
www.nfpaonline.org/

National Indian Child Welfare Association
The only Native American organization in the US focused specifically on issues of child abuse and neglect and tribal capacity to prevent and respond effectively to these problems. .
5100 SW Macadam Ave., Ste. 300 | Portland, OR 97239 | www.nicwa.org

Juvenile Justice & Racial Disparities in Juvenile Justice Systems
Campaign for Youth Justice
Dedicated to ending the practice of trying, sentencing, and incarcerating youth under 18 in the adult criminal justice system.
1012 14th St., NW, Ste. 610 | Washington, DC 20005 | (202) 558-3580
www.campaignforyouthjustice.org

The National Juvenile Justice Network
Promotes the reform of America's critically flawed juvenile justice system at every level.
1319 F St., NW, Ste. 402 | Washington, DC 20004 | (202) 467-0864 | www.njjn.org/

PFLAG National - Parents, Friends and Family of Lesbians and Gays
The largest US organization for parents, families, friends, and straight allies united with people who are lesbian, gay, bisexual, and transgender.
1828 L St., NW Ste. 660 | Washington, DC 20036 | (202) 467-8180 | www.pflag.org

REPORT: "No Place for Kids: The Case for Reducing Juvenile Incarceration."
The report from The Annie E. Casey Foundation offers an array of juvenile crime statistics and other evidence to demonstrate that incarcerating kids doesn't work.
www.aecf.org/OurWork/JuvenileJustice/~/media/Pubs/Topics/Juvenile%20Justice/Detention%20Reform/NoPlaceForKids/JJ_NoPlaceForKids_Full.pdf

REPORT/DATA: "Reducing Youth Incarceration in the United States" Data Snap Shot Kids Count by Annie E. Casey Foundation (February 2013)
The report found that the number of incarcerated youth in the US fell more than 40 percent from 1995 to 2010, with no decline in public safety.
www.aecf.org/~/media/Pubs/Initiatives/KIDS%20COUNT/R/ReducingYouthIncarcerationSnapshot/DataSnapshotYouthIncarceration.pdf

The W. Haywood Burns Institute for Juvenile Justice Fairness & Equity
Helps protect and improve the lives of youth of color and poor youth by promoting and ensuring fairness and equity in youth-serving systems.
180 Howard St., Ste. 320 | San Francisco, CA 94105 | (415) 321-4100 | www.burnsinstitute.org

KINSHIP FOSTER CARE

Allegheny County Department of Human Services
Consolidates the provision of human services across Allegheny County in Pennsylvania and refers and/or provides a range of prevention and reunification services to families.
www.alleghenycounty.us/DHS/index.aspx

Center for the Advanced Studies in Child Welfare · University of Minnesota
Brings together the county, tribal, state and community social services to improve the lives of children and families involved with public child welfare.
205 Peters Hall | 1404 Gortner Ave. | Saint Paul, MN 55108 | (800) 779-8636
blog.lib.umn.edu/cascw/policy/foster-care-policy/

Child Welfare League of America
A coalition of private and public agencies serving vulnerable children and families.
2345 Crystal Dr., Ste. 250 | Arlington, VA 22002 | www.cwla.org

Children's Defense Fund
Advocates nationwide on behalf of children to ensure they are always a priority.
25 E St. NW | Washington, DC 20001 | (800) CDF-1200 | www.childrensdefense.org

Florida Kinship Center, University of South Florida School of Social Work
Serves kinship care families living in Florida.
The University of South Florida, School of Social Work | 4202 East Fowler Ave., MGY 132
Tampa, FL 33620 | (800) 640-6444 | www.cas.usf.edu/~krisman/

Kinship Caregiver Coalition
Health and social services agencies that work on issues and problems facing kinship caregivers.
1 Elizabeth Pl., | West Medical Plaza, Ste. 110 | Dayton, OH 45417 | (937) 775-8245
www.med.wright.edu/chc/kinship/

Kinship Care Services: Los Angeles County Department of Children and Family Services
Provides information, resources, services and support to relative caregivers and their children to enhance the family unit, promote permanency, safety, and reduce reliance on detentions.
Kinship Support Division | 9834 Norwalk Blvd. | Santa Fe Springs, CA 90670
(323) 298-3515 | http://dcfs.co.la.ca.us/kinshippublic/default.html

Kinship Care Resource Center at Michigan State University
A central location where relative caregivers for children and professionals can receive assistance.
254 Baker Hall | East Lansing, MI 48824 | (800) 535-1218 | www.kinship.msu.edu/

National Resource Center for Permanency and Family Connections at Hunter College, School of Social Work
Provides training, technical assistance, and information services to strengthen the capacity of state, local, Tribal and other publicly administered or supported child welfare agencies.
www.hunter.cuny.edu/socwork/nrcfcpp/info_services/kinship-relative-care.html

State Child Welfare Database
Provides state-by-state policy information on a range of child welfare topics.
www.childwelfarepolicy.org/

State of New Jersey Parent Link: The Early Childhood, Parenting and Professional Resource Center
Improves the accessibility, coordination and delivery of information and services to parents
www.nj.gov/njparentlink/

The Urban Institute
The institute gathers data, conducts research, evaluates programs, offers technical assistance oversees, and educates on social and economic issues that foster sound public policy and effective government.
2100 M St., NW | Washington, DC 20037 | (202) 833-7200 | www.urban.org/

LEGISLATION/POLICY

National Resource Center for Permanency and Family Connections
Maintains a website on the Fostering Connections to Success and Increasing Adoptions Act of 2008, including resources on kinship/guardianship.
www.nrcpfc.org/fostering_connections/kinship_guardianship.html

Placement of Children with Relatives (A Report)
Summarizes state statutes regarding relatives for placement or guardianship, requirements for placement, relatives who may adopt, and the requirements for adoption by relatives. (July 2010)
www.childwelfare.gov/systemwide/laws_policies/statutes/placement.cfm

Relative Foster Care Licensing Waivers in the States: Policies and Possibilities
An overview of Title IV-E and licensing for relatives (September 2010)
www.clasp.org/admin/site/publications/files/Relative-foster-care-licensing-waivers-in-the-states101810.pdf

REPORT: State Kinship Care Policies for Children that Come to the Attention of Child Welfare Agencies – Findings from the 2007 Casey Kinship Foster Care Policy Survey
Interviews with state child welfare agencies about their kinship care practices.
www.hunter.cuny.edu/socwork/nrcfcpp/info_services/kinship-relative-care.html

REPORT: Stepping Up for Kids: What Government and Communities Should Do to Support Kinship Families (2012)
Explores the increased number of children living with extended family and close friends.
www.aecf.org/KnowledgeCenter/Publications.aspx?pubguid=%7b642BF3F2-9A85-4C6B-83C8-A30F5D928E4D%7d

MEDIA

Equal Voice
Published by the Marguerite Casey Foundation - reports on the lives of families living in poverty in the US..
www.equalvoiceforfamilies.org/

Journalism Center on Children & Families
An online resource that serves as a link to experts, journalists, data and original content on critical topics, including child and family.
Room 1100, Knight Hall | University of Maryland | College Park, MD 20742
(301) 405-8808 | www.journalismcenter.org/

Youth Today
Nationally distributed newspaper for professionals in the youth service field.
www.youthtoday.org

STRESS AND TRAUMA

Center for Pediatric Traumatic Stress
This multidisciplinary center addresses medical trauma in the lives of children and families.
34th Street and Civic Center Blvd. | Philadelphia, PA 19104 | (267) 426-5205
www.chop.edu/professionals/pediatric-traumatic-stress/home.html

Pittsburgh Action Against Rape
The only organization in Allegheny County dedicated exclusively to victims of sexual violence.
81 South 19th St. | Pittsburgh, PA 15203 | (866) END-RAPE | www.paar.net/

UNIVERSITY RESOURCES, RESEARCH, EDUCATION, AND TRAINING

Child Welfare Training Centre, California State University, Long Beach
Trains social workers from the LA County Department of Children and Family Services.
6300 State University Dr., Ste. 180 | Long Beach, CA 90815 | (562) 985-7383
www.csulb.edu/colleges/chhs/departments/social-work/child-welfare/

The Center for Advanced Studies in Child Welfare at The University of Minnesota
The Center brings the University together with county, tribal, state and community social services in a partnership dedicated to improving the lives of children and families involved with public child welfare.
Center for Advanced Studies in Child Welfare, | University of Minnesota | 205 Peters Hall
1404 Gortner Ave., | Saint Paul, MN 55108 | (800) 779-8636
www.cehd.umn.edu/ssw/cascw/

University of Chicago, Chapin Hall: Policy and Research
A research and policy center focused on improving the well-being of children and youth, families, and their communities.
University of Chicago | Chapin Hall | 1313 East 60th St. | Chicago, IL 60637
(773) 753-5900 | www.chapinhall.org/about

University of Houston: Graduate College of Social Work

A member of the Title IV-E Child Welfare Agency/ University Partnerships that help prepare undergraduate and graduate students for work in public child welfare and provides high quality in-service training to practitioners in public child welfare agencies.

www.sw.uh.edu/community/cwep/title-iv-e/index.php | (713) 743-2255

University of Pittsburgh: Pennsylvania Child Welfare Resource Center

A collaborative of the University of Pittsburgh, School of Social Work, the Pennsylvania Department of Public Welfare, and the Pennsylvania Children and Youth Administrators. It trains direct service workers, supervisors, administrators, and foster parents in providing social services to abused and neglected children and their families.

403 E. Winding Hill Rd. | Mechanicsburg, PA 17055 | (717) 795-9048 | www.pacwcbt.pitt.edu/

The University of Vermont, College of Education and Social Services: The Vermont Child Welfare Training Partnership

Training and professional development to strengthen the child welfare system in Vermont.

College of Education and Social Services | 528 Waterman Building | Burlington, VT 05405 (802) 656-3131 | www.uvm.edu/~socwork/vcwp/

PHILANTHROPIES AND CHILD WELFARE

Administrative Office of the Courts (California)

The staff agency of the Judicial Council, the policy-making body for the state court system.

www.courts.ca.gov

The American Legion Child Welfare Foundation

Provides nonprofits with a means to educate the public about the needs of children.

PO Box 1055, Indianapolis, IN 46206 | (317) 630-1202 | www.cwf-inc.org/

Annie E. Casey Foundation

Works to build better futures for disadvantaged children and their families by fostering better public policies, human service reforms, and community supports.

701 St. Paul St. | Baltimore, MD 21202 | (410) 547-6600 | www.aecf.org

Anschutz Family Foundation
Supports Colorado nonprofit organizations that assist people in helping themselves while nurturing and preserving their self-respect.
555 17th St., Ste. 2400 | Denver, CO 80202 | (303) 293-2338
www.anschutzfamilyfoundation.org

Association of Black Foundation Executives
Established in 1971, this independent membership orrganization has a mission to promote effective and responsive philanthropy in Black communities.
333 Seventh Ave., 14th Floor | New York, NY 10001 | (646) 230-0306
www.abfe.org

Arizona Community Foundation
The foundation works to improve the quality of life by promoting and facilitating effective philanthropy.
2201 E. Camelback Rd., Ste. 405B | Phoenix, AZ 85016 | (800) 222-8221
www.azfoundation.org/

Arizona Grantmakers Forum
A regional forum that provides educational resources, research and networking opportunities for grantmakers.
2201 E. Camelback Rd., Ste. 405B | Phoenix, AZ 85016 | (602) 977-2756
www.arizonagrantmakersforum.org

Bezos Family Foundation
Supports rigorous, inspired-learning environments for young people, from birth through high school, to put their education into action.
(206) 275-2048 | www.bezosfamilyfoundation.org/

Bill & Melinda Gates Foundation
Guided by the belief that every life has equal value, the Gates Foundation aspires to help all people lead healthy, productive lives.
500 Fifth Ave. North | Seattle, WA 98102 | (206) 709-3100
www.gatesfoundation.org/

Black Male Donor Collaborative

A funding initiative seeking to reduce the academic achievement gap and raise the academic performance, graduation rates and college readiness of Black males in New York City.

333 Seventh Ave., 14th Fl. | New York, NY 10001 | (646) 230-0306

www.abfe.org/FCDOCS%5CSchott_Foundation_Funder_Profile.html

Blue Cross and Blue Shield of Florida Foundation

A philanthropic affiliate of Blue Cross and Blue Shield of Florida. It works to improve the health and well-being of Floridians and their communities and accomplishes grant-making.

4800 Deerwood Campus Parkway, DCC3-4 | Jacksonville, FL 32246

(800) 477-3736, ext. 63215

Blue Ridge Foundation

Connects people living in high poverty communities to the opportunities, resources, and support they need to fulfill their potential.

150 Court St., 2nd Fl. | Brooklyn, NY 11201 | (718) 923-1400

www.brfny.org/

Busch Foundation

Acatalyst for sustainable solutions to public problems and vitality in communities across the states of Minnesota, N. Dakota, S. Dakota and the 23 Native nations that share the same geography.

332 Minnesota St., Ste. East-900 | St. Paul, Minnesota 55101 | (651) 227-0891

www.bushfoundation.org/

California Child Welfare Co-Investment Partnership

A collaborative group working to improve the lives of children and families who are in or are at risk of entering the state's child welfare system.

(415) 616-3930 | www.co-invest.org

California Department of Social Services

The mission of the department is to serve, aid, and protect needy and vulnerable children and adults.

(877) 846-1602 | www.childsworld.ca.gov

The California Endowment

A private, statewide health foundation, expands access to affordable, quality health care to underserved communities.

1000 N. Alameda St. | Los Angeles, CA 90012 | (800) 449-4149 | www.calendow.org/

Casey Family Programs

The nation's largest operating foundation, is focused entirely on foster care and improving the child welfare system in the United States.

2001 Eighth Ave., Ste. 2700 | Seattle, WA 98121 | (206) 282-7300 | www.casey.org/

Marguerite Casey Foundation

Since 2001, has strategically focused its grant-making – and non-grant-making work – on nurturing a movement of families advocating in their own behalf for change.

1425 4th Ave, Ste. 900 | Seattle, WA 98101 | (206) 691-3134 | www.caseygrants.org/

Harold K.L. Castle Foundation

A mission of closing the achievement gap in public education for all of Hawaii's children.

1197 Auloa Rd. | Kailua, HI 96734 | (808) 263-7073 | www.castlefoundation.org/index.htm

Center for Children & Youth Justice

A private nonprofit dedicated to reforming the state's juvenile justice and child welfare systems.

615 Second Ave., Ste. 275 | Seattle, WA 98104 | (206)696-7503 | www.ccyj.org

Charles Stewart Mott Foundation

A private philanthropy committed to supporting projects that promote a just, equitable and sustainable society.

Mott Foundation Building, | 503 S. Saginaw St., Ste. 1200, | Flint, Michigan 48502-1851 (810) 238-5651 | www.mott.org/

Clark Foundation

Supports primarily local nonprofits and programs in the fields of education, human services, employment, and children/youth services, focused on economically disadvantaged youth.

135 East 64th Street | New York, NY 10065 | (212) 288-8900 | www.rsclark.org/index.php

The Edna McConnell Clark Foundation
The Foundation seeks to transform the life trajectories of America's most vulnerable and economically disadvantaged youth.
415 Madison Ave., 10th Floor | New York, NY 10017 | (212) 551-9100 | www.emcf.org/

Colorado Association of Funders
A nonprofit organization for private foundations, community foundations, family foundations, corporate funders, federated funds and workplace giving programs.
600 S. Cherry St., Ste. 1200 | Denver, CO 80246-1712 | (303) 398-7404
www.coloradofunders.org

Colorado State University
Among the nation's leading research universities.
www.sc.colostate.edu | (970) 491-6444

Colorado Trust
A grant-making foundation dedicated to achieving access to health for all Coloradans.
1600 Sherman St. | Denver, Colorado 80203-1604 | (888) 847-9140 | www.coloradotrust.org/

The Community Foundation (Boulder County)
Exists to improve the quality of life in Boulder County and to build a culture of giving.
1123 Spruce St. | Boulder, CO 80302 | (877) 744-7239 | www.commfound.org

The Communications Network
Resources, guidance and leadership to advance the practice of communications in philanthropy.
1717 North Naper Blvd., Ste. 102 | Naperville, IL 60563 | www.comnetwork.org/

Community Corrections Improvement Foundation
Builds solutions for safer communities in the state of Iowa.
951 29th Ave. SW | Cedar Rapids, IA 52404 | (319) 730-1173 | www.bezosfamilyfoundation.org

Community Foundation of Greater Atlanta
Works to strengthen the region's nonprofits.
50 Hurt Plaza, Ste. 449 | Atlanta, GA 30303 | (404) 688-5525 | www.cfgreateratlanta.org/

Community Foundation of Greater Birmingham

More than 450 charitable funds established by individuals, families and businesses.

2100 First Ave. North, Ste. 700 | Birmingham AL 35203-4223 | (205) 327-3800

www.foundationbirmingham.org/

Community Foundation of South Alabama

Works to improve the quality of life in South Alabama by assisting individuals, families, corporations and nonprofit organizations with charitable giving.

PO Box 990 | Mobile, AL 36601-0990 | (251) 438-5591 | www.communityendowment.org/

Community Foundation of Southeast Michigan

Exists in perpetuity to enhance the quality of life of the citizens in southeast Michigan.

333 West Fort St., Ste. 2010 | Detroit, MI 48226-3134 | (313) 961-6675 | www.cfsem.org/

Community Foundation of Texas

Partners with local individuals, families and businesses to raise the region's quality of life.

5500 Caruth Haven Ln. | Dallas, TX 75225-8146 | (214) 750-4222 | www.cftexas.org

The Compound Foundation

Founded by Shaffer "NE-YO" Smith and his business partner Reynell "Tango" Hay, works to enhance the well-being of youth growing up in foster care and group homes.

Khalilah Abdul-Baqi | Executive Director

www.compoundfoundation.org/

Conference of Southwest Foundations

Provides a forum for the exchange of ideas, experiences, and expertise among grant makers.

624 N. Good-Latimer Expressway., Ste. 100 | Dallas, TX 75204 | (214) 740-178

www.c-s-f.org

The Conrad N. Hilton Foundation

The Foundation provides funds for non-profits working to improve the lives of disadvantaged and vulnerable people.

30440 Agoura Rd. | Agoura Hills, CA 91301 | (818) 851-3700

www.hiltonfoundation.org/

Consuelo Foundation
Operates and supports programs in Hawaii and the Philippines that prevent and treat abuse, neglect and the exploitation of children, women and families.
110 N. Hotel St. | Honolulu, Hawaii 96817 | (808) 532-3939 | www.consuelo.org

County Welfare Directors Association of California
Represents human service directors from 58 counties in CA and promotes a human services system that encourages self-sufficiency of families and communities, and protects vulnerable children and adults from abuse and neglect.
925 L Street, Ste. 350 | Sacramento, CA 95814 | (916) 443-1749 | www.cwda.org

Daniels Fund
Operates the Daniels Fund Grants Program and the Daniels Fund Scholarship Program in Colorado, New Mexico, Utah, and Wyoming.
101 Monroe St. | Denver, CO 80206 | (877) 791-4726 | www.danielsfund.org/home.asp

Dave Thomas Foundation for Adoption
Find homes for children who are waiting to be adopted from foster care in North America.
716 Mt. Airyshire Blvd., Ste. 100 | Columbus, OH 43235 | (800) ASK-DTFA or (800) 275-3832 | www.davethomasfoundation.org/

David & Laura Merage Foundation
Focuses on venture philanthropy.
18 Inverness Pl. | East Englewood, CO 80112 | (303) 789-2664 | www.merage.org

David Rockefeller Foundation
Supports work that expands opportunity and strengthens resilience to social, economic, health and environmental challenges in the United States and around the world.
420 Fifth Ave. | New York, NY 10018 | (212) 869-8500 | www.rockefellerfoundation.org/

Delaware Valley Grantmakers
A membership association of funders dedicated to advancing philanthropy in the greater Philadelphia region.
230 South Broad St., Suite 402 | Philadelphia, PA 19102 | (215) 790-9700 | www.dvg.org/

The Denver Foundation
Aims to inspire people and mobilize resources that help people give back to the Denver area.
55 Madison St., 8th Fl. | Denver, CO 80206 | (303) 300-1790 | www.denverfoundation.org/

Doris Duke Charitable Foundation
Grants to improve the quality of life through supporting the performing arts, environmental conservation, medical research and the prevention of child abuse.
650 Fifth Ave., 19th Floor | New York, NY 10019 | (212) 974-7000 | www.ddcf.org/

Doris Duke Endowment
J.B. Duke established the Endowment to serve the people of the Carolinas.
650 Fifth Ave., 19th Fl. | New York, NY 10019 | (212) 974-7000 | www.ddcf.org/

Early Learning Ventures
Believes all children have the right to develop strong learning foundations through universal access to high-quality early care and education.
Merage Foundations | 18 Inverness Place | East Englewood, CO 80112 | (303) 789-2664
www.merage.org/Early-Learning.aspx

El Pomar Foundation
Funds nonprofits and government equivalents involved in charitable endeavors in Colorado.
10 Lake Circle | Colorado Springs, Colorado 80906 | (800) 554-7711 | www.elpomar.org/

Empire Health Foundation
Works to improve the health of communities in eastern Washington.
111 North Post Street, Ste. 301 | Spokane, WA 99201 | (509) 315-1323
www.empirehealthfoundation.org/

The Falk Foundation
Works to achieve a tolerant, just and inclusive society by reforming racially discriminatory policies and practices, promoting inclusion, increasing access to opportunity, and ensuring fair allocation of public resources.
3315 Grant Building | 330 Grant Street | Pittsburgh, PA 15219-2395 | (412) 261-2485
|www.falkfund.org/index1.html

Florida Philanthropic Network

A statewide association of more than 100 grant makers working to build philanthropy.

1211 N. Westshore Blvd., Ste. 314 | Tampa, FL 33607 | (813) 983-7399 | www.fpnetwork.org

Foundation for the Mid-South

Brings together the public and private sectors and focuses resources on increasing social and economic opportunity for those living in the states of Arkansas, Louisiana, and Mississippi.

134 East Amite St. | Jackson, MS 39201 | (601) 355-8167 | www.fndmidsouth.org/

Foundation for Early Learning

A non-profit that supports the learning of children, birth through age five across Washington State.

615 Second Ave., Ste. 525 | Seattle, WA 98104 | (206) 525-4801 | www.earlylearning.org/

Fundación Comunitaria de Puerto Rico (The Puerto Rico Community Foundation)

Develops the capacity of communities in Puerto Rico to achieve social and economic transformation.

PO Box 70362 | San Juan, PR 00936-8362 | (787) 721-1037 | www.fcpr.org

Geiss Foundation

A private, not-for-profit foundation, which sponsors research on China's Ming dynasty (1368-1644).

www.geissfoundation.org

Giddens Foundation

Supports activities and programs that benefit neglected and abused children and youth, with a particular, but not exclusive, interest in serving youth in the Seattle metropolitan area.

600 N. 36th St., Ste. 326 | Seattle, WA 98103 | (206) 905-1450

www.giddensfoundation.org

Grantmakers for Children, Youth and Families

A membership association of grant making institutions.

8757 Georgia Ave., Ste. 540 | Silver Spring, MD 20910 | (301) 589-GCYF

www.gcyf.org/

Grantmakers for Education

Use philanthropy to improve outcomes and expand opportunities for all learners.

720 SW Washington St., Ste. 605 | Portland, OR 97205 | (503) 595-2100 | www.edfunders.org/

Grantmakers for Effective Organizations

A coalition committed to building strong and effective nonprofit organizations.

1725 DeSales St., NW, Ste. 404 | Washington, DC 20036 | (202) 898-1840 | www.geofunders.org

Heckscher Foundation for Children

Serves the needs of youth through programs in education, college access and persistence, workforce training and jobs access, health, recreation, social services, juvenile justice and the arts.

123 East 70th St. | New York, NY 10021 | (212) 744-0190 | www.heckscherfoundation.org

The Heinz Endowments

Support projects to improve the quality of life in southwestern Pennsylvania and to address challenges it shares with communities across the United States.

30 Dominion Tower | 625 Liberty Ave. | Pittsburgh, PA 15222-3115 | (412) 281-5777
www.heinz.org

Hispanics in Philanthropy

Invests in Latino leaders and communities to build a more prosperous and vibrant America and Latin America.

414 13th St., Ste. 200 | Oakland, CA 94612 | (415) 837-0427 | www.hiponline.org

Independent Sector

The leadership network for nonprofits, foundations, and corporate giving programs committed to advancing the common good in America and around the world.

1602 L St., NW, Ste. 900 | Washington, DC 20036 | (202) 467-6100 | www.independentsector.org

The Kapor Center for Social Impact

Formerly the Mitchell Kapor Foundation, pursues creative strategies that will leverage information technology for positive social impact. It primarily works with underrepresented communities, focusing on closing academic, political, health, and economic gaps.

2201 Broadway, Ste. 725 | Oakland, CA 94612 | (510) 488-6600 | www.kaporcenter.org/

Kirlin Charitable Foundation
A catalyst and partner in positive social change, helping children and their families become-lifelong learners and thoughtfully active, compassionate members of our global community.
2607 2nd Ave., Ste. 300 | Seattle, WA 98121 | (206) 686-8226 | www.kirlinfoundation.org

John S. and James L. Knight Foundation
Supports transformational ideas that promote quality journalism, advance media innovation, engage communities and foster the arts.
200 South Biscayne Blvd., Ste. 3300 | Miami, FL. 33131-2349 | (305) 908-2600
www.knightfoundation.org/

The Jacob and Valeria Langeloth Foundation
Promotes and supports effective and creative programs, practices and policies related to healing from illness, accident, physical, social or emotional trauma, and to underserved populations.
275 Madison Ave., 33rd Fl. | New York, NY 10016 | (212) 687-1133 | www.langeloth.org/

Lumina Foundation for Education
An independent, private foundation committed to increasing the proportion of Americans who have high-quality, college-level learning.
www.luminafoundation.org/

Medina Foundation
Funds human service organizations that provide direct support to Puget Sound residents.
801 Second Ave., Ste. 1300 | Seattle, WA 98104 | (206) 652-8783
www.medinafoundation.org

Meadows Foundation
Assists the people and institutions of Texas improve the quality and circumstances of life for themselves and future generations.
3003 Swiss Ave. | Dallas, TX 75204-6049 | (800) 826-9431 | www.mfi.org/

Meyer Foundation
The foundaytion invests in visionary leaders and effective community-based nonprofits working to create improvements in the lives of low-income people in the Washington, DC

metropolitan region.
1250 Connecticut Ave., NW, Ste. 800 | Washington, DC 20036 | (202) 483-8294
www.meyerfoundation.org/

Michael and Susa Dell Foundation
Inspired by their passion for children and a desire to improve the lives of children.
PO Box 163867 | Austin, TX 78716 | www.msdf.org/

Mid-Iowa Health Foundation
Serves as a catalyst and partner for improving the health of vulnerable people in Des Moines.
3900 Ingersoll Ave., Ste. 104 | Des Moines, IA 50312 | (515) 277-6411
www.midiowahealth.org

Mile High United Way
Partners with hundreds of local nonprofits, government agencies, policy-makers and businesses to deliver the building blocks for a good quality of life for all.
2505 18th St. | Denver, CO 80211 | (303) 433-8383
www.unitedwaydenver.org

Minnesota Philanthropy Partners
A network of charitable affiliates that includes The Saint Paul Foundation, Minnesota Community Foundation, F.R. Bigelow Foundation, and the Mardag Foundation.
55 Fifth St. East, Ste. 600 | St. Paul, MN 55101-1797 | (800) 875-6167 | www.mnpartners.org/

Native Americans in Philanthropy
This group includes a growing circle of nonprofits, tribal communities, and foundations committed to the beliefs, traditions and gifts of Native peoples.
2801 21st St. South, Ste. 132D | Minneapolis, MN 55407 | (612) 724-8798, ext. 2
www.nativephilanthropy.org/

New York Community Trust
NYS's community foundation. It is one of the largest private funders of City nonprofits.
909 Third Ave. | 22nd Floor | New York, NY 10022 | (212) 686-0010
www.nycommunitytrust.org

New York Foundation
A supporter of community organizing and advocacy in New York City.
10 East 34th St. | 10th Floor | New York, NY 10016 | (212) 594-8009 | www.nyf.org/

New Yorkers for Children
Supports child welfare and programs that focus on the needs of young people in foster care.
450 Seventh Ave., Ste. 403 | New York, NY 10123 | (646) 257-2930 |
www.newyorkersforchildren.org/

Norlien Foundation
A private foundation that initiates strategic projects to enhance the quality of life for Canadians, particularly those living in Alberta.
1100 I St., SE, Ste. 540 | Calgary, Alberta | T2G Canada | (403) 215-4490 | www.norlien.org/

Northland Foundation
The Foundation is a regional philanthropy serving the communities of northeastern Minnesota.
202 West Superior St., Ste. 610 | Duluth, MN 55802 | (800) 433-4045 | www.northlandfdn.org/

Nsoro Education Foundation
A mission to nurture and inspire emancipated foster care youth and provide non-merit based academic scholarships.
2859 Paces Ferry Rd., Ste. 600 | Atlanta, GA 30339 | (404) 574-6763 | www.thenf.org

Open Society Foundations
Works to build vibrant and tolerant societies whose governments are accountable and open to the participation of all people.
224 West 57th Street | New York, NY 10019 | (212) 548-0600
www.opensocietyfoundations.org/

The Philadelphia Foundation
Works to improve the quality of life in Bucks, Chester, Delaware, Montgomery, and Philadelphia counties through funds established by its donors.
1234 Market St., Ste. 1800 | Philadelphia, PA 19107 | (215) 563-6417
www.philafound.org

Philanthropy New York
The principal professional community of philanthropic foundations in the NYCC region.
79 Fifth Ave., 4th Floor | New York, NY 10003-3076 | (212) 714-0699
www.philanthropynewyork.org

Philanthropy Northwest
Promotes, facilitates, and drives collaborative action by philanthropic organizations to strengthen communities in our region.
2101 Fourth Ave., Ste. 650 | Seattle, WA 98121 | (877) 769-2752 | www.philanthropynw.org

Pinkerton Foundation
Programs for children, youth and families in economically disadvantaged areas in NYC.
610 Fifth Ave., Ste. 316 | New York, NY 10020 | (212) 332-3385
www.thepinkertonfoundation.org/

The Pritzger Traubert Family Foundation
Invests in people and programs that enrich the life experiences of Chicago's children.
www.ptffoundation.org

Prospect Hill Foundation
Strives to advance the human experience while ensuring the well-being of the earth. Its grant and program areas include reproductive health & justice, and juvenile justice.
99 Park Ave, Ste. 2220 | New York, NY 10016-1601 | (212) 370-1165 | www.prospect-hill.org/

Quicken Loans Foundation
Helps coordinate the company's support of 250 non-profits and charitable organizations throughout southeast Michigan, northeast Ohio, and the Arizona community.
www.quickenloans.org/about.html

Raikes Foundation
A catalyst for innovative, collaborative and pragmatic solutions to help young people reach their full potential.
4616 25th Ave. NE, #769 | Seattle, WA 98105-4183 | info@raikesfoundation.org
www.raikesfoundation.org

Rees-Jones Foundation
Works to defend the welfare of children suffering from abuse or neglect.
5956 Sherry Ln., Ste. 1603 | Dallas, Texas 75225 | (214) 751-2977 |
www.rees-jonesfoundation.org

Robert Wood Johnson Foundation
The Foundation's mission is to improve the health and health care of all Americans.
PO Box 2316 | Rt. 1 & College Rd East | Princeton, NJ 08543 | (877) 843-RWJF | www.rwjf.org

Rose Community Foundation
Makes grants to organizations and institutions serving the Greater Denver community in the areas of aging, child and family development, education, health and Jewish Life.
600 S. Cherry St., Ste. 1200 | Denver, CO 80246-1712 | (303) 398-7400 | www.rcfdenver.org

San Diego Grantmakers Association
One of 33 members of the Forum of Regional Associations of Grantmakers.
5060 Shoreham Pl., Ste. 350 | San Diego, CA 92122 | (858) 875-3333
www.sdgrantmakers.org/ |

Sauer Children's Renew Foundation
Uses its resources to improve the lives of disadvantaged children and their families.
2655 N. Innsbruck Dr., Ste. A | New Brighton, MN 55112 | (651) 633-6165
www.scrfmn.org

The Schott Foundation for Public Education
Seeks to develop and strengthen a broad-based and representative movement to achieve fully resourced, quality, pre-K-12 public education.
675 Massachusetts Ave., 8th Floor | Cambridge, MA 02139 | (617) 876-7700
www.schottfoundation.org/

The Seattle Foundation
One of the nation's largest community philanthropies, fosters giving in King County.
IBM Building | 1200 Fifth Ave., Ste. 1300 | Seattle, WA 98101-3151 | (206) 622-2294
www.seattlefoundation.org

Sherwood Foundation
Promotes equity through social justice initiatives enhancing the quality of life in Nebraska.
3555 Farnam St. | Omaha, NE 68131 | (402) 341-1717 | www.sherwoodfoundation.org/

Sierra Health Foundation
This private Foundation's mission is to invest in and serve as a catalyst for ideas, partnerships and programs that improve health and quality of life in Northern California.
1321 Garden Highway | Sacramento, CA 95833 | (916) 922-4755 | www.sierrahealth.org

Skillman Foundation
The Foundation's mission is to improve the lives of children in Detroit.
100 Talon Centre, Ste. 100 | Detroit, MI, 48207 | (313) 393-1185 | www.skillman.org

Southern California Grantmakers Association
A diverse community of philanthropists from Los Angeles, Orange, Riverside, San Bernardino and Ventura counties who are committed to making a difference.
1000 N. Alameda St., Suite 230 | Los Angeles, CA 90012 | (213) 680-8866 | www.socalgrantmakers.org/

Southeastern Council of Foundations
A membership association of grant makers working together to promote and increase philanthropy in 11 southeastern states (AL, AR, FL, GA, KY, LA, MS, NC, SC, TN, VA).
50 Hurt Plaza, Ste. 350 | Atlanta, GA 30303 | (404) 524-0911 | www.secf.org/

Stoneleigh Foundation
The foundation exists to improve the life outcomes of vulnerable and underserved children and youth.
123 S. Broad St., Ste. 1130 | Philadelphia, PA 19109 | (215) 735-7080
www.stoneleighfoundation.org/

Stuart Foundation
Dedicated to the protection, education and development of children and youth.
500 Washington St., 8th Fl. | San Francisco, CA 94111 | (415) 393-1551
www.stuartfoundation.org

The Keith and Judy Swayne Foundation
Engages younger family members in philanthropy and addresses issues and needs in the community, especially those of the most vulnerable.
www.swaynefoundation.org

Temple Hoyne Buell Foundation
Supports the positive development of children through grants and partnerships primarily on the state of Colorado.
1666 S. University Blvd., Ste. B | Denver, CO 80210 | (303) 744-1688
www.buellfoundation.org/

Timothy & Bernadette Marquez Foundation
A partner and strategic investor in student achievement, success in public schools, higher education, and in expanding access and options in healthcare and human services for those who are underserved and/or under-represented in these critical areas.
PO Box 44354 | Denver, CO 80201 | (303) 583-1609 | www.tbmfoundation.org

The Jim and Carol Trawick Foundation
Assists local health and human service and arts non-profits in Montgomery County, Md. reach people in need.
7979 Old Georgetown Rd. | 10th Fl. | Bethesda, MD 20814 | (301) 654-7030 | www.trawick.org/

Topfer Family Foundation
Helping people connect to the resources needed to build self-sufficient and fulfilling lives.
3600 N. Capital of TX Hwy. | Bldg. B, Ste. 310 | Austin, TX 78746 | (866) 897-0298
www.topferfoundation.org

Tow Foundation
Supports nonprofit organizations and systems that help vulnerable populations and individuals.
50 Locust Ave. | New Canaan, CT 06840-4737 | (203) 761-6604 | www.towfoundation.org

United Way of Central Iowa
Creates opportunities for a better life for all by focusing on education, income, and health.
www.unitedwaydm.org/

United Way Network

A leadership and support organization for the network of nearly 1,800 community-based United Ways in 45 countries and territories.

www.apps.unitedway.org

Virginia G. Piper Charitable Trust

A private foundation, the Trust works to strengthen the health and quality of life of people residing in Maricopa County, Arizona, a region that includes Phoenix.

1202 East Missouri Ave. | Phoenix, AZ, 85014 | (855) 948-5853 | www.pipertrust.org

Wal-Mart Foundation

Meets the needs of the underserved by directing charitable giving toward hunger relief and healthy eating, sustainability, women's economic empowerment, and career opportunity.

702 SW 8th St. | Bentonville, AR 72716-8611 | (479) 273-4000 | www.foundation.walmart.com/

Walter S. Johnson Foundation

Assists youth in Northern California and in Washoe County, Nevada, to become successful adults by promoting positive change to the policies and systems that serve them.

505 Montgomery St., Ste. 620 | San Francisco, CA 94111 | (415) 283-1854 | www.wsjf.org/

The Washington Foundation

The faith-based Foundation works for equality on behalf of individuals and their families in the criminal justice system who would otherwise be without support.

PO Box 42508 | Houston, TX 77242 | (713) 266-6427 | www.thewashingtonfoundation.org

Washington Philanthropist's Forum

Some of the nation's most influential and generous funders of child welfare and juvenile justice reform projects opportunities for collaborations at the Center for Children & Youth Justice.

The Center for Children & Youth Justice | 615 Second Ave., Ste. 275 | Seattle, WA 98104 (206) 696-7503 | www.ccyj.org/initiatives/philanthropist-s-forum/

The Weingart Foundation

A nonprofit that seeks to build better communities by providing assistance to people in need.

1055 W. 7th St., Ste. 3200 | Los Angeles CA 90017 | (213) 688-7799 | www.weingartfnd.org

W.K. Kellogg Foundation
Works with communities to create conditions for vulnerable children so they can realize their full potential in school, work and life.
Headquarters | One Michigan Ave., East | Battle Creek, MI 49017-4012 | (269) 968-1611
www.wkkf.org/

William Caspar Graustein Memorial Fund
Connecticut's children are the focus of the Fund's grantmaking. It works with rural, urban and suburban communities, and public and private schools.
One Hamden Center | 2319 Whitney Ave., Ste. 2B | Hamden, CT 06518 | (203) 230-3330
www.wcgmf.org

Winthrop Rockefeller Foundation
Works to improve the lives of people in Arkansas through education, economic development, and economic, racial and social justice.
225 E. Markham St., Ste. 200 | Little Rock, AR 72201 | (501) 376-6854
www.wrfoundation.org

Xcel Energy
A major U.S. electricity and natural gas company with regulated operations in eight Western and Midwestern States.
414 Nicollet Mall | Minneapolis, MN 55401
www.xcelenergy.com/

Youth Transition Funders Group
A network of grantmakers working to help all youth make a successful transition to adulthood by age 25.
207 E. Ohio Street, #392 | Chicago, IL 60611 | www.ytfg.org

Zellerbach Family Foundation
Serves as a catalyst for constructive social change by initiating and investing in efforts that strengthen families and communities.
575 Market St., Ste. 2950 | San Francisco, CA 94105 | (415) 421-2629
www.zellerbachfamilyfoundation.org/

YOUTH MENTORING ORGANIZATIONS

Adoption & Foster Care Mentoring
The only community-based mentoring program in Massachusetts that exclusively serves youth with foster care or adoption experience.
727 Atlantic Ave., 3rd Fl. | Boston, MA 02111 | (617) 224-1300 | www.afcmentoring.org/

BEST Kids
Focuses exclusively on foster care children in Washington, DC and provides volunteer mentors.
515 M St. SE, #215 | Washington, DC 20003 | (202) 397-3272 | www.bestkids.org

Camp C.O.P.E.S. (Children Optimizing Personal Experience through Sports)
An award winning summer program of A Second Chance, Inc. that uses basketball to mentor and teach leadership skills to youth ages 12 to 18.
A Second Chance, Inc. | 8350 Frankstown Ave. | Pittsburgh, PA 15221 | (412) 342-0600
www.asecondchance-kinship.com/home.html

Concerned Black Men, National
Provides guidance, support and encouragement to children, while stabilizing families and positioning them to lead healthy productive lives.
1313 L St. NW, Ste. 111 | Washington, DC 20005 | (202) 783-6119 | www.cbmnational.org/

National CARES Mentoring Movement
CARES matches adults with vulnerable youth.
5 Penn Plaza, 23rd Fl. | New York, NY 10001 | (888) 990-IMIN | www.caresmentoring.org/

MENTOR/National Mentoring Partnership
Serves as a champion for youth mentoring in the United States.
201 South St. | Sixth Fl. | Boston, MA 02111 | (617) 303-4600 | www.mentoring.org

Youth Mentoring Connection
Generates mentoring programs that are site-based and have a group dynamic.
1818 S. Western Ave., Ste. 505 | Los Angeles, CA 90006 | (323) 731-8080
www.youthmentoring.org/

YOUTH AND FOSTER CARE

Jim Casey Youth Opportunities Initiative
Ensures that young people make successful transitions from foster care to adulthood.
222 S. Central Ave., Ste. 305 | St Louis, MO 63105 | (314) 863-7000 | www.jimcaseyyouth.org/

Johnson C. Smith University, Foster Care Initiative
The Initiative includes the "Phasing Up to New Possibilities" program, which works to ease the transition for youth phasing out of foster care.
100 Beatties Ford Rd. | Charlotte, NC 28216 | (704) 378-1000
www.jcsu.edu/about/foster-care-initiative

Orphan Foundation of America
Supports foster teens across the United States. Services include offering college scholarships and connections with mentors and internships.
21351 Gentry Dr., Ste. 130 | Sterling, VA 20166 | (571) 203-0270 | www.fc2success.org/

San Diego State University, Guardian Scholars Program
Helps students who are exiting the foster care system, are wards of the court, under legal guardianship or unaccompanied homeless youth earn a college degree.
(619) 594-6298 | www.eop.sdsu.edu/Content/Guardian%20Scholars.html

APPENDIX A: Overview of Integrated Service Delivery for Kinship Care Programming at A Second Chance, Inc.

Point of Contact POC	Point of Contact is our nationally recognized, full-service, kinship care case management program. POC takes the family on a personal journey of empowerment to ensure safety for the child and family. The program also provides a plan for permanency while ensuring that the placement meets state and other requirements. *Kinship Emergency Response (KER)* is our modified kinship program. It stabilizes the placement and licenses a family, so their case can be later managed by another service provider.
Kinship Caregiver Educational Enrichment Training	ASCI's training department offers educational enrichment workshops, using our SARKS™ Curriculum (Standards for Assessing and Recognizing Kinship Strengths). It provides training for kinship caregivers who want to become licensed (certified) foster parents.
Families And Children Together FACT	This 90-day intensive reunification program focuses on empowering birth parents with the skills and knowledge they need to reconnect with their children.
Subsidized Permanent Legal Custodianship SPLC	Through SPLC, we support kinship caregivers who seek legal custody for the child in their care, allowing birthparents to still maintain their parental rights.
Pre/Post Permanency Program Respite and Support Groups Services	As a StateWide Adoption and Permanency Network (SWAN) affiliate, ASCI assists our kinship care families throughout the pre/post-permanency process (e.g., SPLC and adoption). Included in the program are respite services for families needing a short break from caregiving. Respite services help to enhance permanency in families. In addition, ASCI facilitates various support groups that also meet the needs of our families.
The Family Services Unit	Emergency respite services (e.g., a temporary alternative placement for the children in their care) are provided for ASCI families.
In-Home Clinical Services	An in-home clinical support service offering referrals, consultations, counseling and assessment of mental wellness needs.
Kinship Community Collaborative	This is a referral and support service for informal kinship caregivers and birth families at risk of entering the child welfare system.
Kin Link	KINLink (Kinship care Informational Network) is a web-based informational network/resource developed specifically to address the needs of kinship care families. | www.kinlink.org

Architects rendition of existing A Second Chance, Inc. corporate office in Pittsburgh, PA.